IN ACTION

D1285306

Creating the Learning Organization

VOLUME 1

TWENTY-TWO

CASE STUDIES

FROM THE

REAL WORLD

OF TRAINING.

ASTD
AMERICAN SOCIETY
FOR TRAINING AND
DEVELOPMENT

JACK J. PHILLIPS
SERIES EDITOR

KAREN E. WATKINS
VICTORIA J. MARSICK
EDITORS

Copyright © 1996 by the American Society for Training and Development.

All rights reserved. No part of this publication may be reproduced, distributed, or transmitted in any form or by any means, including photocopying, recording, or other electronic or mechanical methods, without the prior written permission of the publisher, except in the case of brief quotations embodied in critical reviews and certain other noncommercial uses permitted by copyright law. For permission requests, write to ASTD, Publications Department, 1640 King Street, Box 1443, Alexandria, Virginia 22313-2043.

Ordering information: Books published by the American Society for Training and Development can be ordered by calling 703/683-8100.

Library of Congress Catalog Card Number: 96-83346

ISBN: 1-56286-052-6

Table of Contents

Section 1: Introducing the Learning Organization

Section 2: Changing Whole Systems Toward Learning

Section 3: Capitalizing on Continuous Learning

Section 4: Team and Action Learning Programs and the Learning Organization

Section 5: Organizational Restructuring as Prelude to the Learning Organization

Section 6: Lessons Learned and Future Prospects for the Learning Organization

Introduction to the *In Action* Series

As are most professionals, the people involved in human resource development (HRD) are eager to see practical applications of the models, techniques, theories, strategies, and issues the field comprises. In recent years, practitioners have developed an intense desire to learn about the success of other organizations when they implement HRD programs. The Publishing Review Committee of the American Society for Training and Development has established this series of casebooks to fill this need. Covering a variety of topics in HRD, the series should add significantly to the current literature in the field.

This series has the following objectives:

- *To provide real-world examples of HRD program application and implementation.* Each case will describe significant issues, events, actions, and activities. When possible, the actual names of the organizations and individuals involved will be used. In other cases, the names will be disguised, but the events are factual.
- *To focus on challenging and difficult issues confronting the HRD field.* These cases will explore areas where it is difficult to find information or where the processes or techniques are not standardized or fully developed. Also, emerging issues critical to success in the field will be covered in the series.
- *To recognize the work of professionals in the HRD field by presenting best practices.* Each book in the series will attempt to represent the most effective examples in the field. The most respected organizations, practitioners, authors, researchers, and consultants will be asked to provide cases.
- *To serve as a self-teaching tool for people learning about the HRD field.* As a stand-alone reference, each volume should be a very useful learning tool. Each case will contain many issues and fully explore several topics.
- *To present a medium for teaching groups about the practical aspects of HRD.* Each book should serve as a discussion guide to enhance learning in formal and informal settings. Each case will have questions for

discussion. And each book will be useful as a supplement to general and specialized textbooks in HRD.

The topics for the volumes will be carefully selected to ensure that they represent important and timely issues in the HRD field. The editors for the individual volumes are experienced professionals in the field. The series will provide a high-quality product to fill a critical void in the literature. An ambitious schedule is planned.

If you have suggestions of ways to improve this series or an individual volume in the series, please respond directly to me. Your input is welcome.

Jack J. Phillips, Ph.D.
Series Editor
Performance Resources Organization
P.O. Box 380637
Birmingham, AL 35238-0637

How to Use This Casebook

Much has been written about the concept of a learning organization—the capacity of the organization as a whole to learn and to transform itself. The idea of a learning organization has intellectual roots that are not new, but only recently have companies consciously used this framework to guide organizational change.

There is no one best formula for creating a learning organization. We use the metaphor of sculpting because creating a learning organization is as much an art as a science. Michelangelo spoke of sculpting as chipping away that which does not belong to the essence within the sculpted material. Unlike sculptures, however, learning organizations are ever changing. Learning organizations are socially created; the visionary leader serves a role not unlike that of the sculptor who releases the inner essence of the creation.

These case studies—whose authors intentionally describe themselves as creating a learning organization—advance both theory and practice. The cases in this book move beyond the rhetoric of what authors think a learning organization, in general, should look like to what practitioners are creating uniquely for their companies. They answer practical questions of implementation such as the following: Who needs to be involved? Where does one start? Which learning strategies are best suited to different purposes and industries? In what ways do organizational structures and policies need to change? What barriers should be expected? What allies may be counted on? How can success be measured?

The cases represent innovative practices. They are not always the best or ideal solution for each reader, however, nor were they always the best solution for the case author at the time. Those who are creating learning organizations are breaking new ground and acting within the constraints of a particular situation at a particular moment in time. It is unlikely that every step taken will always have the desired results. The essence of the learning organization depends, in part, on the ability to learn from one's experience, whether or not an action was 100% successful. These cases show positive results. They also show how unanticipated or negative results can be used intelligently to redirect the change effort.

Organization of This Book

In section 1 we elaborate definitions and models of the learning organization as a prelude to illustrating different ways in which organizations are approaching its implementation. Several of these models are represented in this book.

Sections 2 through 5 present the cases. Table 1 shows key features of these cases in the order in which they appear in four sections of this book. We place these cases in categories by level of intervention, but we recognize that real life is messy and can never be poured into categories without some overlap. The cases in Section Two feature the fullest interventions; cases in the other three sections describe interventions aimed more directly at individual, team, or organizational levels of learning and change.

- Cases in the first set show integrated examples in which the whole system is involved in a coordinated learning strategy.
- Cases in the second group illustrate continuous learning interventions that aim to enhance the learning capacity of individuals or a particular group of people.
- Cases in the third section illustrate learning within and among teams to catalyze individual and/or organizational changes.
- Cases in the fourth grouping use organizational restructuring to create a new environment in which individuals and larger groups of people learn and change.

In all cases, the initiative involves some kind of partnership among stakeholders, line management, and specialists in the areas of learning, organizational change, and technology. Table 1 can serve as a quick reference for readers who want to identify examples that relate to companies in a particular industry or sector (private, public, non-profit, community), by location or size, by target audience, or by type of intervention.

Section 6 draws lessons learned from the cases to answer the question: What are we learning about the way in which companies are sculpting their learning organizations? We identify themes that emerge from the cases that may assist practitioners in thinking more critically about selecting ideas and strategies from the cases in this book for use in their own organizations.

Using the Cases

There are several ways to use this book. The cases provide a reference for those who seek real-life examples to guide their thinking and practice. We recommend the following uses for the following people:

- *Specialists in HRD, OD, or learning—and the line managers with whom they work—who are already familiar with this concept and/or who are in the middle of interventions designed to create the learning organization.* These individuals can use the lessons learned by others for practical advice in planning steps that need taking, tips on how to jump their own learning curve when creating learning organizations, and warnings about traps that they might avoid.
- *Specialists in HRD, OD, or learning—and the line managers with whom they work—for whom the idea of a learning organization is new.* These individuals can use these cases to decide whether they want to become a learning organization, and if so, which strategies are being used in companies that are comparable in some way.
- *Participants in seminars and workshops on the learning organization.* Those for whom the idea of a learning organization is new can use these cases to find out what the learning organization looks like and how it is being implemented.
- *College and university students enrolled in HRD or management courses.* Those who teach about and are enrolled in the learning organization can use this book of cases as a supplement to textbooks on training and development, organization development, and management.
- *Scholars and researchers.* These cases provide data about actual experiences that can assist in teaching and scholarship about the learning organization, even though the cases represent the views of the authors and are not typically based on research data from many people or sources within the organizations represented.

Each case author has suggested questions that can be used to initiate discussion. Each case is unique. What has worked well for one organization may not work well for another. We do not recommend that readers simply duplicate the approaches presented here. However, the book does provide readers with a variety of approaches and strategies from which to develop one's own approach.

To provide a wide variety of examples, cases may be shorter than both the authors and the editors might prefer. If additional information on a case is needed, the lead author may be contacted directly. The address is listed at the end of each case.

Table 1. Overview of the case studies by industry and location, intervention, audience, and organization size.

Case	Industry and location	Nature of intervention	Audience	Organization size
	Integrated, whole system learning cases			
Intermedics Orthopedics, Inc.	Medical devices, Texas	Strategic visioning process and follow-up interventions	Everyone (*N*=600)	600
Johnsonville Foods	Sausage & food products, Wisconsin	New reward systems for learning	Everyone (*N*=600)	600
British Insulated Callender Cables	Copper cable manufacturing, Manchester, U.K.	Learning to support redesign of business strategy and structure	Everyone (*N*=300)	300
Morrison Communications	Publishing company, Tennessee	Leadership as modeling learning	Everyone (*N*=165)	165
Land O'Lakes	Dairy and farm supply, Midwest	Learning to support total quality management	Everyone (three divisions *N*=6,000)	6,000

Continuous learning cases

Nortel	Telecommunications, Tennessee	Skills development initiative	Everyone in Information Systems group (N=1,400)	1,400
Rohm and Haas Company	Specialty chemicals and plastics, global	Computer-based learning guide	100 global market managers	10 business units
The Virtual School	Teachers and educators network, Tennessee	Interactive computer network linking teachers	Teachers (N=2,500)	10,000
Ultrasound Coronary Systems	Intravascular ultrasound imaging, California	Focus groups to learn from groups with experience	Engineers (N=19)	125
AMEV Nederland	Insurance, Netherlands	On-the-job learning and training	New client administrators	2,450
A British multinational corporation	Subsidiary of multinational, United Kingdom	Creation of personal development plans	Top executive team	4,000
Fretwell Downing	Software specialist, United Kingdom	Linking learning between individual and organization	Managing director	100

Table 1 (continued). Overview of the case studies by industry and location, intervention, audience, and organization size.

Case	Industry and location	Nature of intervention	Audience	Organization size
Team and action learning cases				
Volvo Truck Corporation	Trucks, global, Sweden	Action reflection learning	Top managers (N=100)	22,000
Grace Cocoa	Chocolate products, global, Connecticut HQ	Action reflection learning	Top managers (N=58)	1,800
Ford Motor Company (EFHD) with Washtenaw Community College	Automotive components and community college, Michigan	Learning model taught through course and application to real world problems	As many as possible	6,135 EFHD members + members in community
Coca-Cola	Beverages and bottling, multinational, Atlanta HQ	Leadership development for global managers	Top managers, international division	(not specified)
Middle & Southwest Georgia Communities	Economic and community development, Georgia	Collaborative community-wide learning projects	Cross section of 50 people	Two communities

Organizational restructuring cases

Alberta Labour	County government, Alberta, Canada	Learning to support customer-focused reorganization	Everyone (N=700)	700
Environmental Protection Agency	National government, Washington DC	Learning through Future Search and reorganization	Human resource group (N=190)	190
New York City Bureau of Exams	City government, New York City	Learning to support reorganization to self-managed teams	Everyone (N=100)	100
Fowler Products Company	Beverage and packaging, Athens, Georgia	Learning to support total quality initiative	Everyone (N=80)	80
Swiss Postal Service	National government, Switzerland	Learning to support privatization and restructuring	Top managers (N=100)	39,000

Acknowledgments

First, we want to acknowledge the authors of these cases for their part in creating this fascinating look at learning organizations. They have inspired us with their incredible efforts, creativity, and inspiration. Without their willingness to respond to our call, there would be no story to tell. We have learned from these cases, and we hope you will, too.

We thank the American Society for Training and Development and Series Editor Jack Phillips for their interest in our work, and we thank Tammy Bush for her support and responsiveness in preparing these manuscripts for publication. Victoria is especially grateful to Rebecca Jones and Todd Holzman, two students at Teachers College who spent many hours helping her edit several chapters. We have both benefited from the support of our colleagues and our departments at the Department of Adult Education at the University of Georgia and the Department of Adult and Higher Education at Teachers College. We appreciate the opportunity to work in environments that stimulate us to grow and learn and that support us in our work.

The love of family is by far the most important *terra firma* from which we fly. Karen is anchored firmly to the ground by her ties to her son Tyson and to her daughter Tanya (who is newly married to Aaron). This marriage brought an element of joy and celebration to this writing period. Karen glimpses the experience of these organizations through the shared life histories of her siblings, Connie Schilling, and Jerry and Jim Carncross. And she is bolstered by the love of her parents, William and Elizabeth Carncross.

Victoria stays centered through the wit, warmth, and editing assistance of her husband, Peter Neaman. And father Edwin Marsick reminds her to "get real" and to stay sane.

Karen Watkins
Athens, Georgia

Victoria Marsick
New York, New York

November, 1995x

Section 1:
Introducing the
Learning Organization

A Framework for the Learning Organization

Victoria Marsick and Karen Watkins

The authors discuss the idea of a learning organization and introduce their model for understanding how this idea is implemented. They discuss action imperatives that foster individual, team, and organizational learning, and show how their framework helped them to organize the cases presented in this book.

The Need for Learning Organizations

In the last decade, organizations have experienced wave after wave of rapid transformation as global markets and external political and economic changes make it impossible for any business or service—whether private, public, or nonprofit—to cling to past ways of doing work. Organizations have had to learn new ways to keep in touch with customers, take advantage of innovations in technology, cross national boundaries, and restructure work. Unions are rethinking the way in which they represent members and bargain on their behalf (Marsick, Scully, and Woolis, 1995). Governments are changing policies and "reinventing" themselves (Gore, 1993). Workers have had to change the way they think about their jobs, careers, and lifelong learning.

A learning organization arises from the total-change strategies that institutions of all types are using to help navigate these challenges. The fundamentals of the learning organization are not new. What is new is the way in which its advocates think proactively of using learning in an integrated way to support and catalyze growth for individual workers, teams, and other groups, entire organizations, and (at times) the institutions and communities with which companies are linked. Peter Senge (1990) popularized the learning organization phenomenon in the United States. However, as is often the case, he spoke for the many scholars and practitioners who had simultaneously begun to identify the characteristics of learning organizations in their own work.

Our Model of the Learning Organization

An organization of people who learn is not a learning organization per se. A learning organization must capture, share, and use knowledge so its members can work together to change the way the organization responds to challenges. People must question the old, socially constructed and maintained ways of thinking. Learning must take place and be supported in teams and larger groups, where individuals can mutually create new knowledge. And the process must be continuous because becoming a learning organization is a never-ending journey.

We define a learning organization as "one that learns continuously and transforms itself.... Learning is a continuous, strategically used process—integrated with and running parallel to work" (Watkins and Marsick, 1993). In our earlier study of learning organizations, we created a model that reflects features common to a learning organization (see Figure 1). The model depicts two intersecting triangles: The lower triangle represents the people who comprise an organization; the top triangle represents the structures and culture created by the social institution of the company. (The triangles are fixed in this diagram, but we should think of them as in motion, as the forces that each represents interact with one another during change.) In the figure, learning becomes increasingly complex as we move from the bottom to the top, because individuals must interact within successively larger social units. In other words, individuals learn first as individuals, but as they join together in organizational change, they learn as clusters, teams, networks, and increasingly larger units. In addition, while individuals can initiate some changes on their own as a result of their learning, the organization must create facilitative structures, policies, and cultures to support learning in larger groups and throughout the organization.

A precondition for creating the learning organization in our model is assessing the organization's present capacities and disabilities. From there, the organization needs to decide which strategies to use to implement the learning organization. The action imperatives in Figure 1 are such strategies and can measure progress toward the ultimate goal of becoming a learning organization. We use the action imperatives to organize the cases in this book. Moving from the bottom to the top of Figure 1, they include four levels.

Figure 1. Model of the learning organization.

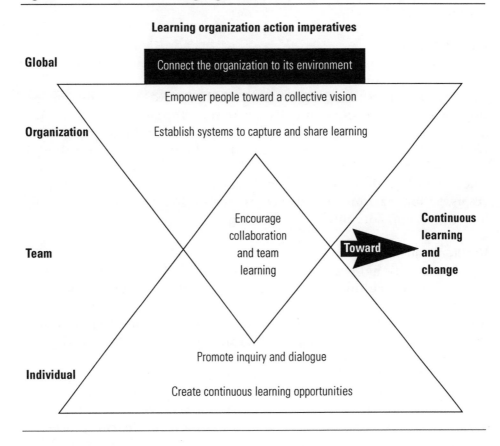

Learning organization action imperatives

Global — Connect the organization to its environment

Empower people toward a collective vision

Organization — Establish systems to capture and share learning

Team — Encourage collaboration and team learning — **Toward** — **Continuous learning and change**

Promote inquiry and dialogue

Individual — Create continuous learning opportunities

The Individual Level

At this level, we define learning as the way in which people make meaning—how members in the organization acquire knowledge and skills. We also identify the learning and cultural infrastructure that must be in place to support this learning.

CREATE CONTINUOUS LEARNING OPPORTUNITIES. Learning should be on-going, used strategically, growing out of the work itself. Strategies that organizations have used to implement this step include skills assessment against future needs, desktop learning programs that are interactive and cumulative, personal development programs, informal learning, on-the-job training programs, and tuition reimbursement plans.

PROMOTE DIALOGUE AND INQUIRY. The organization should create a culture of questioning, feedback, and experimentation. Strategies to implement this action include dialogue circles, action learning, action science that combines advocacy with inquiry, and culture change processes to end blaming.

The Team Level

Team learning is the mutual construction of new knowledge and the capacity for concerted, collaborative action.

ENCOURAGE COLLABORATION AND TEAM LEARNING. This action imperative focuses on the spirit of collaboration and the collaborative skills that undergird the effective use of teams in the learning organization. We do not focus solely on teamwork, but also on the added value of learning as a team. Strategies to implement this action imperative include cross-functional teams, self-directed work teams, work-out programs, action learning, and direct instruction to all employees of skills for negotiation, consensus, and meeting management.

The Organizational Level

Organizational learning is captured in standard operating procedures, policies, culture, work processes, and the information systems that connect virtual teams and maintain the memory of the organization. This learning is exhibited by a new vision of what the organization might be or by new knowledge of the organization's strategies, its new products or markets, and ways to conduct business.

ESTABLISH SYSTEMS TO CAPTURE AND SHARE LEARNING. Most organizations struggle when they reach this stage. Although many organizations successfully implement the individual and team levels of the learning organization, few are able to effectively sustain the learning beyond this. Strategies that organizations are using to capture learning include use of the following: software such as Lotus Notes or Microsoft Access to capture ideas across dispersed teams and divisions; electronic "water coolers" to solve problems; journals of lessons learned; computerized maintenance and production histories; "town hall" processes for collaborative development of new visions, structures, competencies, markets, or other organizational directions so that all are involved in cocreating knowledge before using it; and celebration events to share new findings across geography, function, time, and experience.

EMPOWER PEOPLE TOWARD A COLLECTIVE VISION. Organizations realize more and more the power of vision-driven change. In this type of change, an organization creates processes to share its vision and to get feedback from its members about the gaps between current organizational practice and the new vision. Strategies to implement this action include using groupware to gain organizational consensus and commitment around a shared vision, forming self-directed work teams, contracting for performance, having task forces identify and change elements that are inconsistent with the vision, holding ceremonies to mourn the passing of the old culture or skits to depict the new, and having an artist create a rendering of the new vision. Measures of how well this action works are the degree of alignment within the organization around the vision and the degree to which everyone in the organization actively participates in creating and implementing the changes that come from the vision.

The Global Level

Learning at the global level is thinking globally; crossing boundaries of environmental or societal impacts, including those that affect the quality of life afforded organizational members by the organization.

CONNECT THE ORGANIZATION TO ITS ENVIRONMENT. This action imperative varies from organization to organization. Global organizations have to learn to think of themselves as one company with one workforce in a shared-market environment. Smaller organizations must interface with all functions and stay close to their internal and external customers. Strategies that organizations have used to accomplish such actions include the following:

- building global leaders with action learning programs (e.g., in which future leaders are taken to different regions and asked to solve a significant, real problem for the host company)
- training for customer service
- having those who manufacture a product train customers in its use
- conducting employee opinion surveys to monitor the internal quality of life
- using benchmarking and computer data bases for environmental scanning
- creating virtual and interpersonal networks that cross geographical, organizational, or other boundaries and that bring the environment into the organization and vice versa
- creating programs that bring organization members and community groups together.

USE LEADERS WHO MODEL AND SUPPORT LEARNING AT THE INDIVIDUAL, TEAM, AND ORGANIZATIONAL LEVELS. Leaders who model learning are key to the learning organization experiments we've studied. They take human learning processes into account in the design of changes. They think strategically about how to use learning to create change and to move the organization in new directions or new markets. And they consciously raise the knowledge capital of the organization—both in terms of the number of new patents, products, processes, and markets —and in terms of the skills or knowledge of organizational members.

Contrasting Learning Organization Frameworks

Three frameworks—namely, those of Watkins and Marsick (1993); Pedler, Burgoyne, and Boydell (1991); and Senge (1990)—undergird the learning organization experiments reported in this volume. Our framework is the primary lens through which we've explored these cases, and this is the model used in the Nortel case. It has also indirectly influenced the cases described by Rogers and Woolis. Two cases—BICC and Fretwell Downing—incorporate the Pedler, Burgoyne, and Boydell framework. Senge's five disciplines form an explicit model for the work at Ford and Land O'Lakes.

This section contrasts the frameworks and the cases based on these models. Each discussion begins with a definition of a learning organization. In all cases, the essence of the model defines a learning organization as one that learns continuously and that can transform itself.

The Fifth Discipline, by Peter Senge (1990), director of the systems thinking and organizational learning program at MIT's Sloan School of Management, defines the learning organization as an organization with not simply an adaptive capacity but with "generativity"—the ability to create alternative futures. He proposes an organization characterized by continuous learning and the ability to "run experiments in the margin." Senge identifies the five disciplines of a learning organization as follows:

- developing personal mastery, with an emphasis on clarifying a personal vision
- using mental models that distinguish data from assumptions and that test assumptions
- building shared visions
- understanding the power of team learning
- systems thinking.

Systems thinking, the fifth discipline, is the glue that holds the others together. He suggests that the problems organizational members now face come from early training to analyze and dissect. This training teaches people to fragment the world and to distance themselves from the consequences of their actions. Learning organizations, according to Senge, are places "where people continually expand their capacity to create the results they truly desire, where new and expansive patterns of thinking are nurtured, where collective aspiration is set free, and where people are continually learning how to learn together" (Senge, 1990, p. 3).

Another model of the learning company (that we believe is also quite compatible with ours) was developed by Pedler, Burgoyne, and Boydell. These authors define the learning company as "an organization that facilitates the learning of all of its members *and* continuously transforms itself in order to meet its strategic goals" (Pedler, Burgoyne, and Boydell, p. 1). They identify 11 areas that must be monitored and transformed: using a learning approach to strategy, participative policy making, informating, formative accounting and control, internal exchange, rewarding flexibility, enabling structures, using boundary workers as environmental scanners, intercompany learning, learning climate, and self-development for everyone. In effect, they have taken the traditional elements of management and reconceived them in a manner that is consistent with and supportive of learning. They define this model more fully in the BICC case. You can find the third and final model of a learning organization in the section in the chapter titled "Our Model of the Learning Organization."

Action imperatives, strategies, or disciplines enable continuous learning and transformation in an organization. Senge's focus is primarily cognitive; he wants to develop personal and organizational shared visions, while changing mental models to a more critical and systems perspective. In his model, teams are the vehicle for integrating individual and organizational visions. We also view teams as the bridging mechanism between individuals who collectively learn and create new knowledge and the organizational visions that these teams enact.

Although not in itself sufficient for organizational learning, team learning builds the skills and structures that foster collaboration and the mechanisms for capturing learning. These in turn enhance the organization's overall capacity to change.

Like Pedler, Burgoyne, and Boydell, we emphasize learning habits such as continuous learning; a collaborative mindset; and increased autonomy, participation, and empowerment to increase the potential for flexible, spontaneous, yet concerted action in the organization. Senge looks at the deep structures, or root shifts of mind, needed to promote learning in the organization. Pedler, Burgoyne, and Boydell reframe existing organizational elements and current managerial practices from a learning perspective. We focus on the nature of learning at three levels—individual, team, and organizational or system learning—and look for ways to leverage each type of learning in the organization.

Looking at the cases arising from these frameworks, we are not surprised to note that the experiments seldom incorporate theory as a whole. Each of these cases, however, emphasizes continuous improvement through work-related learning, discusses the use of teams to support and disseminate the change, describes strategies to increase organizational flexibility, and shows a holistic attempt to drive business results through vision-led experimentation.

Among those cases using one of these three learning organization frameworks, BICC and Intermedics Orthopedics Inc. appear to be the most mature and comprehensive implementations. The Senge framework does not lead to as comprehensive a change process as the other two, because of its limited cognitive focus. However, experiments in Ford and Land O'Lakes show that implementation of Senge's model can be augmented to engage people in learning and action teams that could eventually lead to structural change. Without changes to the structure, learning infrastructure, and culture, the organization itself does not change. If learning and cognitive shifts occur in 100 individuals, and 50 of them leave or are dispersed, what changes will persist in the organization? As is true for several of these cases, learning experiments that are more limited in scope must be supported by other changes if they are to lead to systemwide learning.

Models of the Learning Organization: How Are They Alike or Different?

If we look at various learning organization models (including some represented in this book), we can conclude that the models share several characteristics:

- It is not enough for individuals to learn; learning organizations must focus on organizational learning and transformation.
- Structures and systems must be created to ensure that knowledge is captured and shared for use in the organization's memory.
- Leaders and employees at all levels must think systemtically about the impact of their decisions and work within the total system.
- Learning must be built into work structures, policies, and practices.
- Learning must be transformative in some way, although it is likely that some new learning will also be adaptive.
- Learning has a greater impact when it involves a greater percentage of the employee population.
- Organizational systems and policies must be structured to support, facilitate, and reward learning for individuals, teams, and the organization.
- New reward systems are needed to promote and reward learning.
- New measurement systems are needed both to benchmark current knowledge and culture and to monitor progress toward becoming a learning organization.

Models also differ for a variety of reasons. Sometimes, differences arise because of the type or size of industry with which the developer works or from the mental models that the developer brings to the task from his or her professional background and training. Models also differ according to the assumptions that their developers hold about organizational change, models of organization, theories of learning, and different target groups (e.g., managers, unions, professionals, shop floor workers, or support staff).

Organization of This Casebook

We have used the learning levels in Figure 1 to cluster cases by learning intervention. Section 2 presents integrated cases in which all levels of learning—individual, team, and organizational—are typically represented. Interventions in sections 3, 4, and 5 lean toward learning at one or two of the three learning levels. In addition, section 3 cases highlight exemplary continuous individual learning strategies (although interventions are often linked to team or organizational changes). Section 4 features team learning, where individuals learn, often by joining with others to learn in intact or cross-functional teams or through special-purpose learning teams created for the intervention. Section 5 cases feature organizational restructuring and focus first on helping the organization learn new responses to the environment.

Each section represents what we believe is an effective example of an experiment to change the organization in a certain direction, at a given level, and consistent with the concepts of the learning organization. As in any case history of a change process, both the organization and the change will have evolved before the book is in print. We hope that you, the reader, will find these glimpses useful in sculpting your own organic learning organization.

The Authors

Victoria J. Marsick is an associate professor of adult and continuing education at Teachers College, Columbia University, and chair of the Department of Higher and Adult Education. She holds a Ph.D. in adult education from the University of California, Berkeley, and an M.P.A. in international public administration from Syracuse University. Through Partners for the Learning Organization, Victoria currently consults with both the private and the public sectors on planning an design of strategies to create learning organizations and to monitor progress toward that goal. Through the Institute for Leadership in International Management, she assists in the design and implementation of Action Reflection Learning programs aimed at management development and organizational change. Victoria's books, coauthored with Karen Watkins, include *Sculpting the Learning Organization* and *Incidental Learning in the Workplace*. She has coedited *Professionals' Ways of Knowing* with H.K. Morris Baskett and has edited *Enhancing Staff Development in Diverse Settings* and *Learning in the Workplace*. She can be contacted at the following address: Teachers College, Columbia University, 525 West 120th Street, New York, NY 10027-6625.

Karen E. Watkins is associate professor of adult education at the University of Georgia and director of graduate programs in human resource and organizational development. She is the author, with Victoria Marsick, of *Sculpting the Learning Organization: Lessons in the Art and Science of Systemic Change* (Jossey-Bass, 1993) and *Informal and Incidental Learning in the Workplace* (Routledge, 1990). she is the author of more than 50 articles and chapters and two additional books in the areas of human resource and organizational development. Watkins is the immediate past president of the Academy of Human Resource Development. Her most recent research and consultation activities have included learning organization projects with Ford Motor Company and Nortel, Inc. She can be contacted at the following address: University of Georgia, Adult Education Department, 403 Tucker Hall, Athens, GA 30603.

References

Gore, A. (1993). *Creating government that works better and costs less: The report of the National Performance Review.* New York: Plume.

Marsick, V., Scully, E., and Woolis, D. (1995). Bargaining by other means and on other matters: Learning organizations and the new union strategy. (unpublished manuscript.)

Pedler, M., Burgoyne, J., and Boydell, T. (1991). *The learning company: A strategy for sustainable development.* London: McGraw-Hill.

Senge, P. (1990). *The fifth discipline: The art and practice of the learning organization.* New York: Random House.

Watkins, K., and Marsick, V. (1993). *Sculpting the learning organization: Lessons in the art and science of systemic change.* San Francisco: Jossey-Bass.

Section 2:
Changing Whole Systems
Toward Learning

When Visioning Becomes Organizational Learning

Intermedics Orthopedics, Inc.

Renee Rogers

The CEO of a small, entrepreneurial medical device manufacturing company used organization-wide visioning (Vision Quest) to launch a change journey to build a new future. This case study explores learning challenges as managers took next steps toward culture change—collaborative planning, defining core competencies, and a return to Vision Quest sessions aimed at team learning.

Background

In April 1992, Intermedics Orthopedics, Inc. (IOI), began a process to develop a shared vision for the year 2000 throughout the company. The process was initiated by the CEO, Jerry Marlar, to prepare the company to navigate the rough waters of change in the health care industry.

A history of rapid growth posed the first major challenge. IOI first entered the orthopedic market in 1981. The company grew from 12 employees in 1984 to almost 600 in 1994. Product development for IOI increased from one hip replacement line in 1984 to more than a dozen prostheses for hips, knees, and shoulders. The company continued to show a compound annual growth rate in sales of more than 25 percent from 1990 to 1995.

Other major events underscored the need to bring people together if IOI was to be successful in the wake of change. In 1988, IOI was purchased by Sulzer Corporation, a 160-year-old Swiss multinational

This case was prepared to serve as a basis for discussion rather than to illustrate either effective or ineffective administrative and management practices.

company. With this change, IOI moved into the global marketplace, becoming a part of the Sulzermedica USA group, a leading developer of medical devices, instruments, and biomaterials for the orthopedic, cardiovascular, and dental implant markets worldwide.

Jerry Marlar became the president of IOI in February 1992, following the retirement of the former president, who had been at the helm for 10 years. Two months into Marlar's tenure, one-half of the executive team walked out of IOI to start a competing company. During the previous seven years, the stated purpose of IOI had been to reach $100 million in sales. At the time of the executive team's breakup, IOI had accomplished this goal. Many employees throughout the company wondered what was next.

The Visioning Process

As the new leader in this environment of turbulent change, Marlar asked George Land of Leadership 2000 to facilitate IOI's visioning process using creative techniques, experiential learning, and a computer-assisted groupware technology (CoNexus). The executive staff and one sales agent met for four days in April 1992 to develop the first statement of the company's purpose, mission, values, and strategies for the year 2000. From the very beginning, Marlar included the author (the company's organization development specialist) as the internal facilitator/coordinator of the process. In doing this, Marlar legitimized the participation of organization development in defining and implementing strategic direction for the organization.

In early May 1992, 23 middle managers and two sales agents met for three days to confirm, add to, and modify the work of the executive team. Shortly thereafter, both the executive team and middle management met for four days to combine and integrate their work. The process led to a purpose statement, service and economic mission statements, a values statement, and prioritized strategies for achieving the purpose, mission, and values.

The new purpose statement portended a significant shift in the company culture. For the first decade of the company's history, the informally stated goal of those involved in the enterprise had been to be highly profitable. Under Marlar's direction, the explicit company purpose shifted to a more inclusive, service-oriented stance: To improve the quality of life by advancing orthopedic medicine and creating a model learning organization. Marlar influenced the company culture even further by advocating the separation of the company's service and economic missions. In his words, "If we do good, we will do well."

The advocacy to include becoming a model learning organization in the purpose statement began with Jerry Marlar. He firmly believed that the orthopedic industry was moving into a time of turbulent change and that the company would have to do dramatically different things to continue its success. In addition, the early sessions included the company's top sales agents, who described the critical role they played in facilitating learning for their customers—the physicians, physician assistants, and surgical technicians. Over time, the idea of creating a model learning organization stimulated multiple conversations about what this actually means. Two conclusions, however, continued to inform the company's collective understanding of what it means to become a learning organization: 1) IOI must do new things to adapt to the changing marketplace; 2) IOI must continue to create value for its customers by offering services that support learning, information exchange, and knowledge along with orthopedic products.

Reaching Agreement on Key Strategies

To reach agreement on shared values and the priorities of key company strategies, the management team relied on a process that included the use of groupware technology. This process facilitated agreement on the strategic priority of different critical issues facing the company. Because this was the first time that strategic objectives had been defined systematically, a major challenge was the lack of a shared understanding of where to focus large group conversations. To reach this understanding, the facilitator led IOI managers through a set process that intentionally separated divergent and convergent thinking processes. In the divergent phase, participants were led through a force field analysis in which they brainstormed answers to the following questions:

- What are all the things that get in the way of our achieving great success?
- What are all the things that could help us achieve great success?
- Imagine it is the year 2000 and IOI has achieved great success. The company is known by customers for providing products and services that are high quality and meet customer needs. What did IOI do?

Once this list was generated, participants were led through a convergent process in which three group votes were taken to capture the collective understanding of 1) the relative importance of the different ideas, 2) the company's current performance in this area, and 3) whether the idea was "old" for the company or "new." These data were then displayed on a four-square matrix and ideas were interpreted as immediate, midterm, and long-term opportunities; as "maintainers"; or as problem areas.

In addition to identifying average votes, the groupware allowed for the display of individual votes so that disagreement could be processed. Through extended conversation, consensus on different topics was enhanced as participants worked through disagreements rooted in different definitions of terms and uneven access to information.

Vision Quest Employee Involvement

Marlar was committed to broad employee involvement in the company visioning process. He believed that the challenges facing the company were so enormous that success depended on everyone's understanding how he or she could contribute and align individual energies to ensure IOI's long-term success.

In June 1992, a Vision Quest rollout team was formed to plan and implement the employee-involvement stage of the visioning process. The first task of the rollout team was to design, schedule, and implement one-hour meetings to communicate the products of the visioning process and to outline plans for future employee involvement. A 17-minute video was produced to help communicate the Vision Quest experience. The next stage of the project involved a series of two-and-one-half-day Vision Quest sessions conducted by George Land's company, Leadership 2000, with all employees and key external sales agents. These sessions were designed around a model of change described in Land and Jarman's 1992 book *Breakpoint and Beyond: Mastering the Future Today*. These sessions included dialogue and input to the purpose and mission statements, group prioritizing of values, outdoor experiential learning about teamwork, and training in creative problem solving. By mid-1993, all employees in the company and the majority of outside sales agents had attended these sessions.

The Vision Quest Aftermath

Employee expectations were extremely high after Vision Quest. Many people were touched personally by the invitation to contribute. For some, the experiential learning focus of the training challenged them in unexpected and stimulating ways. As is typical of many organizations, a small minority of employees, many of whom who had been with the company the longest, remained skeptical.

Unfortunately, the company's immaturity in terms of established systems and processes for working cross-functionally made it very difficult for individuals to make significant changes in their areas. When individuals came back from training, ready to make a difference, they hit the wall of "the way work had always been done." For example, one of the most important strategies was rapid product deployment. Because IOI was a relative newcomer to the orthopedics market, compared with competitor companies, there was a need to broaden the product line quickly. This was especially critical because the shift in health care was leading to an increase in the number of sales made through contracts wherein a full product line was required for eligibility to bid for business.

When managers and product team members tried to understand their role in rapid product deployment, their contributions were often conceptualized in terms of optimizing speed within each functional department, often through increased technology. At the same time, almost everyone admitted that, by far, the greatest inefficiencies were created by the lack of integration between marketing, product development, and manufacturing. In February 1993, Jerry Marlar, frustrated by the lack of progress on rapid product deployment, made two decisions. First, he assigned Fred Tripp, vice-president of operations, to serve as executive liaison to work with the middle management group in developing the process for new product introductions. Second, he reinforced accountability by mandating that 50 percent of the merit review be based on team performance in introducing new products on time. With Marlar's decision, IOI began its journey toward compensation and rewards based on team results.

As the executive liaison, Tripp interviewed and listened to numerous employees at all levels who were part of new product introductions. He agreed with others in the company that IOI lacked a formal system for managing multiple projects, and so IOI eventually contracted with a consultant who specialized in project management, would facilitate learning, and would design IOI's process. A small team of middle managers who managed the key resources for new product introduction met regularly from March 1993 until the process was implemented in April 1994. During this time, the group expanded to include other managers of groups who played support roles, but whose resources were often not included in the project planning. By 1994, 50 percent of the performance review for any managers of resources assigned to project teams was based on project results.

Learning the Discipline of Collaborative Planning

Vision Quest began as a strategic planning process. The executive team and middle management collectively defined 21 strategies that would take the company to success by the year 2000. In addition, using CoNexus, a creative process/groupware technology, the group was able to reach agreement on the relative priority of these strategies. Still, all levels of the organization struggled with setting priorities in the whirl of activities that consumed employees' energies. The effort required to build a project management system demonstrated the complexity and work required to seriously address even one strategy—rapid product deployment.

The project management process provided a cross-functional, integrated means to plan the major work for new product introductions. The planning process, however, centered exclusively on projects that would result in a product. Many nonproduct projects competed continuously for employees' time. The amount of work required to design and implement the project management system had been underestimated. In addition, to meet a requirement imposed by IOI's Swiss parent company (Sulzer), IOI employees mounted a substantial, successful effort in 1994 to obtain ISO certification. These two efforts contributed to a growing sense that non–product-related work—that is, the work of building the organization—needed to be conceptualized and planned in order for progress to be possible.

In theory, the companywide strategies, first defined in the Vision Quest process in 1992 and updated each year by the executive team, provided the plan for non–product-related work. By the end of the first year, however, managers felt distanced from the strategies. They were no longer sure what the strategies meant or what they themselves needed to do to make progress on a given strategy. Moreover, in both realms of work (product- and non–product-related), the company's level of sophistication in understanding and managing resource requirements was still immature.

By April 1994, the executive team was ready to take on the challenge of translating "high level" strategies into tactical action. At one of the team's quarterly off-site strategic review sessions, they sanctioned a process that became known throughout the company as "three-tier planning," a term coined by the vice-president of operations. His managers first developed an operations tactical plan to achieve world-class manufacturing in 1990, revising it each year. The operations plan, however, preceded the companywide strategies and was not perceived as being well integrated in the company.

To address the need for better integration of work, each vice-president worked with his or her direct reports in sessions (facilitated by the company's organization development specialist) to agree on and plan the work they needed to do over the next two years to make progress on key companywide strategies. The plans developed were three-tier because they described the work to be done in three levels of detail: tactics, action plans, and action items.

The planning process (which began in October 1994 and extended through January 1995) started with the marketing and sales departments working together to understand the dramatic shifts occurring in the marketplace and to conceptualize what needed to be done to thrive in it. Once marketing and sales completed their plans, they passed them on to the other functions. Then, vice-presidents and managers from research and development, operations, finance, human resources, and scientific affairs worked within their own departments to plan their work for the next two years, focusing on making progress on key strategies and supporting the plans of marketing and sales. The awareness of the lack of integration between departments continued to pose dilemmas throughout the process. During the planning, however, enough strategic thinking and information had been shared between the executive team and middle management and between departments that, by the end, many participants agreed that a level of integration had been achieved beyond everyone's expectations. The vice-presidents formalized this integration by developing measurable goals for all their managers based on the three-tier plans. In many cases, managers were given joint measurable goals to underscore the need for cross-functional collaboration.

Defining Core Competencies

During the development of the project management system, some managers began to understand that a well-defined, managed process could free them from the burden of micromanaging projects. At the same time, the project management process underscored their responsibility to assign competent, effective players to project teams. During the three-tier planning process, some managers, aware of this responsibility, directly addressed the need to define core competencies and to develop systems for assessing skills and developing people.

The sales group led the way in this endeavor. In February 1994, eight months before the company adopted three-tier planning, Gary Sabins, vice-president of sales, led his group in developing a three-tier plan. Their success as a group during 1994 provided a great deal of credibility for the three-tier planning process adopted by all the departments in late 1994.

A major objective defined during the first planning process was to identify and develop the critical skills required for regional managers, sales agents, and sales representatives. Jim Abraham, IOI's director of sales, championed this effort by working with a local consulting group, Gumpai of Austin, to adopt a systems approach in defining the core competencies required to enhance the success of the company's sales distribution networks.

The sales group began by gathering data from all levels of stakeholders, including IOI's president, the executive staff, regional managers (who provided a liaison between the corporation and the field), sales agents, and sales representatives. The sales group surveyed and interviewed the stakeholders to gather their perceptions of the core competencies required for IOI's sales distribution networks to succeed in the changing marketplace. Sales training then could be linked directly to the performance improvement seen to be critical to the success of the strategy to extend and enhance the current sales distribution and network. By making this connection, the sales group was able to define three benchmark measures to track the success of the training interventions in achieving the corporate strategy. The goals were 1) to get sales representatives (reps) into production quicker than in the past (i.e., from 12 to 18 months to six to nine months from time of recruitment to achieving a mean level of production); 2) to increase retention of sales reps, who are costly to recruit and train; and 3) to increase the gross business of all sales reps.

Once the core competencies were defined, a series of training events for different groups was developed and implemented. In addition, direct counseling and coaching sessions were provided for all corporate staff involved with the sales team. As these sessions were delivered, survey feedback was elicited on the effectiveness of the training in four areas: activities, attitudes, skills, and results. This feedback was used, along with the original qualitative surveys, interviews, and analysis, to modify programs and interventions in order to improve performance on the benchmark measures. The sales group repeatedly asked the question, "If not, why not?" After 15 months, significant progress had been achieved on all three of the benchmark goals, including increased sales of all agents by $9 million in a declining market. More than half of the increase was generated by new sales reps.

In terms of the company's goal of creating model learning organizations, the sales group's work on core competencies was significant. This piece of work focused specifically on facilitating learning in order to achieve an important companywide strategy. Furthermore, it highlighted the role that learning plays in adapting to market changes and maintaining financial viability.

Moving Beyond Competencies to a Strategic Marketing Focus

One of the more dramatic changes that evolved from the three-tier planning process was a reorganization of the marketing and sales groups. The planning sessions all began with the sharing of information about major shifts in the health care marketplace. The shift away from the physician as the primary customer and toward a more complex selling environment that also included hospital administrators and contracting organizations required a new approach to marketing. At the same time, the need to tightly integrate marketing and sales was more keenly felt than ever before. To address these issues, the vice-president of sales assumed responsibility for both marketing and sales, and a new role was defined for the director of marketing, who would report to the vice-president of marketing and sales. Much of this director's role would revolve around the need to build a more professional, high-powered marketing group positioned to lead the company in coming to understand the customer and in setting the company's strategic direction. The development of the marketing organization will be one chapter of an important story to unfold over the next one to two years.

Repairing the Rift—Managing the Culture Change

While this description of the change process may appear coherent, the reality of everyday life within IOI was considerably more chaotic. The executive team members spent a year of concerted effort building their team, learning to address tough issues, working out solutions, and making difficult and sometimes unpopular decisions. During this process, they struggled through 15-hour days, rigorous travel, a volatile and unpredictable market, increased regulatory complexity, and the unique challenge of being a U.S. subsidiary of a non–U.S.-based global organization. Eventually, a rift developed between this group and the middle managers as each group struggled with different dilemmas.

For middle managers, the pressures of managing heavy workloads and juggling resource constraints posed special challenges. In particular, the demand to extend the company's product lines through new product introductions overextended the resources of marketing, product development, and manufacturing. Even with this demanding workload, employees were often eager and ready to make contributions to improve IOI's systems and work processes. Given the complexity and demanding pace of company life, however, most of the processes and systems were ultimately worked out at the executive and middle management levels. The employees were often distanced from the progress that was being made.

For many employees, the Vision Quest process was a moving and powerful experience. They saw themselves as producers of a product that makes the quality of life better for their customers. While the process produced a vision for the employees' future at IOI, the delayed follow-up by managers and the perceived lack of true organizational commitment left many people unsatisfied. Some employees felt cynical and skeptical about the genuine commitment of management to the process of change and to the company's purpose and mission.

Vision Quest Revisited

Despite the growing cynicism of employees, the executive team continued to believe that nothing was more important for IOI than a shared, collective vision that would enable employees and the company to become winners in the next years and on into the next century. For this reason, the executive team chose to continue the company's commitment to Vision Quest by extending the process to the 80 new employees who were hired in 1993–94. The program content, however, was changed to explore the inherent learning dilemmas more deeply. The program took a close look at what happens when individuals take responsibility for the team learning that is required to "own" a collective vision and effect change within an individual's circle of influence.

During the experience, Jerry Marlar spent time with employees, inviting them to participate in shaping IOI's culture and future. In these conversations with employees, he echoed the sentiments of Max Dupree: "We do not grow by knowing all of the answers, but rather by living with the questions." He admitted that leadership at IOI did not know all of the answers, but they were learning to understand and ask the right questions.

The original Vision Quest employee sessions focused on the dynamics of change and the need for a compelling vision to pull the organization into the future. It also emphasized the need for creativity and individual courage in embracing the change all around. Three years later, this emphasis on the norms of individualism proved to be somewhat problematic as the company continued to hit the limits of its capacity for real teamwork at all levels. Moreover, at the individual level, people were having trouble feeling connected to a top-down "vision" that they had not been directly involved in designing.

For these reasons, the Vision Quest sessions for new employees were designed to facilitate reflection and team learning. During these sessions, employees were invited to challenge their assumptions and practice new behaviors. Some of the critical dynamics explored were the following:

- Does the group function like a team?
- Is communication in this group clear and open?
- Is leadership clearly defined? Is it shared?
- Is there trust between team members?
- Are team members aligned with a general purpose (vision)?

The overarching goal of these sessions was to have employees experiment with the dynamics of collective thinking and dialogue; to foster understanding of the power of intentional group action; to practice the art of balancing task, team, and individual needs; and to experience the phenomenon of building trust in a team through shared learning. The highly experiential nature of the session allowed participants to experience, firsthand, individual and team learning over a period of two and one-half days. Through this experience, employees were able to see how their attitudes and behaviors directly influenced group success or failure. Feedback from employees immediately after the sessions and six months later indicated that the second Vision Quest experience was a very positive one for the participants but, more important, it left them with the perception that their individual attitudes and actions played a major role in the organization's learning process.

Learning Dilemmas

The journey to build a learning organization is not an easy one, and awareness of shortcomings, rather than success, is often common among employees. At times it seems that the greatest challenge for leadership is to embrace the ambiguity of the process of working through a seemingly endless series of paradoxes and dilemmas. At IOI, learning dilemmas have played out in three specific arenas: empowerment, accountability, and teamwork.

The initial decision to champion a process to develop a shared vision was an act of strong leadership by Jerry Marlar. His intent was to lay a foundation for real empowerment, where individuals increasingly could make judgment calls and evaluate their decisions in light of clearly defined purpose, mission, and strategy. His belief was that "governing" through a shared vision, instead of through direct orders, promoted decision making and leadership that did not rest solely with the organization's hierarchical leaders. Paradoxically, however, many people perceived this approach as a lack of leadership because it differed from the previous mode of autocratic decision making. Executive leadership at

IOI has struggled with the middle management perception that they—the executives—are indecisive, when in many cases the executive view is that acts of leadership have often not been recognized or understood.

Another set of dilemmas for the organization arose as leaders and employees learned about the dichotomy of accountability and trust. True empowerment means allowing individuals to be accountable for their performance. The end of patriarchy means that an organization allows people to make mistakes and to take responsibility for their own actions and learning. Establishing true accountability at IOI required building systems and processes to enable people to work effectively and to track the results of their work. Again paradoxically, in the process of building in accountability, individuals sometimes felt they were not trusted. Although the intention was to trust people more than ever before, perceptions and feelings at times played out as resistance to moving toward this goal. Executive leadership has had to live with the tension of the paradox that increased accountability—which is a by-product of entrusting employees—may, at times, diminish trust in the short term. At a personal level, individuals have had to work out issues of trust without lapsing into being punitive or of taking care of others.

A third major dilemma in the journey to building a learning organization is the contradiction of individual versus company goals. Human resource managers responsible for organizational compensation systems live with the challenge of trying to reward both individual accomplishments and team success. At times, these two perspectives can be contradictory. Success in business today requires cross-functional team processes—concurrent engineering, horizontal process integration, "managing the white space" in organizations. These are just some of the phrases that have been used at IOI to describe the need for improved teamwork.

During the early entrepreneurial days at IOI, employees experienced great opportunities to excel and to be rewarded for their individual efforts. As the company has matured, the need for team players, not individual superstars, has changed the criteria for adding value to the enterprise. Moreover, the capacity of the organization to provide individual rewards has been constrained by business realities. In the development of the project management system, Pat Diak, vice-president of human resources, led the effort to revise the company's compensation systems in order to reward project team performance in new product introduction efforts. The introduction of a team scorecard and reward increased pressure within the organization to confront the inadequacies of internal processes that worked against teamwork and against a focus on overall results. The next step was the creation of a middle management task force led by the vice-president of human resources. The task force reevaluated and redesigned the compensation system to better direct the whole organization toward the achievement of company goals.

Lessons Learned

Organizational learning is an ongoing, never-ending process of moving through questions and confusion to moments of clarity and shared understanding that open the door to new questions. The evolving needs of the organization require solutions that, once implemented, pose a new set of problems. At IOI, achieving clarity about our purpose and mission provided the opportunity to define and focus on some key strategies. In doing this, the company faced some major obstacles and became aware of the need for cross-functional processes. Once these cross-functional processes were designed, the company had to wrestle with issues of culture and attitude that sometimes prevented individuals and groups from embracing the concept of teamwork that is so critical for success in today's changing market.

Questions for Discussion

1. What were some of the most important lessons learned by those at IOI?
2. How was IOI affected by its explicit aim to become a model learning organization?
3. What role did planning play in IOI's effort to become a learning organization?
4. How did IOI come to an understanding of the need to define core competencies? Why is this work critical in the process of becoming a learning organization?
5. What learning dilemmas or paradoxes is IOI having to work through? What kinds of learning dilemmas have you experienced in other organizations?

The Author

Renee Rogers is an organization development specialist with Intermedics Orthopedics, Inc., an Austin-based orthopedic device manufacturing company. At IOI, she provides consultation to all levels of the organization to improve teamwork, productivity, and strategic alignment. Before working for Intermedics, Rogers worked as an OD consultant for the City of Austin Electric Utility and designed training for American Airlines. She also taught English for several years in Japan. Rogers holds a master's degree in applied linguistics and a doctorate in human resource development from the University of Texas at Austin. She serves as an adjunct faculty member for the Adult and Human Resource Development Leadership program at the University of Texas. She is a member of the OD Network and the American Society of Training and Development. Rogers can be contacted at the following address: Intermedics Orthopedics, Inc., 9900 Spectrum Drive, Austin, TX 78717.

References

Land, G., and Jarman, B. (1992). *Breakpoint and beyond: Mastering the future today.* New York: Harper Business.

The Great Performance Share

Johnsonville Foods

Linda Honold

The CEO of a small, privately owned sausage company restructured his company in 1982 to put responsibility for decision making in the hands of employees. He left in 1989, and empowerment waned. The CEO returned in 1991 and invited employees to reshape the company. This case study describes their solution—performance contracting between teams and customers that rewards extraordinary learning.

Organizational Profile

Johnsonville Foods began operation in 1945 as a local mom-and-pop meat market in Johnsonville, Wisconsin. It has grown to become a national producer and distributor of sausage and other food products. The company has production facilities in Johnsonville and in Watertown, Wisconsin, as well as in New Haven, Connecticut. It also has an office in Kohler, Wisconsin. Recently, Johnsonville expanded its product line to include precooked, gourmet entrees. A privately held company, Johnsonville has decided not to publish specific financial figures. The company's annual sales, however, are in the range of $150 million, and its profitability numbers outperform the industry average.

Through 1982, Johnsonville had a traditional organizational structure—a strict hierarchy, with family member executives making most decisions. In 1982, the son of the company's founders embarked on a change effort to make the company more customer focused. His goal was to transfer responsibility for performance to the company's approximately 300 line workers. He dramatically changed systems of performance, information, and reward. Although the organization

This case was prepared to serve as a basis for discussion rather than to illustrate either effective or ineffective administrative and management practices.

implemented functional and cross-functional teams, the traditional hierarchy remained in place.

Key Player

The primary role in this case belongs to Ralph Stayer, owner and chief executive officer of Johnsonville. Ralph's transition from a traditional CEO to a philosophical leader began in the early 1980s and continues today. In addition to his roles at Johnsonville, Ralph has headed a consulting firm since 1988. His experiences working with other organizations have helped him come up with many new ideas for Johnsonville.

Description of the Initiative

The following sections describe the key elements of Johnsonville Foods' change initiative.

Performance Responsibility

Until 1982, Johnsonville Foods was a traditional organization whose members had well-defined roles. Executives made all major decisions, managers carried out these decisions, frontline workers did the hands-on physical labor, and supervisors made sure they did. From 1982 to 1989, the company experienced a transformation from which new roles emerged.

By 1989, the leadership team's role was to set the organization's direction and vision. The managers' job evolved into that of assisting people throughout the company in defining for themselves how to accomplish what leadership had directed. Frontline workers were responsible for their own performance. They did their own production and people scheduling, and set their own budgets based on sales projections for their products. To build a dedicated team, they hired their own teammates and worked with coworkers on performance improvement issues.

In 1989, Ralph began to focus more on consulting than on operations. He transferred responsibility for operations to a new president, Mike, who had his own vision and a different definition for what Ralph was trying to achieve. Both Ralph and Mike wanted the business to grow and become more profitable. The difference was that Mike did not share Ralph's belief that employees could interpret and carry out the leadership's vision for the organization. In small ways, Mike began to reverse the empowerment that employees had come to feel throughout the 1980s.

In 1991, Ralph realized what was happening, and he worked with Mike to make his point of view known. He set new criteria for assessing

Mike's success, which had been evaluated on the basis of financial results alone. Now people's growth and empowerment also would come under review. After six months, Ralph realized that he and Mike had drastically different visions, and so he asked Mike to step down from the presidency. When Ralph returned to lead his organization, he found that things had changed substantially and that he would need to work quickly to send a message that he was serious about fixing what had gone wrong. He also knew that it would be contrary to his own philosophy to dictate what in particular must be done.

Summit Conference

Ralph called a meeting of all members of the organization who were in sales or other leadership positions. The Summit Conference, as it was known, included all "managers" (Johnsonville has not used the term "manager" for many years, but it best describes the attendees in a traditional way), coaches, and resource or support personnel. Any other member of the company who was interested in attending was also invited. The meeting was held on a weekend. No one was required to attend, but everyone was informed that this meeting would determine where the company was going and how it would get there. Approximately 120 of about 600 employees attended.

The meeting took place off site. To begin, Ralph announced that the company needed to be fixed and that this group would develop the action plans to fix it. The first item on the meeting agenda was to revisit the goals of the company: Where was it going? Who were its customers? What were the critical measures of success? Participants developed four key goals that would become the focus of all activities throughout the company: great-performing products, great customer service, great financial results, and great people. Except for the financial results, no specifications were made for any of these goals. Financial results are within the purview of ownership; therefore, Ralph retained responsibility for setting those parameters. The other three goals would have different measurements depending on the customers they served, the group or department doing the work, and the individuals in that group who were responsible for results.

The next step was to determine how to achieve demonstrable improvements in each of the four areas. The 120 people broke into smaller subgroups. Each subgroup focused on what it perceived to be the three or four main obstacles to the company's goals. The entire group listed all obstacles and debated which ones were primary. Two main obstacles were identified: 1) there was no adequate way to measure performance, and 2) bonuses under the old system were not tied directly to performance and were awarded too infrequently (twice per year for hourly paid workers and once per year for salaried workers) to have a major influence. People volunteered to serve on action teams to address each obstacle.

At a half-day meeting of the entire company, the results of the Summit Conference were presented. All in attendance were provided the opportunity to join one of the action teams. Before implementing solutions, the action teams needed to bring their recommendations back to the original group to get agreement. This step was not for approval but rather was to ensure that all of the critical questions were answered before implementation.

The Great Performance Share

The solution to the issues of lack of performance criteria and inadequacy of the bonus turned out to be one and the same. The action teams created a system called Great Performance Share (GPS). The following paragraphs describe how this system works.

Each month, functional or project-based work teams or individuals contact internal customers to determine what they need and how they can be better served. A contract, which must fall within one of the four key focus areas, is drawn up based on this information. Development of the contract may take place in direct meetings or via electronic mail. If it is needed, there is negotiation to come to a common understanding. This process ensures that performance is measurable for all persons in the company and is based on the customer's perception of their performance.

The contract may be up to six months long and includes action points for each month. Once the contract is drawn up, the team meets to determine what each individual will do to ensure fulfillment of the contract. Each individual is responsible for carrying through his or her agreed-upon part. At the end of each month, a simple questionnaire is sent to the customer(s) asking, "Are we meeting and/or making progress toward the goals of our contract?" If the response is in the affirmative, the process moves to the next step of GPS distribution.

The exact process of determining how much each share is worth warrants detailed description. The primary determinant is the profitability of the company. For hourly workers, each share is approximately the monthly profits divided by the total number of people working in the company. This provides the value of one GPS share. If the contract is for an entire team, the team gets the equivalent of one share for each individual. Team members then split the team GPS. Some simply divide them equally; others find that certain individuals have contributed more that month and decide to give a greater share to those people. For instance, the sausage stuffing team made a contract with its customers to improve the shelf life of its product. One woman came up with an idea that had a significant influence. Her teammates decided to share 10 percent of their individual shares with her.

Some teams even find that someone has not contributed to success, and they reduce his or her amount. For salaried workers, the process is a bit different; each aims for a target GPS based on the fair market wage for his or her job.

When the customer responds on the survey that the contract has not been fulfilled, the contractees do not get their GPS for that period. They then try to determine what went wrong and how they can overcome any difficulties for the next month's GPS. They may need to renegotiate the contract. This happens very infrequently—never in two consecutive months. Nonperformance is not tolerated in this environment. Nonperformers either figure out how to perform or they leave the company.

This system rewards performance based on the satisfaction of people who use the products or services of the performers. It also requires individuals throughout the organization to be constantly learning. The GPS is provided for performance above and beyond what is required in people's basic jobs. The performer is always looking for what his or her customer needs.

Had this system been in place under Mike, and had he contracted for the services he provided to those he coached, it might have been apparent much more quickly that he was not carrying through on Ralph's intended management style. All contracts are posted on the company's electronic mail system, and anyone can read and comment on the contracts and customers' evaluations.

The GPS is not cast in stone. It is reexamined every six months when the company gathers to determine the next level of activities for the company's focus, using a process similar to the one Ralph used in 1991. In essence, the company is reinvented every six months.

Today, Johnsonville continues to grow. The company has more than 700 employees focused on the organization's long-term success.

Targeted Learning Level

In this change process, the organization, teams, and individuals all learn. From the organizational perspective, the twice-yearly meetings keep the company focused. There is a willingness to admit when something is not working. Every six months there is an opportunity to return to the drawing board. Change has become not only acceptable, but a way of life.

From the team perspective, people have learned they must work together to meet the needs of their customers. Most personality issues have fallen by the wayside, and true teamwork is taking place. Because all contracts must fall into one of the four main focus areas (products, service, financial results, or people), everyone works toward a common goal.

Individuals are also constantly learning. The contracts cannot be merely for what is expected; they are for "great" performance. Actions must be above and beyond the day-to-day job requirements. People are constantly challenging themselves.

Assumptions That Influenced Events

The Johnsonville process has been successful in transcending a stagnated change effort to become a dynamic, focused, high-performance organization. Assumptions are threefold:

- Ralph Stayer believed that he must do something dramatic to reenergize the company.
- Ralph believed that people would do the right thing once they knew what needed to be accomplished and what the rules of the game were.
- There was a belief that the reward system (GPS) must reinforce the performance that was sought.

The intended outcomes of this process were to reaffirm a customer focus, to ensure products of high quality, to assure the stakeholders of desired financial returns, and to transfer responsibility for all of the above to each person in the company. In that respect, it has been quite successful. Profitability has never been better. Johnsonville has the reputation of a high-quality, customer-focused company. The people within the company are achieving things they never thought they would be able to do. Staff turnover was initially high as people determined whether or not this intense focus was right for them, but is now very low.

Strategies for Assessment

Measurement of success for three of the four key areas is relatively easy. Profitability is based on return on assets, dollar-volume sales, and pretax profit. Each of these has a specific criterion. Performance to customer expectations can be measured by meeting contracts successfully. The quality of products can be measured by specific scientific criteria, as well as by repeat and expanding sales.

Measuring the greatness of people is more subjective. Employee turnover is not a helpful measure, because the turnover may come from nonperformers. An employee attitude survey is probably not the answer, either. Attitude surveys imply that someone else needs to fix the environment for the performer to have a better attitude. This runs contrary to the concept of developing personal responsibility. Because the contracts require employees to challenge themselves, people growth might best be measured by follow-through on what the people have agreed to do for their customers.

Key Success Factors

In this case, leadership from the top was critical. The owner wanted to change the organization, and he was committed to doing so. Another critical factor was Ralph Stayer's dedication to practicing what he preached. The fact that Johnsonville had already experienced a great deal of change from 1982 to 1989 was a key success factor. Another was that the managers and supervisors had already begun the transition toward coaching. Their jobs changed from that of directors—telling people what to do—to that of facilitators. Their responsibility was to provide general direction and support so people could do their own jobs.

The alignment of systems of performance, feedback on that performance, and rewards are also key success factors in Johnsonville's transition. Had these major systems not been in alignment, mixed messages would have been sent, and behavior might have been different. In addition, because the people within the organization created the reward system, they worked hard to make it successful.

This type of change effort can be instituted in divisions or departments as well. One needs to obtain a common focus and get everyone working together to obtain that common goal. Without support from the top, there may not be the opportunity to change or add a reward system and there may not be control over some of the corporate-sponsored performance and information systems. The key will be for the unit to work on what it *can* control, and to accept the rest as given for the time being.

The other major obstacle to implementation on the department or division level is that if the rest of the company does not participate, the changing group will always be bumping into old thinking when interacting with other groups. So long as this is known and understood by those making the change effort, success can still be achieved on a localized basis.

Tips and Traps

Perhaps the most significant trap a facilitator of change can run into is becoming a "doer" rather than a facilitator. One of the keys to success is the sense of ownership achieved when the people affected by the change determine how they are going to accomplish it. If the facilitator becomes a doer, this critical element is lost. The key is for the facilitator to understand the goal and the parameters. He or she must then learn to ask great questions so that the people affected by the change come up with their own solutions.

The human resource department or organization development department must become a resource for its customers—those making changes throughout the company. Members of the department can take on the role of facilitator or simply provide access to resources. The key here is the same as for the facilitator: one must not become the doer. If one does, the sense of ownership is lost and the change effort will likely not be successful.

The job of the manager changes as well. He or she must learn to be a resource and to avoid giving answers. The manager must learn to set the direction for the company or the department, and must help people to define that vision for themselves. He or she must also help people understand what the operating parameters are and why they are in place. Finally, the manager must learn to ask questions instead of giving answers. When a person is told the answer, he or she has no sense of commitment to the solution. When someone is asked a question and allowed to think through the answer, that person gains a sense of ownership.

How Is Johnsonville a Learning Organization?

Johnsonville virtually can change all the rules every six months. There is no need to be saddled with a structure that is not working. For instance, at one Summit Conference an organizational structure of customer focus teams was created. Each month, representatives from all areas of the company would get together to focus on the needs of a specific set of customers. Then they would take back this information to their respective functional work areas for information purposes or for appropriate actions. This worked well for six to nine months. It got people from different departments to communicate with each other about customer issues. After a year it was discovered that the conversations were taking place without the formal meeting. At the next Great Performance meeting, the monthly customer focus meetings were abolished. One disadvantage of this decision is that it is sometimes difficult for everyone in the organization to keep up. With things changing constantly and with some people needing to focus on their production jobs, information does not always flow as smoothly as would be hoped.

Another key advantage of Johnsonville's management system is that people are constantly learning. Individuals are doing things they never thought possible. Frontline performers are hiring, meeting with customers, determining and monitoring their own budgets, and assisting in the strategic direction of the company.

One drawback associated with learning is that it may become stressful. Each Great Performance Share contract must be different from the previous one. It must be for performance that is above and beyond what is expected. How far is too far? What happens to the stress levels of people working in such a high-performing organization? Is there a point at which people will be left behind because the stretch is too great? Maybe there isn't. Perhaps as people learn and grow, their potential for learning and growing expands and they can continue to keep up. Only time will tell.

In the meantime, Johnsonville is known as a high-performing organization. Its sausage products are known as premium quality. The people who work in the organization are continually challenged and have a fair amount of control over their own work and how it is done. Learning takes place for everyone on a daily basis.

Questions for Discussion

1. What are the main drivers of performance at Johnsonville Foods?
2. As this company progresses and as levels of performance are continually raised, what happens to stress levels? How long until people are stretched beyond their limits? What happens to them then?
3. With the Great Performance Share reinforcing performance, will the process become too financially oriented? How much is too much? Is the focus moving from having a reward system that is in alignment with performance expectations to one that is the driving force? Is that healthy for the company and for the people who work in it?
4. Are there any other reward systems that might better stimulate learning?

The Author

Linda Honold founded Empowerment Systems in 1990. She is the owner of A Reader's Paradise bookstore and was the coach for member development at Johnsonville Foods from 1985 to 1990. Her job at Johnsonville was to coach the executive team and others in the company during their transition to a totally empowered workforce. At Empowerment Systems, Honold coaches CEOs and management at various companies and organizations to develop a process for transforming their organizations. Her coaching is based on the knowledge and experience she acquired at Johnsonville Foods and while working with Ralph Stayer, CEO of Johnsonville Foods. This process is highly effective for organizational improvement, managing change, and empowering people. Linda has been a keynote or featured presenter at international conferences in the United States, Canada, England, Scotland, and Australia. She has spoken to the Training Directors' Forum, the Self Managed Work Teams Global Networks Annual Conference, the Learning Company Conference, and the National Healthcare Quality Conference. She is a resource person for the Executive Committee throughout the United States. Honold has been a presenter, facilitator, or coach, at corporate meetings for companies in manufacturing, mining, construction, finance, healthcare, retail, food service, agriculture, and public utilities, as well as with social service agencies and governmental bodies. Her article "The Power of Learning at Johnsonville Foods" appeared in *Training* magazine in April 1991. She is currently working on a book of examples of successful empowerment in action. Honold holds a master of science degree in industrial relations from the University of Wisconsin. She can be contacted at the following address: Empowerment Systems, 305 Michigan Avenue, Sheboygan, WI 53081.

Transformation and the Learning Company Project

British Insulated Callender Cables

Tom Boydell

*A consultant describes the steps he took in helping a telephone cable sup-
plier restructure as a decentralized, team-centered company in order to
survive and increase market share while simultaneously building the capacity of employees. Measurement against a "learning company" framework shows the systemic nature of actions taken to build a learning culture and environment.*

Background

British Insulated Callender Cables (BICC) is a large U.K.-based
engineering company. Its name indicates its primary business, although it has diversified into other sectors, particularly civil engineering. Within its cables business there are a number of product-based divisions, specializing in areas such as power transmission, fiber optics,
and copper-based telephone cables. The plant involved in this project
manufactures the latter. The company is located in a somewhat run-
down area of Manchester, in Northern England.

For many years, BICC and two other manufacturers had enjoyed a
"cozy" relationship with the sole U.K. customer for such cables—
British Telecom (BT). A state-owned company, BT had a monopoly on
the provision of telephone systems in the United Kingdom. Therefore,
it was somewhat unconcerned with issues of cost, price, value, and
profitability. Thus BICC and its "competitors" were each allocated approximately equal market shares, were able to charge whatever they

*This case was prepared to serve as a basis for discussion rather than to illustrate either effective or inef-
fective administrative and management practices.*

wished, and were not particularly challenged on issues such as quality and delivery.

This situation changed when BT was privatized and its monopoly position was removed. Suddenly it was interested in cost, price, quality, and delivery. It reallocated the market shares between the existing suppliers, and further, stated that its intention was to deal with two suppliers, and eventually with only one.

For BICC this presented a considerable challenge. Because of BT's perception of the relative merit of the three suppliers, BICC's share was cut to a mere 17 percent, turning a healthy profit into a major loss. It was clear that for BICC to remain in this business, it would have to make major improvements in quality and delivery, and reduce price significantly. At the same time, the total U.K. market for copper-based telephone cable was shrinking, due to increased use of fiber optics. BICC's response to these challenges may be divided into four main phases:
1. Setting the scene (March–August 1992)
2. Removing the barriers and creating the right environment (September 1992–June 1993)
3. Introducing teamworking in manufacturing (April 1993–April 1994)
4. Creating a learning environment (November 1993–).

Phase 1: Setting the Scene

This phase involved deciding if the plant should be kept open, and if so, agreeing on a planning strategy. Specific steps were as follows:
- obtain senior management's commitment
- agree on a strategy and carry out basic planning
- communicate with employees and union representatives.

After much consideration, senior management gave its support to the continuing operation of the plant. A broad business strategy for the copper cables division was formulated, with a related people strategy (Figure 1).

The learning organization strategy was chosen because it was perceived as being particularly appropriate to:
- requiring an integrative, holistic approach
- "learning through" to BICC's own solution in a situation where there was no standard blueprint
- providing the basis for self-sustaining, long-term transformation
- integrating organizational and individual development
- empowering individuals and enabling them to use their considerable insight and skills, hitherto largely ignored.

Figure 1. Business strategy.

Business strategy
■ Short term: Survival return to profitability
■ Medium term: expand, increase share U.K. market, move into key markets abroad

People strategy
■ Obtain competitive edge by reorganizing and fully utilizing employees
■ Secure continuous improvement by moving toward becoming a learning organization

The 11 Characteristics of a Learning Company: A Guiding Framework

In 1991, Pedler, Burgoyne, and Boydell published *The Learning Company*, in which they proposed a systemic framework for characterizing the learning organization.

Boydell (1994; see also Learning Company Project, 1993) modified this framework to include 11 characteristics (Figure 2). These characteristics, used to guide progress throughout the BICC transformation, are described briefly in Table 1.

Phase Two: Removing the Barriers and Creating the Right Environment

Prior to BT's commercialization, it accepted just about anything that was suggested or given to them by suppliers. This relationship was mirrored in the management-union relationship within the factory. Thus, in broad terms, management tended to go along with any requests made by the union, so in many ways the union ran the plant.

BT's new strategies called for a very different relationship between management and the workforce, and for a significant change in the role of the unions. The building of this new relationship has been ongoing. The process started in Phase Two, after an initial communication of the new strategies. It involved the following:

- establishment of a new site management team
- integration of all functions on one site
- head count reductions and outside contracting for services

Figure 2. The eleven characteristics.

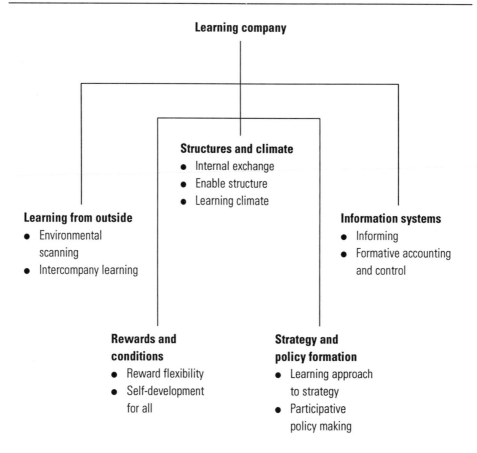

Learning company

Structures and climate
- Internal exchange
- Enable structure
- Learning climate

Learning from outside
- Environmental scanning
- Intercompany learning

Information systems
- Informing
- Formative accounting and control

Rewards and conditions
- Reward flexibility
- Self-development for all

Strategy and policy formation
- Learning approach to strategy
- Participative policy making

Based on cluster analysis of data from 10 organizations

- creation of a single wage scale
- establishment of a "people contract"
- improved working environment
- improved management-employee communications
- changes in the manufacturing management structure to facilitate the introduction of teamworking.

The existing site management team was replaced. At the same time, some of the production functions that were carried out at another site were brought over to Manchester. Elimination of redundancies among the workforce, coupled with the contracting out of certain services, led to a drop in workforce numbers from around 400 to around 300.

Table 1. Eleven characteristics of a learning company.

Structures and climate
- Internal exchange. Internal units and departments see themselves as customers; suppliers contract with each other in a partly regulated market economy.
- Enabling structures. Those which create opportunities for individual and business development, with an emphasis on adaptability and flexibility.
- Learning climate. A learning company has a particular culture and climate which aims to foster learning.

Learning from outside
- Environmental scanning. Addresses the question of how organizations learn from their environments. The learning company involves all its people in scanning the environment for important data.
- Intercompany learning. Refers to the way organizations can learn with and from each other. The learning company is always on the lookout for opportunities to learn with other companies.

Information systems
- Informating. Information technology (IT) is used here to aid the free flow of information and to inform and empower all members of the organization to ask questions and make decisions based on available data.
- Formative accounting and control. The essential control systems of accounting, budgeting, and reporting are structured to assist learning from the consequence of managerial decisions.

Strategy and policy formation
- A learning approach to strategy. Implies that strategic planning and implementation are learning processes.
- Participative policy making. More, rather than fewer, people are involved in the policy or strategy-making process.

Rewards and conditions
- Reward flexibility. Instituting rewards and conditions which reinforce learning.
- Self-development opportunities for all. Resources and facilities for learning are made available for all people in the organization. People are encouraged to exercise self-management of their own career development and learning.

The manufacturing of the cable involved seven sequential processes, each of which was carried out in its own "area." Each area used its own employees, skills, and machinery. The staff of each area would in turn be allocated to specific subtasks, activities, and machines. A cumbersome set of wage scales—more than 30 in all—covered the variety of subtasks, so that even in one area the employees specialized in a limited range of tasks and were paid on a corresponding scale.

Of course, this was a major hindrance to job flexibility, even within a relatively restricted production area, let alone across the plant as a whole. Therefore, one major change was the move to a single, unified wage scale that covered all production employees across all processes and areas. This single-status environment took six months to negotiate. The necessity for job redundancies made this negotiation all the more difficult. Part of this negotiation led to what was termed a "people contract." The contract included the following.

The employer agrees to:
- state expectations and set standards
- comply with legislation
- encourage employees to take the initiative
- provide reasonable facilities
- listen to employees' views and opinions and provide feedback
- increase job-related skills and knowledge and provide further education opportunities
- work with trade unions for the good of the business.

The employees agree to:
- operate the required quality system and standards
- attend work regularly and punctually
- keep their own work areas clean
- participate in problem solving
- provide training to colleagues
- be flexible
- recognize the need to improve productivity continually.

The employer and employees agree to:
- improve quality, increase productivity, review practices regularly, and respond positively and rapidly to uncertainty.

Although the actual manufacturing plant was reasonably modern and in good working order, the general environmental conditions were poor. The site was over 100 years old, in a fairly depressed area of a Northern manufacturing city. Considerable cleaning up and refurbishment was carried out, including the provision of a team room in

Figure 3. Old manufacturing structure.

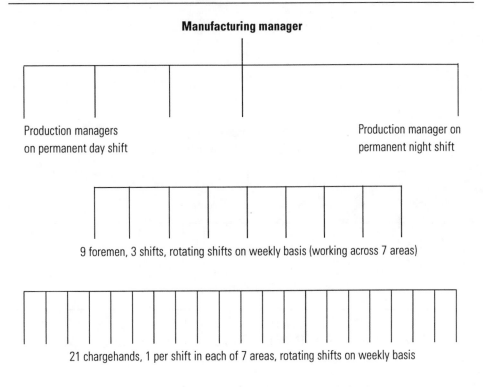

Manufacturing manager

Production managers
on permanent day shift

Production manager on
permanent night shift

9 foremen, 3 shifts, rotating shifts on weekly basis (working across 7 areas)

21 chargehands, 1 per shift in each of 7 areas, rotating shifts on weekly basis

each of the manufacturing areas (to be used for breaks, meetings, and information display) and new information technology production control equipment.

The other major change was the introduction of a new manufacturing structure. In the past the structure looked roughly as in Figure 3, where it is clear that there was no vertical linkage. For example, the daytime production managers worked quite different hours (9 a.m.–5 p.m.) than the supervisors on shifts A and B (6 a.m.–2 p.m.; 2 p.m.–10 p.m.). Because the supervisors rotated shifts on a weekly basis, there was no continuity in their contact with the production managers. Perhaps even worse, there was no horizontal integration until the manufacturing manager level (except at night, when everybody reported to one particular production manager).

The new structure, designed to facilitate both vertical and horizontal integration, is shown in Figure 4. In addition, there were three teams working day shift only; stores, dispatch and engineering mainte-

Figure 4. New manufacturing structure.

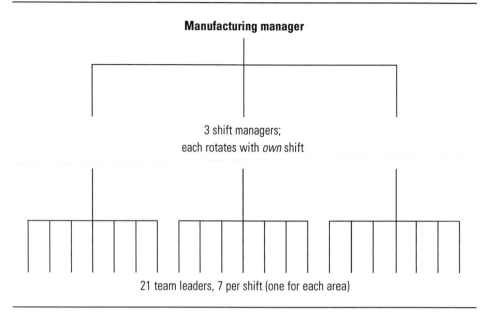

Manufacturing manager

3 shift managers;
each rotates with *own* shift

21 team leaders, 7 per shift (one for each area)

nance (later, stores and dispatch were combined, and engineering maintenance went to a three-shift system).

Phase Three: Introducing Teamworking in Manufacturing

Steps in Phase Three are as follows:
- recruitment and selection of shift managers and team leaders
- off-site training and on-the-job development of team leaders and their teams
- intercompany learning
- improved information system.

Three shift managers were recruited. One had been the permanent night production manager; the other two were external appointments, neither of whom had worked in this industry before. Employees from throughout the plant were encouraged to apply for the post of team leader—of which there were 23 in all (seven areas, three shifts; plus stores and dispatch). As a result, not only did most existing foremen and some chargehands apply, but also others who until now had been direct production workers. Applicants were assessed by a combination of tests, groupwork, and individual interviews. The first round of recruitment led to the appointment of 18 team leaders, so a second round was necessary to bring the number up to the required 23.

Training of the team leaders started with a two-day off-site workshop. Although some of this training involved well-known "artificial" exercises, the main emphasis was on looking at real concerns, issues, and opportunities.

At the first workshop, for example, topics covered included:

- how "teamworking" is at the plant now
- how we would like it to be in the future
- our hopes and fears about the outcomes of the change to teamworking
- what we want senior management to know.

These last two topics were followed by a dialogue with the works and manufacturing managers.

There followed a difficult period when, for various reasons (including last-minute representations from the unions) the actual start of teamworking was delayed for three months. During this time the consultants spent time with "their" team leaders, giving some further training in areas such as listening, briefing, questioning, and running meetings. At the same time, the shift consultants focused on handling feelings of disillusionment that were creeping in as a result of the delay.

After three months, the teamworking system got under way. Every two weeks, one production area initiated teamworking. On the Friday and Saturday before an area formally switched to teamworking, three shift managers and three team leaders, together with most of the teamworkers (a total of 25 to 75 people) went away for some introductory training. We say "most" of the teamworkers because a few (around 10 percent) were unwilling or unable to attend. Although all workers were encouraged verbally and practically (e.g., by arranging transportation) to attend, the training was not compulsory. The training consisted of 25 percent theory (albeit handled in an active way through exercises) and 75 percent real concerns, covering

- issues in an area, within a shift team
- issues in an area, between shift teams
- issues between areas
- issues with senior management.

We used ideas from Roger Harrison's *Role Negotiation*, namely:

- things you (i.e., other team members, other shift teams, other areas, senior management) do that we find helpful; please continue
- things you do that we find unhelpful; please stop
- things you don't do that we would find helpful; please start.

Because 90 percent of the people involved were present, it was possible to initiate dialogue there and then on issues within a team, and between shift teams in the same area. This also applied to issues with senior management, as the works and manufacturing managers attended part of each workshop.

The workshops also provided a good opportunity for the three shift managers to meet, which until then had not happened. (After the seven workshops were over, the shift managers continued to meet every two weeks.) Participants worked on ways to meet with members from other manufacturing areas who were not at the workshop. They also instituted regular meetings with the works manager.

All of these events—the off-site initial workshops and subsequent meetings—called for well-thought-out planning, due to the shift-working system. Team leaders and members made these arrangements themselves. Once the initial wave of workshops was completed, each consultant spent one shift per week with his or her shift (following the normal pattern). During this time, they worked with teams and team leaders to facilitate the resolution of issues, to create opportunities, and to give further direct training to the team leaders. Leaders and some team members were encouraged to visit other companies in which teamworking had been established.

Some of the issues, training competencies, and visible outcomes are shown in Table 2.

Teams were given more authority and autonomy—senior management was very "permissive." Not only were teams encouraged—indeed required—to sort out their own working processes, but they also were given their own budgets and considerable technical and commercial information (e.g., on output, financial performance, and upcoming orders) that in the past had been withheld.

Phase Four: Maintaining the Learning Environment

Phase Three got basic team training and ongoing support well under way. Gradually a number of further initiatives were introduced, including the following:
- establishment of a personal development program (for more basic personal skills, including some literary/mathematical training, foreign languages, and so on)
- creation of an open learning facility on site
- further developments of team leader and team member training, based on a process of self-assessment
- integration of production and maintenance (technical) skills training with nationally recognized occupational qualifications (National Vocational Qualifications)

- establishment of a training and development pro[...] support functions
- launch of a process improvement initiative
- commitment to receive a national award ("Investors in[...]

Summary

Table 1 shows the systemic nature of the transition to [...] organization. Each of the 11 characteristics were addressed, not necessarily in sequence. Rather, certain decisions about [...]gy were made, and other areas were dealt with as the need arose.

The outcomes were excellent, and included the following:
- Employee productivity increased by 113 percent.
- Scrap was reduced by 50 percent.

Table 2. Issues, training competencies, and visible outcomes.

	Issues	Teamworking competencies	Visible changes in BICC
Stage 0 **Getting ready**	Preparation for new teamworking initiative, taking into account previous experiences, attitudes and opinions of actual and potential team members	Briefing, listening, questioning, allaying fears Obtaining resources Networking Recruiting	Focusing on the business imperative (in this case survival of the plant) New salary system—single status agreement Team leaders selected and appointed
Stage 1 **Getting started**	Launching the team; dealing with basic issues, getting down to what is essential and necessary to start working together; identifying areas of concern that are to be dealt with at Stage 2	Listening, questioning, discussing Instructing, making specifications, setting targets, clarifying operational definitions Running meetings—team meetings, briefings	Concerns and fears as well as hopes and expectations about teamworking freely expressed Open discussion and building a picture of what teamworking will be like (no standard blueprint); then an enthusiastic lunch

ınued). Issues, training competencies, and visible outcomes.

	Issues	Teamworking competencies	Visible changes in BICC
Stage 2 Getting going	Sorting out issues, roles and relationships sufficiently to be able to get the task completed	Using investigative procedures, causal analysis Team decision making processes Assertiveness, raising issues, making presentations, presenting cases, handling disagreements	Basic procedures established for operational arrangements, e.g., shift handovers Ground rules drawn up for teamworking Information supplied to teams on scheduling, targets, etc. Team allowed to make arrangements for machine allocation, etc. Increased flexibility Team meetings held on a regular basis—action taken on points raised
Stage 3 Getting results	Becoming effective and efficient, working well as a task-oriented, businesslike unit Becoming ambitious enough to look for areas of improvement Formulating and implementing improvement plans	Performance improvement methods Running special project meetings, e.g., Q.I.T.s Setting and working to performance targets	Priority areas for improvement identified by team members Quality improvement projects initiated Outcomes measured and results recorded and disseminated

Table 2 (continued). Issues, training competencies, and visible outcomes.

	Issues	Teamworking competencies	Visible changes in BICC
Stage 4 **Getting together**	Learning to cooperate and collaborate—requiring that any residual relationship issues be addressed and difficulties worked through	Giving and receiving feedback (positive and negative) Influencing skills Supporting, challenging Handling people with different temperaments	Team members assisting each other, standing in, cooperating without being directed Decisions made more quickly Better decisions made (emphasis on implementation) Team leaders and members take up issue directly with senior management
Stage 5 **Getting through**	Team is working creatively, generating new solutions, trying new methods Team members help each other to become more imaginative and creative	Delegation, mandating procedures for team decision making Positivity Learning to learn, reviewing, monitoring, evaluating	Suggestions for new ways of working, new roles and moves toward self-managed teamworking structure Teams run their meetings, take action, keep records and supply information
Stage X **Getting along** **with others**	Developing better working relationships with customers, suppliers and other teams, internally and externally Cross-functional working	Customer mapping Role negotiation Bargaining	Intershift and production meetings held; actions followed through Customer mapping/supplier mapping leads to improved relationships

- Absenteeism fell by 58 percent.
- The U.K. market share went up from 17 percent to 40 percent (BICC remained as one of the two suppliers to BT).
- Several new export contracts were awarded.

- On-time deliveries were the highest ever (98 percent).
- Loss of more than $1 million was reversed to a profit of more than $1 million.
- More than 30 jobs were saved.

No one intervention, change, or characteristic led to these outcomes. They were the result of the whole system of changes summarized by the 11 characteristics. By working on these changes simultaneously, members of the company could apply their existing knowledge and learn not only about how to make copper cable, but also about how to work together.

Questions for Discussion

1. "From a development point of view, BICC Manchester had the great good fortune to be faced with a shrinking market, strengthening competition, and falling prices." Discuss this suggestion and its relevance to the development of other organizations with which you are familiar.
2. Which of the various interventions at BICC was the most critical? Why?
3. How does the eleven characteristics model of a learning organization compare with others with which you are familiar?
4. How would you find out which of the eleven characteristics is currently most urgently in need of strengthening in your own organization?

The Author

Tom Boydell obtained a degree in engineering before he worked in Guyana with Voluntary Service Overseas, where he became interested in learning and development within organizations. He subsequently obtained postgraduate qualifications, including a Ph.D. in management learning. Tom worked for 20 years as principal lecturer at Sheffield Hallam University, where he was responsible for postgraduate programs in human resource management and organization development and learning. In 1989, together with Mike Pedler and John Burgoyne, Tom established The Learning Company Project with the purpose of carrying out research, writing, and dissemination of ideas about learning organizations. Since then the LCP has also moved into developing research-based products (such as instruments, software, and learning devices) and collaborative consortium-based projects, and as well as the three founding partners it now involves a number of associates. Original research (1988) was followed by *The Learning Company* (Pedler, Burgoyne, and Boydell, McGraw-Hill, 1991; 2d edition, 1996), which appeared in the U.K. roughly at the same time as Peter Senge's *The Fifth Discipline*

(1990). As well as being a partner in the Learning Company Project, Tom runs his own consultancy practice and is a director of Transform IODC Ltd. He has clients throughout Europe, as well as in the United States, Canada, Africa, and the Middle East. He is author or coauthor of more than 35 books on various aspects of self-development and management and organizational learning. He can be contacted at the following address: The Learning Company Project, 28 Woodholm Road, Sheffield S11 9HT U.K.

References

Boydell, T. (1994). *The eleven characteristics: Questionnaire, case paper No. 1: Basic data from 10 organizations.* Sheffield, U.K.: Learning Company Project.

Harrison, R. (1972). Role negotiation: A tough-minded approach to team development. In W. Burke and H. Hornstein (Eds.), *The social psychology of organization development.* La Jolla, CA: University Associates.

Learning Company Project. (1993). *Eleven characteristics questionnaire.* Sheffield, U.K.: Learning Company Project.

Pedler, M., Burgoyne, J., and Boydell, T. (1991). *The learning company: A strategy for sustainable development.* Maidenhead: McGraw-Hill.

The Learning Organization: Awakening a Small Family Business

Morrison Communications

Mary F. Ziegler

The owners of a small family publishing business involved themselves and their company in personal and organizational renewal that awakened them to new visions and possibilities. This case shows that learning is not linear and predictable, but rather a generative process characterized at times by uncertainty and a willingness to explore.

Morrison Communications

Before embarking on their plan to become a learning organization, Morrison Enterprises, as it was formerly called, was a holding company consisting of two operating companies: Morrison Printing and School Calendar. Although the two companies operated separately, their futures became more intertwined as the company began its intensive self-examination process.

History and Background of Morrison Printing

Morrison Printing was started in 1944 when James Cecil Morrison Sr. bought a printing press and started printing tags for the Navy during World War II. Turning a hobby into a business, Morrison began a small, family-owned commercial printing company in East Tennessee. The company developed a loyal base of customers who placed orders for custom printed documents.

Morrison's two sons were exposed to the company from their early youth and began working part-time for their father in the late 1950s

This case was prepared to serve as a basis for discussion rather than to illustrate either effective or ineffective administrative and management practices.

and early 1960s. By age 16, the boys had worked in most of the depart-ments in the company. One of them recalls:

> My father took us throughout different departments in the plant and had us learn. I operated machines, worked in estimating, the art department, the bindery. When I was in high school, I remember melting lead to make type and pouring it into the molds on the weekends. That was good, I guess. Nobody could come up to you and say you couldn't do something.

Like many other children of parents who owned small businesses then, the Morrison sons went to work in their father's company directly after high school. As one of them says, "I didn't go to college and felt like it would have been foolish for me to do anything else...I felt like this [working at Morrison Printing] is what I was supposed to do." Eventually both sons became managers in the printing business. Richard Morrison, the older son, succeeded his father as president of Morrison Printing in 1976. Jadie Morrison, the younger son, became the director of sales for the company.

Morrison Printing, with 24 employees, had a sales volume of $1 million in 1974. In 1994, the company employed 150 people and had a sales volume of more than $12 million. It had evolved from a small, personal family business to what the present owners consider to be a large, complex commercial printing enterprise. Products produced by the company consist primarily of printed materials for the recreational and tourist industries.

History and Background of School Calendar

In the mid-1960s, business founder James C. Morrison took a pho-tograph of his daughter Maudie's marching band and printed it as a poster. He raised donations for the band by selling advertising on the poster. This event spawned what is today a multimillion dollar indus-try—raising money for extracurricular activities in schools by selling advertising space on calendars. In 1968 Maudie, after only a year of col-lege, took a leadership role in School Calendar, a new, separate compa-ny housed in the same building as Morrison Printing. Maudie says that her father told her to "make a million dollars." She enthusiastically de-scribed the early days of School Calendar:

> I started this company when there was just me. And as the company grew in its infant stages, everybody was constantly making changes in the way they did things because there were no written rules. The jobs weren't described.

In other words, the vision was all you had. So in the beginning, that is the way it was. There was constant change and improvement and people's jobs didn't have boxes that they were in. There were no limitations on what you could tackle if you thought it would improve the company's opportunity to do the vision. The vision wasn't written and there was no book written on how you do school calendars. We pioneered the industry. So it was just everybody running around trying to figure out how to do a million dollars worth of ads on calendars.

School Calendar employs more than 60 people on-site. Another 70 independent contractors, located all over the country, are sales representatives who present school activity groups with the idea of creating a calendar as a fund-raiser. Once a school group agrees to sponsor a calendar, the sales representative then sells local advertising on the calendar. The home office completes the artwork, and Morrison Printing prints the calendar. School Calendar also has grown tremendously over the last 20 years. Its present annual sales volume is approximately $6 million.

Both organizational cultures have changed since the inception of the two companies. The Morrison siblings described their father, the companies' founder, as a benevolent patriarch. Employees relied on the elder Morrison for answers to questions and solutions to problems. Richard Morrison said, "Morrison Printing was a true family business. Dad was in charge then....There was no question when you were presented with a situation, you knew just what the company needed to have done." The siblings also characterized that earlier time as less ambiguous and uncertain, with fewer demands for change than at present. In 1982, James Morrison transferred stock equally to his three children—Richard, Maudie, and Jadie—who are currently the sole owners of the business. At that time, a holding company called Morrison Enterprises was formed; it is an administrative entity that houses the two operating companies. At the beginning of the change initiative, the companies operated autonomously with separate workforces, though they shared a human resource department. Before the change initiative began, formal education and training programs were minimal. As with most small businesses, financial constraints and time pressures made it difficult to release workers for training. Because there was no training department, training was the responsibility of the human resource manager. The human resource manager also handled employee concerns, benefits, government regulations, insurance programs, and employee events. Employees who did receive formal training—a course or a special training workshop—did so outside the company. On-the-job training has been, historically, the principal method for teaching new employees.

Events That Triggered the Decision to Change

Although the owners reported many reasons for wanting to change their company, several factors were prominent: 1) lagging profits, 2) loss of family feeling and increasing distance from their employees, 3) lack of workforce involvement, and 4) realization that everyone—not just the owners—was responsible for the future of the company.

Appeal of the Learning Organization

The owners reported that they learned about the learning organization and principle-centered leadership from consultants and from their own reading. The idea of the learning organization appealed to them as a process for overcoming their own and the company's difficulties. Four factors common in the literature about learning organizations appealed to them:

1. A common vision for the company shared by the owners and employees.
2. Empowerment of all employees at Morrison Printing beginning with the owners, managers, and supervisors.
3. Systems thinking—seeing the company, and in fact the two companies, as a whole.
4. Learning, especially learning how to become a different organization.

Despite many foreseen and unforeseen obstacles, the owners decided to begin changing the company by first looking at changing themselves. With the help of a consultant, the three owners met outside the company to examine the assumptions they had about owning the business, the theories they held about management, the principles and values on which the company was based, and their aspirations for the future. They knew they did not want to continue, and in fact could not risk continuing, on the same path they had traveled in the past. They wanted all the managers and supervisors in the company to make the same kinds of self- and company assessments they were making.

Thirty-five executive managers, managers, and supervisors from both companies assembled at the local country club for two seminars. Consultants presented information on such topics as the learning organization, principled leadership, creativity, quality, changing management theories, and global competition. During the seminar, the assembled group began to identify the stakeholders in the company, considered the company's vision and mission, and identified various processes that were in need of analysis and improvement.

Before and after the seminars, the most intensive learning was done by the seven members of the executive committee in their bi-weekly meetings. One meeting was specifically set aside for dialogue. In this meeting, the group examined its own working process, identified problems and their underlying assumptions about the nature of the problems, and reflected on the work they had done to see what could be learned from it. Some of these dialogue meetings were facilitated by the consultant and some were self-facilitated.

Cross-departmental teams were established to analyze particular work processes that had been identified during the seminars as critical. These "process" teams had a member of the executive committee, a process champion, follow their progress. For example, a critical process for Morrison Printing was paper inventory. The process team mapped the process, analyzed areas of difficulties, and recommended solutions. A critical process for School Calendar was communication; a team was formed to study the way communication flowed through the company. Detailed minutes of meetings show how the teams gathered information, discussed all aspects of a problem, and collaboratively decided on recommendations to be given to the executive committee. Small changes recommended by the teams had an immediate positive impact. In addition, individuals serving on teams had the most exposure to perspectives. Richard Morrison noted that the teams had many successes in spite of having selected the most complex processes to work on first. They learned that it might have been easier to develop the teams and learn team skills by tackling simpler processes. The consultant developed training programs for process teams. Several team members attended team training seminars outside the company.

The result of the various seminars, and the many discussions that followed, was the initial identification of what Senge (1990) calls "current reality." The identification of current reality, however, was not the result of a systematic analysis. Awareness grew slowly as the executive committee met to shape the upcoming change, as teams met to discuss work processes, and as managers reflected on their management style. Individuals began to discuss topics that were previously ignored, primarily because they had seemed insoluble. For example, how do you confront a loyal employee who has worked for the firm for many years, who has become a friend of the family, but who no longer has the level of skills needed to manage complicated technological changes in equipment and work processes? Or how do you tell an executive the truth, especially if the truth reveals a shortcoming? For an outsider, the answers to these examples might appear simple. For the owners, the solutions were wrapped in the legacy of family values inherited from their father.

Jadie Morrison said, "Relationships, that's all there is. The rest, well, the rest is easy by comparison." Owners and managers acknowledged the need to change relationships with one another and with the workforce. Changing relationships meant keeping what was valued from the past and using it as a foundation for the as-yet-unimagined and unknown future.

Becoming a Learning Organization

During the first year, only those at the managerial/supervisory level were involved in the change initiative. The owners' goals were for both operating companies in Morrison Enterprises to have a shared vision, an empowered and involved workforce, systems thinking or a "big picture" perspective, and continuous learning. The following factors indicate that the two companies were beginning to achieve their goals.

Owners' Commitment to Learning

It was obvious to an observer that the owners and executive managers were committed to their own learning. The owners and executive managers were reading—one book after another. One supervisor said he knew that the executive committee hated meetings, so if they were meeting this much, then what they were working on must be important. Another person, a long-time employee, said, "The owners have never been this committed to anything before." Because the owners appeared to be so committed to this change effort, others in the company took it very seriously. They made it clear that learning would be an essential part of the change process. The president of the company said that in some ways the company was backward. People were too content with the way things were, and even though profits were slipping, there was little motivation to be involved in thinking about the company's future. The owners' courage to change woke up the entire company.

Openness About Lack of Knowledge

A key to opening the door of learning for the owners themselves was their willingness to say publicly that they wanted to learn. This freed them from the expectation that they had all the answers. At first, a number of managers resisted this notion. They wondered, If the owners do not know where the company is going, then who does? As time passed, however, even these managers realized that it was through the act of suspending certainty that new possibilities surfaced. As company president Richard Morrison said, "Saying 'I don't know' can be a frightening prospect when you are responsible for the future of the company." Yet he explained that new demands on the businesses were increasing in complexity. The industry itself was changing at a dramatic rate. "Recently, more and more problems have ended up on my desk," the president said, waving his hand over stacks of paper. "It's impossible for me to solve them all. I need help." The other two owners expressed similar feelings. Their acceptance of the fact that they did not know what to do, while initially creating anxiety, eventually led them into a far different future than they could have imagined.

Widespread Understanding of Why Change Was Necessary

In the initial stages of becoming a learning organization, a shared vision is far less important than a shared understanding of why change is needed. Believing that change is required fuels learning more powerfully than a written vision statement created at the outset of an intentional change. As one manager said, "The mood of the marketplace has changed. The customers demand much more from us now than they did in the past. The efficiency, the speed—the turnaround time is much shorter than it used to be." Another said, "The sales are there; the volume is there; the percent of profit is not there." This awareness of the need for change helped align managers and supervisors in support of change, whether they liked the idea or not.

Identification of Current Assumptions

Management practices in a 50-year-old family firm did not develop over the years by design. In fact, the theories and assumptions underlying most practices had evolved piecemeal for generations, and were largely tacit and taken for granted. Before deciding on a vision for management, the owners wanted to examine the current management theory and practice at Morrison Enterprises. Theories and assumptions emerged as the executives continually asked themselves, "How did the company come to be this way?" A subtle yet enormously important shift occurred during this process. Current management practices were analyzed with the intention of understanding and naming them. Managers could decide whether the practices, once named, met the needs of the individuals involved and of the company as a whole. If not, the practices could be changed. One management trend identified by the executive committee was the inability of some managers to confront employees, especially long-time employees, who were performing inadequately. The committee realized that the assumption underlying this practice was a high regard for individuals who had worked many years for the firm even if their level of skill fell behind the demands of their jobs. There was a company norm not to hurt people's feelings. Another key awareness arose in an executive committee meeting when the group realized they put off making decisions when there was even slight disagreement. Once the executive committee raised common management practices to the surface, they could explore ways to change them.

Willingness to Establish New Relationships

A significant change at Morrison Enterprises occurred when managers reported they had learned to set a goal with individual employees, but were willing to permit the employees to select the means of achieving the goal. One manager described a situation in which he ordinarily would have made a decision and then told the employee what to do. Instead, both manager and employee discussed the situation to fully understand its meaning. The employee then decided what his next steps would be. A key task for the manager was to learn how to provide the necessary information to the employee so that the employee could make an informed decision. The manager said it had been very difficult to give up control, even when he and the employee had agreed on a goal.

Everybody Wins

Empowerment requires engagement in the struggle of finding the balance between what is good for individuals and what is good for the company as a whole. A team that crossed departments and levels studied the results of a survey of employee needs. Probes by the team explored the reasons why employees viewed their needs the way they did. The team made recommendations to the executive committee for changes in employee policy. One executive experimented with creating a win-win agreement between the company and all of its managers and employees as a way of translating theories of empowerment into practice. The agreement stated specifically which elements constituted a "win" for the company and which elements a "win" for the employee. Rather than job descriptions, a work description is being developed that includes work on the job, work on the business, work on yourself, and work with others.

Awareness of Connectedness

Because of the culture of autonomy at Morrison Printing, the individual departments had developed like grain silos, close together in proximity but completely isolated from one another. As the conviction spread that teamwork would help the companies survive, interest grew in the company as a whole. Morrison Enterprises formed committees and teams from different departments and from different levels. This was the first time most team members crossed over the boundary of their particular silos or departments to view a problem from a variety of perspectives. It was through team meetings, documented in team minutes, that individuals learned about the inner workings of the company.

Big Picture Perspective

The growing awareness that the enterprise was a system with interrelated subsystems caused a shift in thinking. A supervisor at School Calendar said, "I always wondered what happened to stuff after it left my area. But I never checked." Also, by understanding the production process as a system, the belief that only individuals are responsible for error was examined. Rather than blame one another or outside circumstances for problems, focus shifted to a realization that it is poorly designed systems, not incompetent or unmotivated individuals, that cause most organizational problems. Systems thinking presumes that the system must be optimized for individuals to do their best work. This notion appealed to many at School Calendar. Now, when a person makes a mistake, it has become commonplace to ask if there might be a system problem. Teams mapped work areas to illustrate how jobs were interconnected. Work flow to other departments was also reviewed.

Lessons About Crafting a Learning Organization
It Doesn't Always Look Like Learning

Learning at Morrison Enterprises involved making meaning and challenging mental models. These activities looked like confusion, ambiguity, sorting out different ideas, and struggling to make connections between theories in books and the actual experiences in the plant. For example, the owners began changing their company before they fully understood what it meant for their company to be a different organization. Understanding evolved from discussion and reflection on their change process while they were engaged in it. Learning also took the form of identifying mental models. The owners frequently asked, "If this is what we are doing, what is the underlying theory or model that drives our action?" The answer emerged slowly as tacit beliefs were raised to the surface—beliefs as common as the way paper was stored, the length of time underused machinery was kept, or the way products were marketed. A manager illustrated this point when he said, "Every day you walk by this picture of a tree. Then something happens and one day you see a flower at the bottom of the tree. You looked at that picture of the tree every day, but you never saw the flower before."

Learning How

Learning how was especially important at Morrison Enterprises. Developing interpersonal, cognitive, and technical skills furnished the tools needed to engage in generative types of learning activities. For example, knowing how to map a work process was a skill that allowed assumptions to surface and be challenged. Training programs that helped individuals build practical skills were supportive of generative learning. Practical skills included such activities as creating flowcharts, identifying variances, facilitating meetings, and giving feedback.

Meaningful Work

The most effective learning occurs in the process of doing real work that is meaningful. Many managers reported that their perceptions shifted as they worked with other individuals from different departments or from the other operating company to identify and solve company problems. A team was formed to examine ways to improve paper inventory, a long-standing area of concern. Learning occurred in the context of meaningful work, as representatives from different departments discussed their needs and contributed their perspectives to the problem solving. Paper storage, a long-time problem, was completely reorganized to better fit with the work processes. What was learned was not necessarily noticeable as it occurred. It was identified afterward through reflection.

The Gap Between Belief and Behavior

A gap exists between changing beliefs and attitudes and changing behavior. This fact may be evident to most people as they learn in their daily lives. Nevertheless, it often causes pain and frustration in organizational settings. It is possible to be exposed to new ideas, to enthusiastically adopt new ideas, and still to be unable to apply those ideas consistently in practice. Very little is known about this key step of the learning process and the way to bridge theory and action. Jadie Morrison explained the difficulty:

> You are rolling this [new] knowledge through your head when somebody asks you a question. You want to go through your top ten theories and principles and react from one of those. But you don't. You just react. And your reaction is diametrically opposed to the new theories and things you really

believe. Somewhere in there, the connection is not automatic. You have to throw the switch to make it connect and sometimes you cannot get the switch thrown in time. You just do what you did before and you don't even know it until you stop to think about it.

Experiencing the gap was common at Morrison Enterprises. Those who had adopted new beliefs, but found it difficult to put them into practice, became very frustrated with themselves and with the learning process.

Old and New Exist Side by Side

Organizations do not change instantly. Change is developmental and occurs along a continuum. When new thinking occurs, old thinking does not necessarily cease to exist. In one situation, it may be possible to think and act according to a new belief, while in another situation, the new belief may not emerge at all. In the midst of a learning process, inconsistency is common. Jadie Morrison said, "It's like a dual system. People will be listening to you and you will feel pretty good about it. Then you will turn around and run into a 30-year-old situation where you feel like a pawn in some game."

Based on Morrison's experience, stress often caused old behaviors to surface and push new ones aside. For instance, several managers talked about their desire to really listen to their employees. Yet they said it was not uncommon for them to be attentive on one occasion and, on another, appear not to be listening at all.

Everyone Must Be Involved

Creating a learning organization in a family firm in which the family actively participates would be very difficult without the willingness of the family members to engage in their own learning and self-examination. Their commitment to learning must be visible to others in the organization. Beyond owner commitment is the involvement of as many organizational members as possible in the change effort, especially in areas that affect their jobs or work life.

Revisiting Morrison Enterprises

Two years after the change initiative began, Morrison Enterprises is still learning and changing. The two companies, Morrison Printing and School Calendar, have merged to become Morrison Communications. Maudie is president. Richard is secretary/treasurer of the corporation, and Jadie is a senior vice-president. Many managers have changed jobs completely. The physical premises already looks like a single company. Richard Morrison recently commented that the teams come and go so fast that it is hard to keep up with how many are operating at any one time. He also said they are continuing to change, but now it is a norm rather than a rare occurrence.

Questions for Discussion

1. In what ways does being a family business influence becoming a learning organization?
2. What strategies and practices are most effective for dealing with the ambiguity and confusion of the learning process when it is necessary to simultaneously maintain productivity and efficiency?
3. What does it take to fill the gap that people often experience between the adoption of new ideas and the ability to apply those ideas consistently in practice?

The Author

Mary F. Ziegler is associate director and researcher at the Center for Literacy Studies at the University of Tennessee. Her work focuses on public sector efforts for statewide systemic change through collaboration and technology. Mary has done extensive research in organizational learning. She is a founding partner of InterConnect, a consulting firm specializing in organizational learning and development. With a colleague she developed the research-based *Organizational Learning System Analysis*, a comprehensive organizational assessment process for planning and development. She has also developed and published a variety of resources for workforce learning and change. Mary has an Ed.D. from Teachers College, Columbia University. Her dissertation research focused on the learning organization and small business. She can be contacted at the following address: Center for Literacy Studies, Department of Education, 600 Henley Street, Suite 312, Knoxville, TN 37996-4135.

References

Senge, P. (1990). *The fifth discipline: The art and practice of the learning organization.* New York: Random House.

The Journey Toward Becoming a Learning Organization: Are We Almost There?

Land O'Lakes

Mike Driscoll and Hallie Preskill

The executive management group of a farm supply and dairy processing company commissioned a cross-functional task force to reevaluate the company's approach to training in the wake of TQM initiatives. Both groups discovered learning as a strategy for quality transformation. This case describes initiatives taken to implement a learning system model that targeted individuals, teams, leaders, and the organization.

The Company

Land O'Lakes is a farm supply and dairy processing company. Founded almost 75 years ago by a small group of farmers who joined together to market their dairy products, the company has grown to approximately 6,000 employees and close to $3 billion in sales. The company has three main divisions: one manufactures and distributes products used by farmers in crop and livestock production; one procures milk from farmers and processes it into fluid milk, cheese, and spreads (such as butter and margarine); and one (Country Lake Foods) processes and markets fluid milk. Land O'Lakes has developed a strong reputation in the marketplace for its quality products. Most notable is Land O'Lakes butter, a premium product marketed throughout the United States. The company's reputation for animal feed products is equally strong, but agricultural products are marketed primarily in the upper Midwest.

This case was prepared to serve as a basis for discussion rather than to illustrate either effective or ineffective administrative and management practices.

The company is organized functionally. The agricultural and the dairy divisions report to an executive vice-president, who reports to the president. Country Lake Foods and the staff functions (human resources, finance, legal, member relations, and research and technology) also report to the president. This group constitutes the executive steering team, which serves as a coordinator and decision maker on issues that affect the entire company. It provides input to the president regarding the company's strategic direction and governance issues.

The line units are largely autonomous and make their own decisions regarding day-to-day operations. Over the last five years, the company has become decentralized—the line units have developed their own human resources, accounting, and information systems functions, although they still rely on the corporate staff for some assistance. With decentralization has come the tendency for each unit to customize most of its work. Consequently, there is very little uniformity in any of the systems or programs, and very little collaboration in the exchange of information.

Before the Journey Began

Growth during the past several years has been achieved largely through acquisitions, joint ventures, and line extensions. Like many companies, Land O'Lakes has experienced significant pressure to increase its profitability. In response, the company has reduced cost by implementing better inventory management, improving technology, and reducing the workforce. Workforce reductions, one in 1987 and one in 1992, were very painful experiences that adversely affected employee morale.

To measure morale, the company conducted an employee survey in 1989. The results indicated that supervisors were not doing many of the things that employees thought they should do. In particular, employees believed they were not receiving effective feedback about their performance. Not only were supervisors not advising employees on their career opportunities, but the employees also felt that important information about the company was not being communicated. In defense of the supervisors, we note that they were not required to attend training in supervisory skills and abilities. In the survey, employees were critical of the company for not ensuring that supervisors were given adequate training. After several months of study by a cross-functional committee, a mandatory core curriculum was instituted for all employees. There was one set of core courses for supervisory employees (nine courses ranging from a half-day to four days in length, to be completed in a 36-month period) and another set for nonsupervisors (six courses to be completed in 36 months). In introducing the program, the president of Land O'Lakes, Jack Gherty, strongly stated his support and stressed how important it is for employees to keep their skills current.

As can be imagined, there was a great deal of negative reaction to this program. While for several years the company had been offering a variety of supervisory and nonsupervisory training courses, they had never been required. In the Land O'Lakes vocabulary, "mandatory" and "required" were not used often. Many people objected to mandatory attendance, and many complained about what they considered an unrealistic commitment to training time that would interfere with "getting the work done." In Land O'Lakes culture, it was clear that learning was not considered a critical part of the job. Because of the downsizing that had occurred and the pressure on profitability, the focus was on efficiency and cost reduction. Training was viewed as a distraction that took people away from their jobs.

Starting the Journey

At the same time that the core curriculum was being instituted, Land O'Lakes' most financially successful division (animal feed) embarked on an effort to introduce total quality concepts into their operations. This initiative began when the division management recognized that much of the market growth potential had been realized. Because continued growth in profitability would have to come from more efficient operations, total quality seemed like a logical approach. The division hired an outside consultant to train employees in the fundamentals of total quality management (TQM). The effort was launched through a series of seminars that included statistical process control and teamwork. Teams were formed, and process improvement projects were started. As word got around about the quality program in the feed division, other parts of the company began to investigate the potential of the quality process, and several groups began their own efforts to implement total quality management. Some of the efforts were self-directed—led by an enthusiastic individual or group who wanted to make a change. In other efforts, outside consultants were brought in to help make the transition to TQM. Approximately half of the organization was involved in quality transformation. For a year there was a great deal of training; new visions and missions were established and process improvement teams were initiated. Some of the more enthusiastic advocates of TQM began to promote a more coordinated, companywide effort. This larger effort would be necessary, they claimed, if the company were to make a total transformation.

The executive management group, recognizing the need to increase its own knowledge about TQM, began to study the concept with the help of an external consultant. They soon realized the importance of involving the whole company in TQM. Shortly thereafter, Jack Gherty announced in a letter to all employees that the entire organization would indeed be involved in TQM. This decision meant not so much that all the groups in the company would be involved in total quality, but that the "public" commitment to TQM would cause systems and behaviors inconsistent with quality principles to be considered for redesign or exclusion. This raised expectations that everyone in the organization would learn and apply the principles and tools of TQM. One of the first targets for reform was the company's approach to training. The core curriculum was no longer perceived as viable because most of it was built around improving individual performance. The concepts of "team" and "empowerment" embedded in TQM did not fit with this curriculum. Also, the quality training was out of control—with so many groups bringing in consultants or doing their own training, there was no consistency in what was being taught. Each group was developing its own language, and the delivery of TQM training was too expensive. More significant, walls were being built between groups as each conducted its own change effort.

The executive management group recognized the need to reevaluate the company's approach to training. They commissioned an eight-person, cross-functional task force to evaluate the current system and to make recommendations as to how to proceed. The task force was composed of individuals from major business units who were involved in the implementation of TQM and the individual who headed up the company's employee development function. Two vice-presidents from the executive management group—the vice-president of human resources and the chief financial officer—volunteered to serve on the task force.

After an evaluation based on examination of the core courses, study of future needs, and feedback from individuals who were involved in facilitating learning in the groups, the task force came to three conclusions. First, the mandatory core curriculum was not as applicable in 1993 as it had been in 1990. Some of the courses were meaningful, many were not. Second, there was duplication of effort in the training that could have been avoided if people had been willing to work together. Although each group was at a different level in its implementation of total quality and each had many different needs, the task force felt there were some universal needs that could be satisfied collaboratively. Third, the company had developed an overreliance on training as a learning method. When the need for a new skill, knowledge, or change in behavior was identified, individuals would look for a workshop or seminar to attend as their first course of action. They were overlooking many other learning methods, such as small discussion groups, individual research, and sharing articles and ideas.

While the task force was doing its evaluation, members of the executive management group continued to work with their consultant on their own learning. Coincidentally, about the time the task force was completing its evaluation, the management group was learning of how Peter Senge (1990) outlined the five disciplines of a learning organization. The executive group was impressed by the film and the possibility that learning could be a strategic advantage. They also saw learning as a strategy for advancing the quality transformation. They decided that Land O'Lakes should become a learning organization. The task force was given the assignment to lead the effort. They accepted the assignment, and—with questions such as "How long does it take to become a learning organization?" and "How will we know when we have become a learning organization?"—the task force began to develop a new learning system.

Heading Down the Road

The task force began by describing what its members believed to be the most important attributes of a learning organization:
- Learning is considered a lifelong, continuous process.
- There is an environment in which people want to, know how to, and are encouraged to learn; corresponding systems are in place.
- Operating assumptions, theories, and facts on which decisions are made are critically examined.
- Learning is looked for in every situation.
- Appropriate talent is matched with appropriate tasks so that the organization and the individual collectively achieve their objectives.
- Learning is shared and applied for the improvement and success of the overall system.
- The improvement effort is continually evaluated to ensure that the acquisition and application of learning are progressing.

The task force also created a model that targets learning at four levels: individual, team, leader, and organizational (see Figure 1). It identified skills and knowledge required for each of those levels and established a curriculum of courses built around the skills identified in the model. The task force also recommended that each line and staff group develop a learning direction that would indicate that group's learning

Figure 1. Learning system.

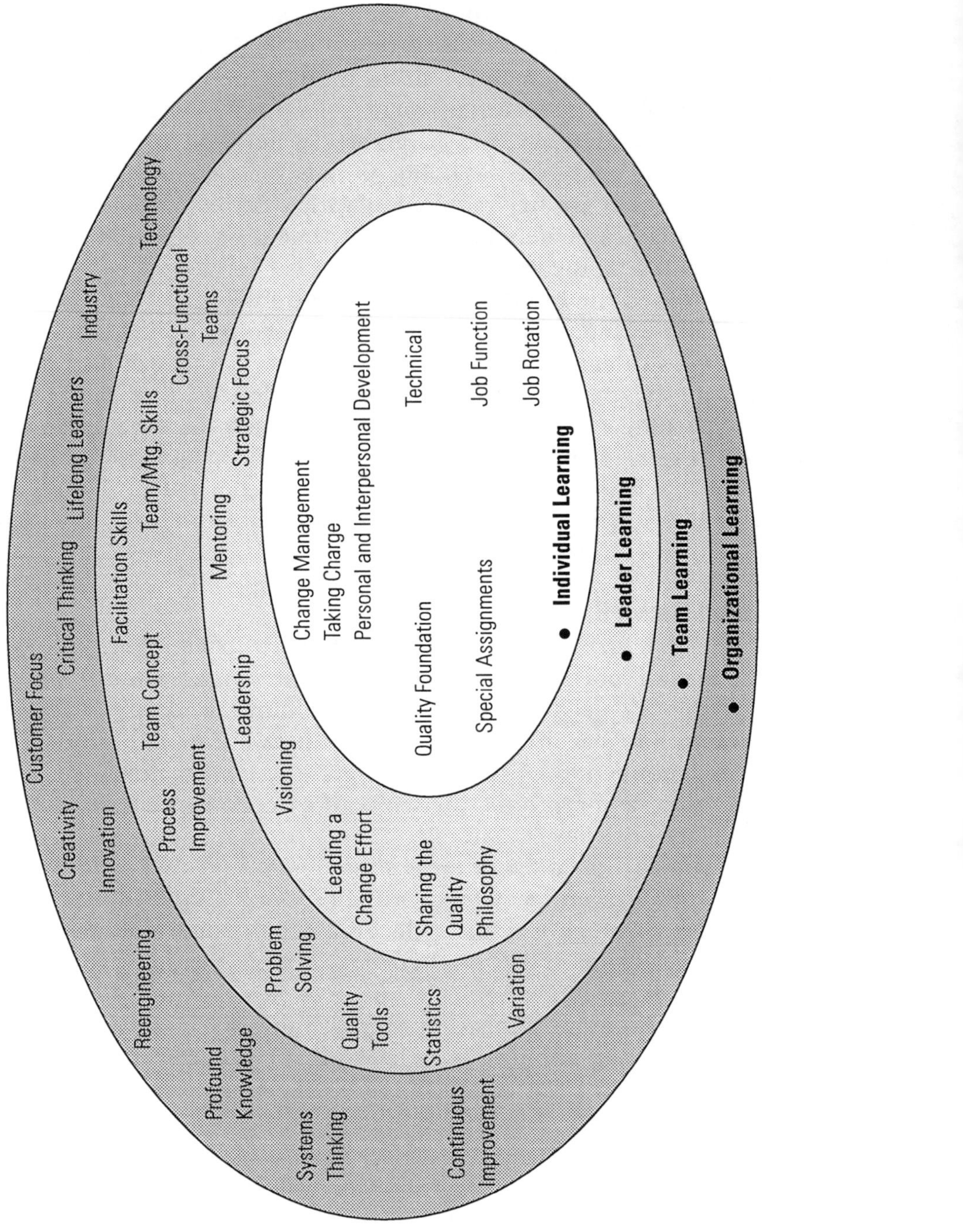

- Individual Learning
  - Change Management
  - Taking Charge
  - Personal and Interpersonal Development
  - Technical
  - Quality Foundation
  - Special Assignments
  - Job Function
  - Job Rotation
- Leader Learning
  - Visioning
  - Leading a Change Effort
  - Sharing the Quality Philosophy
  - Leadership
  - Mentoring
  - Strategic Focus
- Team Learning
  - Problem Solving
  - Quality Tools
  - Statistics
  - Variation
  - Process Improvement
  - Team Concept
  - Team/Mtg. Skills
  - Cross-Functional Teams
- Organizational Learning
  - Reengineering
  - Profound Knowledge
  - Systems Thinking
  - Continuous Improvement
  - Creativity
  - Innovation
  - Customer Focus
  - Critical Thinking
  - Lifelong Learners
  - Facilitation Skills
  - Industry
  - Technology

emphasis for the coming year. In addition, they recommended that each employee develop an individual learning plan congruent with his or her group's learning direction and his or her personal learning needs.

The executive group adopted the system the task force recommended, and in January 1994 Jack Gherty sent a letter to all employees announcing the elimination of the core curriculum and the adoption of the new learning system. In that letter he reemphasized the importance of continued learning: "Our effectiveness as an organization is dependent on our ability to change and respond successfully to the needs of our customers, and our ability to change is dependent on our ability to learn."

As part of the introduction of the new system, the task force made a presentation to the Land O'Lakes management staff at a meeting of the top 125 managers in the company. Most of the meeting was devoted to the task force, which outlined the characteristics of a learning organization and the direction of the courses and learning experiences being developed, explained the model and the concept of individual learning planning, and answered questions about the new system. The reaction was mixed. Some of the managers were enthusiastic and supportive; others reserved judgment. Some managers voiced concerns about this being the "in thing" or the "program of the day." That meeting had one very clear outcome, however: Every manager realized that learning at Land O'Lakes was now a high priority.

Making Some Headway

During 1994 most of the change effort was focused on individual and team learning. Four new courses were developed. Those courses included the philosophy of quality, quality tools and their application, work/life management, and conflict resolution. Some of the courses from the core curriculum are still available. They include courses on problem solving, decision making, and creativity.

Revising the Delivery

A major change has been made in the delivery of these courses, which used to be offered on a "public" basis—anyone from any group could attend. Now they are offered to intact work groups or teams that are working together. This allows the experience to be provided "just in time" using real-life, work-related problems. The outcome is more like a working session than a course. Some information can be obtained without going through the facilitator. For instance, information on quality tools and their application is available on company computers or videos. To facilitate the individual learning planning process, brown bag sessions were held to give employees ideas and suggestions. Specific care has been taken to ensure that the learning plan process is kept simple. Employees generally responded favorably, and a large number developed and implemented their plans.

Searching for Better Data

Another positive outcome is that people are putting their learning to use. There seems to be a greater demand for better data to help in decision making. For example, the feed division instituted a process of regularly surveying customers to learn how they can improve the products and services they provide. Although the feed division has a system in place to stay close to the customer, the current process focuses much more specifically on the customer evaluation of those products and services. It allows the customer to provide more targeted, and potentially more critical, feedback. Instead of feeling threatened by this information, the division embraces the opportunity to learn how it can improve.

Two of the staff units (research and technology, and information systems) have begun to investigate ways to change some of their human resource systems. The process they used began with the formation of cross-functional teams and with a significant effort to learn as much as they could about the principles of these systems and about what other companies have done before making any recommendations for change. In the past the teams would not have been cross-functional. They would have been from the same group, as a result of the prevailing belief that someone from outside the work group would not know enough about the business to make a contribution. These are two examples of the difference in procedures in these divisions as well as in the entire company. There is a definite change in the demand for and use of data from a wider variety of sources. Employees are beginning to recognize the value of information that comes from diverse points of view and experiences different from their own. Many times, they seek opinions from people whose perspectives are sure to be different from their own or who may tell them things that might be difficult to hear.

Learning on Their Own and Sharing With Others

One of the main thrusts of the task force has been to encourage employees to take responsibility for their own learning and to look for new ways to learn. There is evidence that this is happening. A book club was formed in which employees gather to discuss books about quality, process improvement, and learning to learn. One division has been particularly active in promoting brown bag lunches where films are shown or employees make presentations on topics related to quality or organizational learning. Frequently, the information that employees share comes from studies they have done on their own. More and more employees whose primary jobs do not directly involve the facilitation of learning are sharing their knowledge and expertise with others in the company. For instance, one person from the information systems division who recently received a master's degree in business administration makes frequent presentations on the research she has conducted regarding teamwork. A vice-president who is particularly knowledgeable about interpersonal relations and small-group processes shares his knowledge with beginning work teams so that they can get started on the right foot. Employees who are accountants, systems developers, and research and development technicians have been used as instructors and facilitators for several of the company learning experiences.

Sharing Across Division Lines

Another significant example of organizational learning occurred when the management staff of the agriculture division— at the urging of the executive vice-president—held a critical reflection session to discuss an acquisition that had been completed 18 months earlier. Those who participated in the acquisition retraced the process from start to finish, highlighting assumptions made prior to the acquisition, how those assumptions played out, things that went well and did not go well, what they could have done differently, and what had been learned. They shared this information with their peers in the division and with the management of the dairy division. This was the first time that learning of this nature was shared across divisional lines.

This same management group decided to meet together to work through a series of case studies involving companies that have made significant decisions regarding strategic direction. The group is faced with some important strategic directional situations, and its members hope to advance their own learning by using the cases.

Potholes in the Road

Not everything has gone smoothly. There were several tacit assumptions within the new system. One was that a great deal of individual learning and team learning would be translated into organizational learning. Initially it was thought that individual learning would eventually bring about change in the organization. Although there is a lot of change going on in many of the groups and there are some definite changes in how things get done, progress seems slow. Most of the change that is occurring is of an adaptive nature—change as a result of improving an existing way of operating rather than of rethinking assumptions and searching for totally new concepts. New mental models still need to be built.

The second assumption was that "unlearning" would not be a problem. It was assumed that once the use and value of new concepts and ideas were demonstrated, people would implement them. The difficulty of changing entrenched behaviors that have been rewarded for a number of years was underestimated. For example, despite learning experiences in which TQM tools were used in meetings, many meetings continue to be conducted in the same old ways. Despite the emphasis on the need to gather data to make decisions, many decisions continue to be made on the basis of opinion.

Another limitation to learning has been the ever-increasing pressure of competition and the bottom line. The continuous pressure to grow and to improve the bottom line detracts from the pursuit of learning opportunities. It has been difficult at all levels of the organization to make the trade-off in time and effort to learn new skills and tools (which in the long run may make competing easier). Although the people in the company are making progress, many still see the learning efforts not as a good investment, but as an imprudent use of time and money.

Looking in the Rearview Mirror

During the 18 months that Land O'Lakes has been working toward becoming a learning organization, its employees have learned a great deal. They have learned the value of building the infrastructure and of having an effective evaluation process. They also have begun to recognize the importance of generative learning as well as the need to include middle managers in this change effort.

Infrastructure

First, any good system needs the proper infrastructure. The infrastructure represents the tools, processes, resources, and mechanisms on which the system is built. At first, it is hard to recognize all the necessary parts of the infrastructure, but it is important to keep looking at it and building it. At Land O'Lakes, some pieces of the infrastructure were in place. There was a very supportive president and top management group, there were courses available, there were people available to help build the system and put it in place, and there was an executive group and task force to provide a mechanism for input and decision making. The company was fortunate to have had that much infrastructure at the start. What was not available was sufficient help in the form of internal consultants. In the beginning there were only two people who had the background and availability to provide internal consulting. Over the 18 months of working toward becoming a learning organization, Land O'Lakes found it necessary to increase that number to six. Some of those individuals still spend the bulk of their time focusing on their own work groups, but they are available to help provide training and learning experiences throughout the company and are in great demand.

Evaluation

A key process that was absent from the company's infrastructure was a system for evaluating its efforts to become a learning organization. Though data were collected to aid in decision making, the company has not developed a framework helpful in maximizing the usefulness of these data. In retrospect, the company should have built evaluation into the very definition of what it was trying to do. The question, "How will we know when we are there?" should have been the stimulus for building an evaluation process. What better evaluation question could have been chosen? If an evaluation system had been implemented from the start, the process would have enabled the company to develop additional questions and related measures to gauge its successes along the road. The information could have been used to modify and expand implementation efforts throughout the organization.

Had an evaluation process been developed, the company also would have been able to show top management the value of learning much earlier. This would have been especially useful to alleviate the pressure to prove the effects of becoming a learning organization on the bottom line. Whether or not this can actually be done quantitatively is questionable, yet without any data to show the anticipated and the unexpected results of its efforts, the company remains vulnerable to naysayers and cost-cutting initiatives.

Building evaluation into the learning organization's infrastructure would have provided Land O'Lakes with a mechanism to document and make public the successes described in this case. As people in the organization learned of the positive effects of friends' and colleagues' learning, additional support for learning may have come more quickly and broadly. Word of mouth is one of the most powerful forms of communication.

As we look toward the future, we see the need for a greater role for evaluation. Instead of a supplement, it needs to be a catalyst for organizational learning. Evaluation provides the conceptual framework for asking questions about where we're going and how we get there, and facilitates the collection of useful data. We can then make informed decisions and share our learning with others in the company. In short, evaluation should be so interwoven into the process of organizational learning that it becomes invisible.

Organization Structure

In any change process, the organization structure is important. It either facilitates or hinders change. At Land O'Lakes the structure proved both advantageous and detrimental as the company made its journey toward change. The example mentioned earlier of sharing lessons across division lines occurred because the chief operating officer had both the agriculture and the dairy divisions reporting to him. He recognized the opportunity for and the value of sharing learning between divisions. That sort of information exchange did not take place when the divisions reported to different vice-presidents. There was little recognition of the value of information sharing because the divisions were considered to be vastly different.

Organization structure can create barriers as well. The members of the cross-functional task force are challenged with balancing the needs of their own division with the needs of the entire organization. They must carefully allocate their time between efforts of direct and immediate benefit to their respective divisions and task force efforts that benefit the entire company.

A similar conflict is created by the budgeting process, which is directly tied to the organization structure. The task force attempts to pay for the projects they create with equal funding from each division. Some task force members are not authorized to commit their division's money to the projects. This creates a situation that either stops the project or causes other divisions to pay more than their share. Fortunately, the task force at Land O'Lakes has not been prevented from moving ahead with projects. Its members have decided not to let things like structure and budgets keep them from doing what needs to be done. It is important throughout the journey to recognize both the opportunities and the potential limitations that can be created by the organization structure. Learning to use the structure advantageously or at least to keep it from presenting obstacles is an important lesson.

Adaptive Versus Generative Learning

Bringing about any change can be difficult. As was stated earlier, most of the change experienced at Land O'Lakes is adaptive change. Generative change has been much more difficult to accomplish. It has been hard for the company to examine assumptions and beliefs and then adapt them to new ways of acting and thinking. This difficulty in creating generative learning is the reason that change efforts take so long and require so much effort. People have been rewarded for acting according to old paradigms. Rewards that actually encourage rethinking and relearning need to be developed. Unless organizations learn how to learn, bringing about change will continue to take many years, and at best will be incremental and isolated.

Middle Managers

At Land O'Lakes, much of the learning emphasis was placed on top management in order to obtain its support. Even more emphasis was placed on first-line supervisors and workers to ensure their involvement. Middle managers were overlooked. Many of them felt excluded and were unsure of where they fit in. Middle managers can play an important role in communicating information, providing support, and coaching, but an opportunity to have them fill those important needs was missed. Now specific efforts are being made to articulate their role and to provide training and coaching for them so that they also can contribute to the change effort. If specific plans for participation by middle managers are not developed, this group may be unsupportive of learning efforts.

Advice for Others Making the Journey

Getting started is the most important aspect of becoming a learning organization. The key is to recognize the need and to make a commitment to learning new things in order to change. There is no need to wait. You can build the infrastructure as you go, because it will always grow and change. The organization will continue to learn. The important thing is to manage the expectation. It is important to explain that becoming a learning organization is an ongoing journey, and the questions "How long will it take?" and "How will we know when we are there?" are not the right questions. Some better questions to ask are "What are we learning? What do we need to learn? How will our learning change the way we behave?" This is a journey on a never-ending road.

Questions for Discussion

1. Would you consider the Land O'Lakes approach to implementation of the learning organization an adaptive change or a generative change?
2. What did Land O'Lakes do to build the infrastructure to support learning? What else could have been done to build infrastructure?
3. What kind of and how much support did the top management of Land O'Lakes provide in this case?
4. What should be the role of top management in a learning organization?

The Authors

Mike Driscoll is the director of human resources for the Agricultural Services Division of Land O'Lakes in Inver Grove Heights, Minnesota. Mike has spent 26 years in various human resource assignments with Land O'Lakes. For the last 20 years he has been involved primarily in the creation and implementation of the training and development efforts in the company. He has a B.A. in English. He earned his M.A. in human resource development at the University of St. Thomas in St. Paul, Minnesota, where he is a doctoral student in educational leadership. His research interests include organizational and individual learning. Mike can be contacted at the following address: Director of Employee Development, Land O'Lakes, Inc., Minneapolis, MN 55403.

Hallie Preskill, Ph.D., is an associate professor in the Training and Learning Technologies graduate program at the University of New Mexico, where she primarily teaches courses in program evaluation and instructional systems design. Her consulting and research interests include program evaluation theory and methods, organizational learning and culture, and the transfer of learning. She has written several articles on the relationship between organizational culture and evaluation, the role of evaluation in HRD, and has recently coauthored a book on communication and reporting evaluation findings (to be published by Sage, 1996).

References

Senge, P. (1990). *The fifth discipline: The art and practice of the learning organization.* New York: Random House.

Section 3:
Capitalizing on
Continuous Learning

Global Information Systems Organization: Developing Learning Competencies

Nortel Corporation

James A. Hite Jr. and Andrea D'Angelo

Reorganization prompted the Information Systems Group to redesign itself as virtual teams to better serve its customers through "one-stop shopping." This case examines several strategies that supported its shift toward organizational learning: leadership training, an integrated Skills Development Process model tied to competency assessment and individualized learning plans, and integration of learning with performance management.

Industry Profile

The major changes experienced by the global telecommunications industry in recent years can be summarized as a move away from centralization and government regulation. The industry has expanded and is in the process of exploring new waves of technology. Based originally on voice communications and the ability to transmit and switch calls, the industry is now involved in data and video transmission. Telecommunications companies—whether they provide service or equipment—are undergoing rapid change. Their missions have been altered drastically, driven by a need to meet new communications demands and by the increased use of telecommunications networks by customers. Changes in the marketplace have brought about organizational, technological, and product changes that are transforming the entire industry.

This case was prepared to serve as a basis for discussion rather than to illustrate either effective or ineffective administrative and management practices.

Organizational Profile

Nortel, with headquarters in Toronto, Canada, is a major global provider of telecommunications networks. The company has more than 57,000 employees worldwide. Its corporate mission is to deliver market leadership through customer satisfaction, superior value, and product excellence. To support this mission Nortel is organized into four units: corporate staff, North American, world trade, and research and development (BNR).

In 1993, Jean Monty, CEO of Nortel, emphasized two factors important to the success of the corporation: 1) creating a customer/employee satisfaction mindset throughout the company; and 2) effective leadership of people, processes, and organizations. The organizations below the corporate level began to shape themselves and their directions around these central themes. In particular, global information systems (IS) has not only begun to reshape its structure, but has further emphasized the important role that learning plays in attaining Monty's goals. Other organizations within Nortel, in fact, are taking note of the steps IS is taking to strengthen itself as a learning organization.

The global IS organization is a corporate services function, reporting directly to the CEO of Nortel. Global IS employs about 1,400 people worldwide and provides information systems products and services to its internal customers (employees of other corporate functions and the various business units of the corporation). The chief information officer (CIO) is responsible for the IS organization.

Three phenomena led to the evolution of IS as a learning organization: 1) the organization structure changes were themselves powerful incentives for improved organizational learning; 2) employee satisfaction teams focused attention on management and employee issues that were integral to organizational learning and well-being; and 3) the emergence of a skills development team provided the means and opportunity to address organizational learning in a systematic way.

Reorganization

What could be called the catalyst for the development of a learning organization may be traced to the reorganization and revitalization of IS. The reorganization assumed that the world in which IS would operate in the late 1990s, and probably beyond, would be different from the world in which it had been operating. Like other corporate services organizations, IS originally had been constructed to provide services to the entire corporation. With this mission, IS was not immediately concerned with attracting and maintaining customers. The primary emphasis was on providing excellent service and systems that would serve the corporation. By the end of 1993, however, there was an indication that, in the future, corporate services would provide added value to particular customers—their business unit customers within Nortel and BNR. This meant a shift away from the view of corporate services—including IS—as entitlements, and a shift toward thinking of these services as commodities to be treated much like any other product or service. There was an affirmation that real costs were associated with information systems and services and that those costs should be considered by the business units that might use the services or purchase the products. The CIO described the relationship as a "business within a business."

This shift in philosophy influenced the thinking of the CIO and his organization as they redesigned IS from the latter part of 1993 through the early part of 1994. Three major strategic thrusts were announced:

- Global IS would emerge as a "business within a business."
- There would be a migration of services to an infrastructure that would have a common look and feel for the customer.
- The organization would provide "one-stop shopping" for its customers.

In redesigning the IS organization to meet these strategic goals, IS leadership began with the customer as the key point of focus for the entire organization. This structure called for account managers and teams to partner with the customers. Account management would act as the liaison between the customer and the array of resources available within the IS organization. As work was identified, the account managers would assign it to team leaders who would remain in close contact with the account management team, but who also would form strong ties with customers and especially with the end users. The organizational silos were dismantled by the creation of three general categories of work within the organization—researching technology and new processes, languages, and applications; maintaining capability to service existing systems and applications; and managing the enterprise.

As customer needs were identified, projects were formed that would be met not by standing project teams, but by "virtual teams" that could include members of any of the three groups. The strength of the virtual team would lie in the diversity of its experience and capability, brought to bear on a particular customer's problem or need. While the team would have standard tools, each individual project would be shaped to provide the best approaches to a given client's situation. The virtual team itself would partner closely with the customer to design and implement a solution. Behind the team would be subject matter experts and technical experts in systems architecture, programming languages, and hardware, who could contribute as needed to the team's goal. There would also be organized libraries of reusable codes that would simplify the design effort for a given project. The approach would, in essence, make IS a virtual organization, capable of shaping itself to the work at hand and completing it far more efficiently than it might have been able to under more rigid structures. The customers would benefit from this new organization because they would have a single interface with the IS organization (account managers), and their projects would be completed faster and at less cost by IS professionals using the latest and best technologies. In this way, the three strategic aims of the organization would be met. The organization structure itself, then, played a major role in implementing the IS strategy, although structure alone would not be sufficient.

Employee Satisfaction

The findings of the employee satisfaction survey, originally conducted with samples of the population in 1993, became widely available later that year. Within IS, the human resources function facilitated the establishment of regional teams to sift through the findings and to prioritize needs and action plans. The following needs were identified:

- to emphasize diversity, because of the changing nature of the workforce and of the work
- to improve management's ability to manage people, to assist in career development, to lead, and to leverage employee empowerment
- to focus on team structures, teambuilding, and team leadership, in part because of the direction in which the reorganization was moving
- to more clearly define "quality" in the development and delivery of systems to customers.

In response to these needs, the following occurred:

- The employee satisfaction teams continued to work to make change happen at the regional level.
- There was a focus on the evaluation of managers and on ways to improve that process—perhaps integrating an employee feedback capability into the yearly performance management cycle.
- An existing training course for managers was redesigned, and an information session for all IS employees was initiated.

Of these three, the training activities have had the most visibility across the organization.

Becoming a Performance Leader

"Becoming a Performance Leader," a management course originally developed by Nortel's Learning Institute and modified by IS, was introduced in November 1994. In his introductory letter to IS managers, the CIO emphasized that the need for change was immediate. The intent of the course was to

- Help IS managers understand the link between organizational changes they were experiencing and similar change, upheaval, and increased pace in the industry in general
- Help each IS manager assess his or her individual ability to lead according to the Nortel core competencies, through use of a 360-degree personal assessment instrument
- Help IS managers become aware of the need to build strong teams, and to teach them to form effective teams as quickly as possible
- Help IS managers understand the increased role that organizational learning would play in the new IS organizational model.

The course, therefore, was designed to play a strategic role in moving the managers forward. They had to learn to manage in a work environment that differed significantly from that with which they had previously been familiar. The emphasis was on new ways to motivate and work alongside employees. Managers would learn of an "emerging employment agreement," which, in essence, removes emphasis on job security and paves the way for new relationships between managers, employees, and customers. These relationships, in turn, would call for new emphasis on team operations, empowerment, and learning across the organization.

It was at this point that two of the three significant events in IS began to overlap. In late 1994, when the new organization's architecture was beginning to be realized, managers began to understand the implications of the new approach. At the same time, the work of the employee satisfaction teams was beginning to influence thinking in the organization and the direction of managers' development.

Skills Development

The third major factor in the shift in emphasis toward increased organizational learning was the emergence of a skills development initiative in the spring of 1994. The work of the team assigned to this initiative significantly affected the IS organization throughout the first year. The team

- initiated one of the design changes to "Becoming a Performance Leader," adding a session on the concept of the learning organization

- designed a half-day session, "Making Learning Work," to introduce all IS employees to the learning organization concept
- investigated and supported the implementation of a software package to review scanned resumes, which provided managers with an initial look at perceived skills and capabilities across the organization
- elaborated a skills development process model to provide a core for learning in the IS organization
- launched projects with two key IS roles—account management and project management—to prove the concept of the skills model and to get early results.

The key result of this work was the development of an integrated skills development process model. The model represents four stages of activity: service definition, competency definition, learning, and employee development.

In the first stage, IS roles are defined by the service they provide to the larger Nortel organization. The definition of any role at this stage would link it firmly to three shaping forces: 1) customer needs and wants; 2) the IS organization's strategic direction, as shaped by the corporate direction; and 3) innovations in technology. The term "role" is preferred over "job" because IS views a job as a boundary within which one or more roles may be involved. The concept of "role" allows employees and managers to get away from the fixed and limited "job" concept—with a narrowly defined set of responsibilities—and helps them avoid stereotyping people in terms of skills associated with particular job titles.

Once a service definition is achieved, a corresponding competency definition can be established for the role. The purpose of defining competencies is twofold. First, the IS organization is able to forecast the appropriate development activities for the role and prepare training events and learning support materials as needed. Second, the competency definitions and related behavioral descriptions serve as the basis for assessment. This assessment provides individuals with a clear sense of direction for their personal development, and provides management with a concrete register of capabilities across the organization. In an organization that is on the front line of corporate change and reengineering efforts, this ability to capture and review IS competencies presents a strategic advantage.

Competency assessment leads to the third stage—the provision of learning support. For people who want to upgrade their skills or add roles to their professional careers, learning is self-motivated. For skill enhancement dictated by management, incentives and rewards can help motivate workers. By providing a strategic approach to competency needs identification and development, this model will ultimately reduce dependence on the selection process in order to secure needed competencies in the organization. The learning support itself may take several forms: coursework, reading and outside study, special projects, and community service. In all instances, these interventions can be tied directly to competency definitions, which, in turn, are tied directly to the role definition. Learning support is targeted to valued work, is measurable, and lends itself to evaluation processes that test influence on the work itself.

The fourth stage in the model involves integration of learning and measurement of performance into an existing corporate performance management system. Both individuals and their managers will have competency definitions available to them, along with development guides for the competencies. These tools will improve the managers' ability to coach employees in development activities that are sure to have a payoff for the company. A person in an account management role, for instance, will be able to acquire skills rapidly because development needs can be assessed and met by using highly practical tools. There is also a guarantee of consistency—the account management role will look pretty much the same in European IS operations as it does in North American IS operations. Even if differences do emerge, those differences can be linked to distinct data about how the role is intended to operate, and any differences in competencies will be documented. This final stage benefits the individual employee personally. He or she will come to see what skills Nortel's IS organization considers important. It will be possible, based on the competency and role definition data, to plan career changes that will keep the individual "marketable." This marketability will prove advantageous to the employee as he or she develops a career and career path, and will allow the company to make the best use of the skills available.

The work produced by the skills development initiative and by the employee satisfaction teams, along with the structural changes in IS, combined to produce a powerful organizational transformation. Learning is clearly a requisite for success in all three areas. Employees must understand the rationale underlying the structural changes and must adjust their activities to match those changes. Employee satisfaction teams are introducing new ideas that will change the way the organization works together. The skills development model will serve as a touchstone for training, education, and development.

Strategies for Assessment

No single set of measurement techniques has emerged to assess the effect of these activities, although the employee satisfaction survey will provide one instrument for monitoring success. The measures taken in 1993 and 1994 provide baseline data. The changes that have been and will be made are, to some degree, responses to problems and opportunities identified through that survey.

The flexibility of employees will be another measurement tool. As competency data are collected, combined flexibility statistics for each role can be compiled, so that management will have a clear picture of its success in meeting immediate as well as subsequent personnel needs.

A third area of measurement will involve the individual capabilities of employees. Not only should IS see greater flexibility for the various competencies associated with its roles, but it should also see individuals acquiring wider sets of skills and abilities. This will ensure that employees undertake development that will benefit their careers as well as their current jobs and tasks. This measure also will benefit succession and replacement planning, and it may eliminate costly selection activity.

Management should expect to see a reduction in the time it takes to effectively form a team. It is important in a virtual team environment that the initial stages of team structure be achieved quickly. In an organization with few managers, the proof of employee empowerment will be the ability of employees to structure complex teams, sometimes involving customers and contractors, with minimal assistance or oversight from management. While baseline data will be difficult to quantify, qualitative data should be available from the teams themselves, as well as from managers and customers.

A key area of measurement will be the rate at which qualified employees become available for work in new skill and technology areas through the internal development process. The need for external selection will provide a measure here, as will any delay in projects because of lack of qualified staff.

Finally, the IS organization has begun to use a standard instrument titled "Readiness for the Learning Organization." This instrument, consisting of 42 items, provides attitudinal data about the success of IS in implementing the practical, concrete changes that, taken together, shape the ability of the organization to learn. Base data will be collected, and periodic repetitions of the instrument will provide success measures.

Key Success Factors

Specific to the skills development initiative are the following key success factors:

- Employees perceive themselves to have the highest level of marketability in the industry.
- Industry perceives that Nortel employees have the highest marketability in the industry.
- Nortel is perceived as the employer of choice.
- Nortel increases its ability to source skills internally.
- IS employees know what skills they need and want, and will know where to get them just in time.
- IS employees understand and apply learning tools and processes.

While the organizational, employee satisfaction, and employee development initiatives will support the strengthening of the IS learning organization, much work remains. For example, managers who are participating in the "Becoming a Performance Leader" course have suggested a number of changes in the organization—in one instance, by writing a class letter to the CIO. Further, managers have pointed out that a traditional approach to team building is not sufficient in a decentralized, customer-focused environment. They are less likely to form structured teams and more likely to be part of customer teams or to partner with vendors in different forms of relationships. These "learnings," among others, provide the seeds for future change and growth.

Above all, it will be important for the information systems organization, from top to bottom, to acknowledge the role that learning plays in their work life. This is perhaps the key success factor that must continually be emphasized throughout the organization. In a decentralized work environment, in which IS professionals may report directly to customers, the consistency, quality, and standards necessary to maintain the IS function globally will depend on IS professionals learning from each other.

Questions for Discussion

1. What role did the CEO of Nortel and the Nortel executives play in the organizational changes made in the global information systems function?

2. How did the CIO and his team go about the work of reorganization in such a way that it encouraged the development of a learning organization?

3. What information systems employees or groups were involved in moving the organization toward the development of a learning organi-

zation? What specific actions did they take that encouraged organization learning?

4. What evidence do you see that organizational learning is already occurring in this function?

5. If you were the HRD manager for this function, what would you advise the CIO to do next to encourage and reinforce learning in the information systems function?

The Authors

James A. Hite Jr. is a manager of human resources development with Nortel's Learning Institute. His chief responsibility is to provide a link between the Learning Institute and the functions and business units with which he works. In this capacity, he provides a wide range of HRD consulting services to his client organizations. Prior to his experience with Nortel, he managed professional training for Phillips Petroleum Company's exploration and production group. His responsibilities included HRD consulting in both training and OD, management of instructional systems development, and facilitation of management training. Jim has also worked as an HRD consultant, providing OD and training services to clients that include International Harvester, Searle Pharmaceutical, and International Paper. He has published articles on HRD practice and has provided HRD advisory and training services to several schools in Tennessee. He holds a master's degree in English from Georgia State University. He can be contacted at the following address: Nortel, 200 Athens Way, Nashville, TN 37228.

Andrea D'Angelo is the manager of the Information Systems (IS) Learning Center for Nortel's Raleigh, North Carolina, operations. She has been associated with Nortel for three years. Andrea is currently focusing on open systems and client server technologies using alternate delivery methods for training and learning within the Raleigh area IS organization. She is also heavily involved in the leadership of the IS skills development initiative, which serves as a catalyst for change in the IS global organization. Andrea has more than 11 years of experience in information systems application development, encompassing a variety of mainframe computing environments, including IBM, HP, and DEC. Her technical background spans programming, analysis, design, project management, and customer engagement. She has business experience in the insurance, utility, and telecommunications industries. Andrea holds a B.S. degree in business administration, with a specialization in management information systems, and is currently working toward a masters of education degree, with specialization in training and development.

A New Tool for Continuous Learning: The Electronic Learning Guide

Rohm and Haas Corporation

Virginia W. Denny, Debbie Gibson, and Jay Gulick

Market managers at Rohm and Haas needed a learning strategy that would overcome the organizational, geographical, and time barriers inherent in their work. Using data from a benchmarking teleconference, from the work profiling system, and from jobholders, consultants developed a competency profile of the market manager position and a 360-degree feedback assessment. The electronic learning guide is designed around a spreadsheet and is organized according to the 12 competencies. The guide lists a variety of formal and informal learning resources, and users update the guide by adding books, training, and other resources they have found helpful.

Background

Economic changes dictated a detailed analysis of the marketing function at Rohm and Haas Company, a manufacturer of specialty chemicals and plastics (and the inventor of Plexiglas) with sales in excess of $3 billion. The market manager position, responsible for managing and marketing specific product lines, was becoming more and more critical to the company's competitiveness. These managers now were being asked to reach beyond the scope of their previous roles and contribute to corporate competitiveness in new ways. To meet these demands, they would need to learn and develop continuously. As Arie P. DeGeus, former planning director for the Royal Dutch Shell Group, concluded, "The only competitive advantage the company of the future will have is its managers' ability to learn faster than their competitors."

This case was prepared to serve as a basis for discussion rather than to illustrate either effective or ineffective administrative and management practices.

Although the managers were highly skilled and creative, two barriers made their transition to leadership positions difficult:

- The organizational structure impeded informal learning and information exchange. More than 100 market managers in this company were spread among 10 business units throughout the world. The managers had different specialties, educational backgrounds, and experience. The functional isolation and physical distance were serious barriers to shared learning.
- Time was also a significant barrier. Most market managers function in an intense atmosphere in which learning time is considered a luxury, and information can become outdated before it is shared.

Clearly, these market managers needed a new understanding of the demands of their work as well as a strategy for learning that would overcome the organizational, geographical, and time barriers inherent in their work.

In 1993, the Rohm and Haas marketing board, a cross-business group of marketing professionals, created a document titled *Dimensions of Marketing Excellence* that defined the four pillars of functional excellence: customer satisfaction, strategy development and implementation, resource management, and profit and asset management.

This document became the foundation when the marketing board hired Miller Consultants—a management and strategic human resources consulting firm based in Louisville, Kentucky—to create a competency model for the market manager position worldwide. As Rohm and Haas corporate vice-president Harold Floyd explained, "The dimensions of marketing model helped us identify the common threads of a very complex set of responsibilities so that the marketing community could focus on some very key areas of skill and knowledge." The idea was to take the dimensions, define them in terms of human performance competencies, and expand them, if necessary, based on an external benchmarking study of marketing trends and a list of measurable outcomes.

Key Players and the Process

A diverse group of internal and external professionals tackled the issues. They included the marketing board, under the direction of Dan Murad; Miller Consultants, under the direction of its president, Kathy Miller; and CCI Assessment and Development Group, under the direction of Larry Cipolla.

Major steps in the process included
- identifying critical outcomes
- benchmarking top marketing functions at other organizations to provide future dimensions

- collecting data relevant to the position via a standardized job/task analysis instrument and through a 360-degree feedback tool
- developing a competency model profiling the competencies required to achieve excellence in the position
- creating a curriculum designed to help individual market managers develop these competencies through formal and informal learning.

Critical Outcomes

We began by achieving consensus on the desired outcomes of the function from an internal group of marketing experts. We wanted to ensure that the outcomes were future-oriented and that they could be achieved through improved human performance—that is, the enhancement of knowledge, skills, and attitudes. The marketing experts identified the following outcomes:
- growth in business—defending current business and capturing new business
- consistent and long-term revenue generation
- improved profitability
- defined mix of satisfied customers
- global coordination.

Benchmarking

Next, we examined what leaders in marketing considered to be critical outcomes and selected three companies for benchmarking: Hewlett-Packard; Corning, Inc.; and 3M. During teleconferences, all the participants acknowledged that the marketing function was undergoing a tremendous transition in each of their organizations. The skills and knowledge needs of marketing personnel were greatly increasing, with more and more marketers needing competencies in leadership, teamwork, and budgeting/finance. The shift to more globally focused marketing was also a common thread.

Data Collection

Meanwhile, we used the work profiling system, a job/task analysis tool that uses a structured questionnaire and task cards to identify key competencies required by personnel. Ten market managers at the corporate headquarters in Philadelphia participated in the analysis, which yielded a set of task categories critical to the position, such as planning, assessing/evaluating, deciding, and influencing. It also profiled key human attributes, such as verbal skills, number skills, creative thinking skills, and assertive personalities. From these data, Miller Consultants began constructing key competencies.

Still, we needed more detailed information on the specifics of the market managers' work and more qualitative data on the environment in which they work. We interviewed a sample of jobholders individually and in focus groups to uncover additional detail. This process yielded some of the most valuable information for creating a new learning tool.

We learned that the market managers had a powerful need to identify "best practices" in their jobs and learn from each other to implement these practices. Jobholders talked about a strong feeling of isolation, and wanted to be able to communicate more easily and more often with their managers. They complained that traditional classroom training often failed to meet their needs because the information was neither tailored nor timely. In fact, the managers consistently stressed the importance of time. They needed a system that did not waste precious time and that allowed them to access information quickly and on their schedule. Flexibility was also a key concern—market managers wanted to approach learning on their own terms.

In addition to the needs they expressed, we knew the managers would need resources and learning strategies to help them address competency weaknesses identified by their 360-degree feedback tool.

New Directions—The Genesis of the Learning Guide

These diverse needs called for a nontraditional approach to learning and development that would benefit the individual jobholders while introducing a new dimension of organizational learning.

Most market managers are sophisticated computer users, so an electronic medium was appropriate to address the need for up-to-the-moment information and shared learning. They are also accustomed to using a resource guide to locate training, books, and other learning tools related to their work. We married the two tools, and the Electronic Learning Guide was born.

This interactive, computer-based resource is designed to

- put information about learning and development opportunities at the market managers' fingertips
- increase cross-business information exchange among market managers and others who contribute to marketing efforts
- reduce or eliminate expenditures for low-value training programs (e.g., to identify and eliminate vendor training that is found to be of low value)

- encourage a more strategic approach to learning and development evidenced by constructive use of learning plans, increased interaction between jobholders and managers, and employment of nontraditional learning approaches, such as strategic mentoring
- provide a structured process for responding to 360-degree feedback and the subsequent professional development planning that puts ownership of learning in the hands of the jobholder.

A cross between a data base and a computer-based learning tool, the guide allows market managers to leverage one another's competencies and share their wide range of experiences. It is designed to be altered over time, to be immediately accessible to the jobholders, to be current, and, most important, to be relevant to their needs.

How the System Works

First-time users are greeted with a welcome letter and orientation. Users can then engage in a variety of activities. They can
- self-assess their current level of proficiency in 12 core competencies
- identify learning resources indexed by competency and medium (e.g., book, tape, video, computer)
- add learning and resources from their experience
- analyze 360-degree feedback
- learn about the competency model
- open a new jobholder orientation package.

The options are grouped under four main menu buttons. Within each, users find a wealth of information and options. Table 1 summarizes the menu options, contents, and features.

Customized Learning Saves Time and Money

Market managers can identify their distinctive developmental needs in several ways on the system. If they have not yet received 360-degree feedback, they can select a self-assessment option that helps them analyze their skill level in each of 12 competencies. They work through a self-assessment instrument and complete exercises to analyze the results and develop a learning plan. If they have received a 360-degree feedback report, they can bring up a self-paced learning tool that will help them analyze their results and help them discuss the results with their managers. The guide takes them step by step through the process of identifying their preferred learning styles and helps them develop a customized learning plan that features resources from the data base. Worksheets can be printed or used on screen.

Table 1. Summary of the electronic learning guide.

Main functions	Purpose
Resource guide	This function contains a data base that can be sorted by competency. Supporting documents help jobholders refocus their thinking about professional development. It addresses change and continuous learning in the context of their work. Also in this section, they can analyze feedback, discuss learning needs with their managers, and develop learning strategies and plans for enhancing skills. It urges them to take control and ownership of their own learning.
Market manager directory	This data base allows users to locate or identify other Rohm and Haas market managers organization-wide.
About the learning library	This section provides some history of the tools they are using, a copy of the competency model, and some new market manager orientation materials.
How to get the most out of learning	This collection of brief how-to pieces encourages job holders to learn strategically.

Note: The examples in this table demonstrate the flexibility of the system, its usefulness in saving time and training dollars, and its ability to make the most of shared learning.

If a market manager needs to develop a specific competency, the system allows the manager to use his or her preferred learning method and work on his or her own schedule. For example, one market manager may determine that he needs to develop his planning and organizing competency, and he knows that he learns best by reading articles and talking with others. He would go to "resource tools" in the main menu, and then select "article." The data base lists all related articles. Selecting "mentors" provides a list of people willing to coach him on planning and organizing or to answer his questions.

Interactive Features Enhance Shared Learning

An interactive component will eventually be introduced to allow market managers to add resources themselves or to add comments about specific resources. For example, one market manager may find a specific article especially helpful, and so she would enter a comment encouraging others to read the article. She might also request others to contact her to form a cross-business discussion group around the world via e-mail and conference call. The potential for saving training dollars is significant, but at this point the system is too new to show definitive cost-saving figures.

On-Line Orientation Demonstrates Flexibility of System

Market managers must learn a lot before they can become fully productive. Currently, it takes many months before they can acquire the knowledge, skills, and experience to perform all aspects of their jobs.

An on-line resource, currently under development, will give market managers a series of learning activities tailored to their specific needs. It will introduce them to the competency model, provide simple tasks to help them to start learning directly from others, and encourage discussions with their managers about the business of learning. It will rely heavily on learning from others and on capturing that learning for the organization. Jobholders warned us that a critical element will be the skills and preparedness of coaches and mentors.

So Will They Use It?

Two significant questions remain: Will jobholders see the value of such a system? Will they continue to use it over time?

We interviewed a small sample of jobholders and asked them whether they expect to use the system often. Most were very enthusiastic about the resource, but were quick to say that the system would have to be very simple and easy to use.

We expect recipients of the newly instituted 360-degree feedback reports to be strongly motivated to locate resources and develop learning plans to address deficiencies in key competencies. Therefore, the Electronic Learning Guide was rolled out in conjunction with a session on interpreting 360-degree feedback. All those who attended the session received training on the Electronic Learning Guide. When they returned to their own computers, they had the resources to further interpret the results and identify learning resources to improve key competencies.

Other evaluation measures are being designed and may include cost of classroom training and other traditional learning methods, time required for new jobholders to become functional, communication patterns among jobholders, and satisfaction levels of users. A series of phone interviews and surveys (probably via e-mail) will be used to track use in the early stages and target areas for improvement.

Details

The guide was set by Greg Stewart of Rohm and Haas in a spreadsheet data base using Microsoft Excel and Microsoft Access. Currently, the system is made available on disk, so jobholders have immediate and simple access to it on their laptops day and night. A system administrator will update the data base regularly, issuing new disks to market managers as things change. Ideally, the system will be real-time, on-line, and accessible via a shared server. After the learning guide is tested and evaluated at this stage, further efforts will likely be made to transfer it on-line.

Conclusion

Learning organizations have been defined as "enterprises committed to the continuous enhancement of their employees' knowledge and skills and to their own collective improvement" (Aubrey and Cohen, 1995). The Electronic Learning Guide seeks to support that vision. Its basic premise is to give market managers throughout the company the opportunity to teach one another continuously and also to gain access to the wealth of knowledge and experiences that have been largely unused. It is our hope that the learning guide becomes a "living document" that may be continually updated by the market managers themselves to help meet their specific needs in a timely and cost-effective manner. Thus, the base of knowledge continues to grow and to contribute to Rohm and Haas's "collective improvement." If successful, this electronic learning tool will make information and learning available quickly enough to add value to the clients of every Rohm and Haas business worldwide.

Lessons Learned

THE BEST INFORMATION, THE CLEAREST INFORMATION, AND THE SPARKS OF NEW IDEAS ALMOST ALWAYS COME FROM THE JOBHOLDERS THEMSELVES. This is one lesson that we encounter again and again, and it was clearly evident in this project. Knowing the right questions to ask—not knowing the answers—is what leads to new ways of thinking. Collaborative learning was a familiar theme throughout this effort.

GROUP EFFORTS TAKE EXTRA TIME AND CONCENTRATION, BUT THEY ARE WORTH IT. Working with a group such as the marketing board meant taking time to discuss concepts, rethink next steps, and work through differing perspectives. These varying perspectives led to new ways of thinking for all of us.

HAVING A CHAMPION OR TWO MAKES ALL THE DIFFERENCE, ESPECIALLY WHEN BREAKING THROUGH OLD PARADIGMS. The vision of new approaches is best carried by an internal advocate who can describe it in terms meaningful to others. This effort had at least two champions, and they made the entire project possible.

DON'T OVERLOOK PROCESS WHEN CREATING A NEW PRODUCT. The outcome of this project was a new tool that we hope will influence organizational learning; the process itself, however, is equally important. The users of this system helped develop its content, and the process of drawing expertise and ideas from them was critical to its successful long-term use. Helping them identify and appreciate the value of learning was integral. If such a tool were dropped into an organization that did not understand organizational learning or strategic professional development, it is unlikely that the same results would be achieved.

TECHNOLOGY IS OPENING NEW WORLDS. Perhaps this is the most intriguing lesson learned. We discovered that some pretty simple technological tools such as Excel and Access have the potential to revolutionize the way people learn at Rohm and Haas. As the World Wide Web and the Internet become more commonly used, as computerized data bases and e-mail become ordinary, new worlds present themselves to those of us in the human and organizational development professions. It tempts us to think ahead to next steps now, before the project is even fully implemented.

Questions for Discussion

1. How can companies ensure that methods used to develop competencies remain viable as the competencies themselves change?
2. What other methods could be used to create resources that tap into the jobholders' knowledge and skills?
3. How can emerging technologies be used more effectively to ensure that the methods grow as the jobholders grow?
4. How can some of the principles applied in the Electronic Learning Guide be applied in your organization to boost organizational learning?

The Authors

Virginia Denny and Debbie Gibson are consultants with Miller Consultants, and Jay Gulick is a former consultant with the firm. Based in Louisville, Kentucky, Miller Consultants' major services include organizational development, workforce planning, training systems, and trends research. Their international list of clients includes IBM; Rohm and Haas; AT&T; Procter and Gamble; Miller Brewing; Courtaulds Coatings, Inc.; and Borden.

Virginia Denny currently focuses on new learning systems that place strategic learning in the hands of individuals helping organizations meet the demands of a changing workplace. Her affiliation with the Telecommunications Research Center at the University of Louisville helped spark the concept for the Electronic Learning Guide. She can be contacted at the following address: Miller Consultants, 1141 E. Broadway, Louisville, KY 40204.

Debbie Gibson specializes in communication and marketing strategies for Miller Consultants. Debbie is also the principal for Copywrite, a strategic communications firm based in Lexington, Kentucky. She has received more than 50 national, regional, and local awards for communications.

While at Miller Consultants, Jay Gulick was responsible for studying global business trends and their sociopolitical and economic implications for national, regional, and local communities and the workforce. Jay is now a freelance writer based in Louisville, Kentucky.

References

Aubrey, R., and Cohen, P.M. (1995). *Working wisdom: Timeless skills and vanguard strategies for learning organizations.* San Francisco: Jossey-Bass.

Virtually There: Emergence of a Learning Organization

Tennessee Virtual School

Jeff Kenyon and Susan Kuner

Since its inception in 1991, the Virtual School, an on-line network of Tennessee educators, has grown from a group of 20 teachers into an organization with 10,000 members. This case shows how computer-mediated communication provided the fuel for informal problem solving and learning. Work and learning organized the people, rather than the other way around.

Overview

We believe we are looking at the emergence of a learning organization. Emergence is a term we have borrowed from what now is being called "the new science." It describes a phenomenon that occurs when a system organizes itself even though its members initially engage in random behaviors (Waldrop, 1992; Wheatley, 1992).

The Virtual School has emerged from the bottom up, organized by learning, particularly informal and incidental learning (Marsick and Watkins, 1990). A question is posted on-line; a dialogue begins around a problem that needs to be solved; someone asks for help. Members group and regroup around learning events, inspired by the information they are drawn to or that they have contributed. In the Virtual School, learning is an act of organizing. But, in this case, work and learning organize the people rather than the other way around.

Nohria and Berkley (1994) describe the virtual organization as an organization that has replaced traditional structure and methods of communication with computer technology in a way that creates un-

This case was prepared to serve as a basis for discussion rather than to illustrate either effective or ineffective administrative and management practices.

precedented flexibility, spontaneity, and openness to the environment. We believe that what we are seeing in the Virtual School has been made possible only through computer-mediated communication.

We wrestled with many questions as we developed this case. Admittedly, we initially were skeptical about whether the Virtual School was even an organization, let alone a learning organization with a past, present, and future that is relevant for HRD practitioners. After comparing it with accepted definitions and theory, however, we have determined that this is a valuable case that provides an opportunity to look at a virtual organization and extract the principles, conditions, and behaviors that inspire its members, sponsors, and constituents to learn.

This case has moved us to consider an addition to the definition of a learning organization. Besides being an organization that systematically transforms itself through continuous learning, we see the learning organization as an organization structured around individual and collective learning, which benefits its immediate and encompassing systems. Thus, we want to add that in a well-developed learning organization, learning takes into account the well-being of its members, its customers, its community, and the environment.

Background and History

Individual schools tend to operate within cultures of isolation. Teachers have limited time to interact professionally with their colleagues. There is limited teacher-to-teacher contact between individual schools in school districts, and virtually none between distinct school districts. What professional interaction that does occur may not provide opportunities to explore innovative ideas or share strategies. With little time available for interaction, face-to-face communication often involves administrative coordination, the cathartic sharing of war stories, and commiseration over the difficulty of the job.

The Virtual School was initiated by Vanderbilt University Chancellor Joe B. Wyatt. A pioneer in computer networking in the late 1950s, Wyatt later was one of the Harvard University researchers who helped to develop the ARPANET—the first national electronic network to send information in "packets." This technological innovation was instrumental to the formation of today's information superhighway. Because his mother, sister, and daughter were all school teachers, he also understood some of the unique challenges of the teaching profession.

He and Jacqueline Shrago, then Vanderbilt's director of technology transfer, conceived the idea for the Virtual School in an attempt to share Vanderbilt's extensive computing resources with all K–12 teachers in middle Tennessee. The program start-up offered any teacher in the area a free account on the school's network, which included Internet access. The accounts, however, were given only to teachers who completed a three-hour training session on networking basics that was provided for free by Vanderbilt. The program objectives were threefold:

- to teach computing skills
- to overcome the isolation teachers experience in the classroom
- to connect teachers with peers and other experts in the university and business community.

Approximately 20 teachers were invited to the first training session held in November 1991. They learned how to send and receive electronic mail, how to access bulletin boards on the Vanderbilt network, and how to use the modem. To navigate the network, they had to use complicated mainframe computer-language commands that bore little resemblance to English. The technology was decidedly "user-unfriendly," and the prevailing reaction to the session was, "Big deal!"

The training sessions continued, though, and more teachers were encouraged to participate. At the same time, attempts were made to eliminate initial participation barriers. For example, some teachers who were trained reported that they had trouble remembering some of the procedures. So a few volunteers created a manual that provided step-by-step instructions on networking procedures to accompany the hands-on training.

By May 1992, even though there were a few hundred users on the network, only a small percentage of those trained actually were using the Virtual School. Four years later, this continues to be a concern. Approximately 25 percent of those trained are actively participating in the Virtual School. Not only has the system been awkward, but teachers have had limited access to computers and phone lines.

Profile of Ingram Distribution Group

Ingram Distribution Group Inc. is the world's largest wholesale distributor of trade books, prerecorded videocassettes, and microcomputer hardware and software. Ingram has donated space and organized volunteers to test computers donated by the city of Nashville's Chamber of Commerce and the state of Tennessee. They also donated modems and packaged equipment for delivery to teachers. Special-needs high school students are bused in every day to learn workplace skills as they sort parts and clean monitors, CPUs, and keyboards. The Ingram refurbishing program serves as a model for community citizenship throughout the state. The company's efforts have resulted in the donation of nearly 3,000 used computers to the Virtual School, including 1,000 given to teachers.

To encourage more use, Vanderbilt paid a few teachers to do summer research on the Internet to see what resources were available and useful for teachers. In an effort to make the Virtual School more user friendly, a volunteer from the computer center created a menu to make navigating the mainframe easier. As the system became more relevant and user friendly, a few teachers began sharing their lesson plans and other such materials retrieved from the Internet.

Gradually, teachers began telling other teachers about the Virtual School. With little or no formal publicity, requests for information began to increase. Soon it was necessary to increase the number of classes per month from one to two.

In 1993, with Chancellor Wyatt's influence, the program was adopted by the city of Nashville's Chamber of Commerce. This group led an effort to collect outdated computers, which then were completely refurbished and fitted with modems and communications software. These computers were loaned to teachers who completed the Vanderbilt Virtual School training. Teachers were welcome to use the computers at home or to install them in their classrooms. Because of greater access to equipment and a more user-friendly system, Virtual School membership began to grow rapidly.

Training was held on as many Saturdays as possible, with classes booked six months in advance. Teachers called from around the state. Many got up at 4 a.m. to drive to Nashville for the 9 a.m. session. By the beginning of the 1993 Fall semester, there were more than 2,000 teachers participating in the Virtual School.

The rapidly growing demand for training soon overwhelmed Vanderbilt's staff and volunteers. In late 1993, Pellissippi State Community College in Knoxville and Memphis State University agreed to become Virtual School training sites. The Tennessee Department of Education sponsored a toll-free number so that every teacher could have access

---

Profile of Virtual School Member

Ellen Rust is an elementary school counselor. A computer novice when she was trained, she has since mastered the technology. Rust began a Virtual School forum for counselors soon after her training. It became so successful that she took it out on the Internet, where she developed the International Counselor Network—an e-mail discussion list of more than 500 school, university, and private-practice counselors. Through her writing in counseling newsletters and journals, she is persuading universities to include telecommunications in their counseling curriculum and is encouraging technophobic counselors to overcome their fears.

without long distance costs. By December 1994, 7,400 teachers had completed the three-hour Step 1 training. A Step 2 training program, which introduces trainees to the Internet, has also been developed.

The Virtual School continues to grow through the donations of sponsors and the efforts of volunteers. Initially Vanderbilt provided the free computer accounts and maintained the network. Now the Tennessee Board of Regents and the state's Department of Education fulfill this role. South Central Bell has provided grants to promote ISDN subscription. Businesses donate used computers, and volunteers continue to conduct the training and come to the sessions to help as "guardian angels." They also continue to support the school's members by answering teachers' questions via e-mail.

Learning

Virtual School members experience the learning organization action imperatives (Watkins and Marsick, 1993) in this virtual organization much more strongly than in their traditional schools, where time, bureaucracy, and exhaustion may stand in the way of collective inquiry and dialogue.

The Virtual School gives its members free access to their peers and to information sources anytime, anywhere. They can learn individually and collectively in the middle of the night at home while wearing their pajamas if they wish. It is interactive and asynchronous. Learning is voluntary, self-directed, uninhibited, and unrestricted. It can be related to specific objectives, or it can be exploratory. Learning is the fundamental force for organizing within the boundary of the Virtual School.

Inquiry and dialogue are promoted through electronic mail and interest-specific bulletin boards, which also serve to capture and share learning. Such collaboration and team learning opportunities as curriculum development projects and group problem-solving also are encouraged.

Virtual school members are taking collective action to support their organization as well. When news got out that the state of Tennessee was not going to include networking in its K–12 technology plan, for example, teachers lobbied successfully for its inclusion. This has changed the department of education's strategy and vision for technology substantially. The Virtual School is connected to its environment by linking teachers, students, parents, educators, and businesspeople through computer-mediated dialogue and information sharing.

The systemic, interconnected, emergent nature of the learning in the Virtual School creates a situation in which this case study affects the learning that occurs. By going on-line with the announcement of this case study, the authors add information to the Virtual School. We are initiating learning by asking for responses to an on-line survey that, while it elicits information, introduces the concepts of the learning organization and the virtual organization to the members. Interested members will organize temporarily around the ensuing discussion. Tangential discussions will spin off with individual members joining in or disengaging as they see fit.

Several assumptions have held true and have influenced the emergence of the Virtual School as a learning organization. One is that, given the opportunity and adequate support, teachers would use the technology to support their practice, to engage in dialogue with colleagues, and to search for instructional materials. Also key is the assumption that finding the resources necessary to maintain the Virtual School could be a community-wide effort, and that such an effort would be advantageous to the organization and the community.

Key Success Factors

An important factor in the success of the Virtual School has been the elimination of barriers that teachers encountered when they tried to use the technology. Making the system easy to use, providing computer terminals to teachers, and instituting a toll-free telephone service all have helped to eliminate these barriers. Still, only about one-fourth of those trained are actively using the Virtual School. Further study is required to identify those conditions that prevent teachers from taking advantage of this opportunity.

These skills represent a new literacy. This literacy involves a form of communication, the implications of which are just beginning to be understood by information theory experts. Nevertheless, just as learning to read and write provides new opportunities for learning—and changes the way learning occurs—so does this new literacy. Cur-

---

Profile of Virtual School Member

At Jere Baxter, an inner-city middle school, the faculty created an electronic bulletin board exclusively for themselves. With little time to communicate during the day, they use the board to exchange information relating to their profession, discuss organizational topics, share news of interest, and catch up on the details of each others' lives. Combined with other professional programs that emphasize research and learning, "Virtual-Baxter" has become an important forum for mentoring colleagues. It offers a level of professional and personal support that would not exist otherwise.

---

rently, members require further training and support to control the amount and the significance of the cyberspace information they generate and retrieve.

Also contributing to the success of this project is the asynchronous nature of communicating through this medium. The absence of a time constraint emancipates previously isolated teachers. Computer-mediated technology gives them their first real opportunity to engage in continuous professional dialogue.

Perhaps the most significant factor for success is making the training open to any teacher in the school system. This kind of self-selection for training increases participants' buy-in. The diversity of the Virtual School population also promotes the growth of the school and results in rich contributions of new information. This, too, generates more on-line learning.

Recommendations for HRD Practice

Based on our review of the Virtual School, here are some suggestions for HRD practitioners who are working with—or toward—building on-line learning communities within their organizations:

- Facilitate full Internet access through a network that is accessible only to members of the organization.
- Teach and support information discrimination skills. Network access inevitably causes information overload.
- Identify and assess the learning that occurs, and share those results on-line.
- Initiate and facilitate on-line discussions about learning.
- Provide support for on-line learning by recruiting and identifying experts, by collecting and posting successful practices, and by disseminating knowledge of where to go for information.
- Identify and remove barriers to learning and to network use.
- Monitor network activity and encourage dialogue: "You know, you should e-mail Jane about that. She is working on a similar project."
- Encourage learning that reaches outside the organization.

Conclusion

The Virtual School is more than a learning resource and more than a place to organize for learning. It is both of those things to be sure, but the interconnected nature of Virtual School activity makes it look more like a brain. As with the human brain, much of the learning that occurs is informal and incidental. As with humans, such learning can be influenced but not controlled. In the immediate future, influencing learning, and then conserving and exploiting it, may become more important skills for HRD practitioners than directing and controlling it.

One definition of "control" is "to check the roll, or roster." Our favorite definition of influence is "an ethereal liquid emanating from the stars acting upon the mind and senses." Of the two, the latter better seems to express the spirit of the Virtual School and the attributes of leadership that we believe are important for contemporary HRD professionals.

Questions for Discussion

1. What "virtual" characteristics contribute to the success of the Virtual School?
2. Is it a learning organization as such organizations are contemporarily defined? If it is, what levels of learning are occurring?
3. What are the implications of this case for more traditional (physical, temporal) organizations?
4. What questions haven't we thought of? What have we missed?

The Authors

Jeff Kenyon has 20 years of experience as a manager, educator, speaker, and consultant in the United States and Canada. His company, the Corporate Learning Group (CLG), conducts research and provides services in the design, delivery, and evaluation of training and organizational development. CLG specializes in improving organizational effectiveness and competitiveness by building individual and collective learning systems. He can be contacted at the following address: Vanderbilt University, 7441 Highway 70 South, #408, Nashville, TN 37221.

Susan Kuner coordinates Vanderbilt University's collaboration with the Virtual School. She conducts network training and designs projects connecting university research and innovation to the K–12 environment. She supports teachers as they develop curriculum applications, and has helped to secure two Eisenhower Math/Science grants for their work. She is a consultant and a founder of Arcomp, a computer-training company in South Florida. She received her M.Ed. from Vanderbilt and is completing her doctoral studies. Her area of research is the technology of the learning organization.

References

Marsick, V., and Watkins, K. (1990). *Informal and incidental learning in the workplace.* New York: Routledge.

Nohria, N., and Berkley, J. (1994). "The virtual organization." In C. Heckscher and A. Donnellon (Eds.), *The post-bureaucratic organization,* (pp. 108–128). Thousand Oaks, CA: Sage.

Waldrop, M. (1992). *Complexity.* New York: Touchstone Simon & Schuster.

Watkins, K., and Marsick, V. (1993). *Sculpting the learning organization: Lessons in the art and science of systemic change.* San Francisco: Jossey-Bass.

Wheatley, M. (1992). *Leadership and the new science: Learning about organization from an orderly universe.* San Francisco: Berrett-Koehler.

The Implementation of a Learning Organization Process in a High-Technology Company

Ultrasound Coronary Systems

Michael Albert

A consultant describes the second phase of an organizational change project with a high-technology medical manufacturing and marketing company that emphasizes learning from past successes and failures. The case highlights the creation of new mental models for understanding organizational events and taking action.

Organizational and Industry Profile

Ultrasound Coronary Systems (UCS) develops, manufactures, and markets intravascular ultrasound imaging catheters and systems to aid in the diagnosis and treatment of cardiovascular disease. The company was founded in 1986 and introduced its products for commercial use in the United States in 1989. The company's products include imaging consoles, which project ultrasound images of the interior heart on video screens, and a family of disposable ultrasound imaging catheters, which are inserted into a vein in a patient's leg and skillfully moved toward the heart arteries.

The company's strategic goal is to become the leading worldwide producer of disposable imaging catheters. As of 1994, the market for intravascular ultrasound was small at $25 million, but growing rapidly. There has been a widespread belief in the securities industry that the total market will grow to $100 million–$200 million within three to five

This case was prepared to serve as a basis for discussion rather than to illustrate either effective or ineffective administrative and management practices.

years. As of 1994, UCS had between 40 and 45 percent of the market. Only two other companies currently compete in intravascular ultrasound: Endosonics, with between 10 and 15 percent of the market; and Hewlett Packard and Boston Scientific, together controlling about 45 percent of the market (HP manufactures the ultrasound system and Boston Scientific manufactures the catheters). In 1994 UCS sales reached $14 million, a 73 percent increase from 1993; sales had grown by 33 percent in 1992.

The organization is functionally structured, with vice-presidents for finance, operations, research and development, and sales and marketing, as well as a director of quality assurance and regulatory affairs, all of whom report to the CEO/president. Various engineering project managers report to the operations or research and development executives. Company personnel grew from 100 in 1993 to 125 by June 1994.

The Learning Organization: Preliminary Events

Prior to the learning organization intervention, 29 executives, managers, and key staff were involved in an organization development (OD) process of assessment, planning, and implementation. Company-wide task forces developed and implemented recommendations based on data they collected. I was their external organization development consultant from May 1993 through June 1994. This first phase of the intervention planted the seeds for a new model for understanding and action-taking throughout the company.

In the past, people in the organization did not share much information about the implications of past events. Executives discussed issues and made decisions from a closed systems perspective, without adequate input from other managers and key staff. For example, problems in the new product development process would be viewed as isolated events specific to a department—for example, "Look what engineering is doing. Why doesn't marketing do this? Research and development is causing problems by doing this." For the most part, there was little or no dialogue, listening, or appreciation of each other's views.

With the first broad-based organization assessment firmly in place by mid-October 1993, I began to think about a second major intervention. I met with the CEO and explained that what he was doing was consistent with the concept of a learning organization. The success of the first phase created an appreciation for learning from actual events. A new model emerged in which executives, project managers, and staff began to share information in a more open and candid manner.

Had they not experienced success with the first intervention, UCS would not have accepted the idea of a learning organization. Like most rapid-growth companies, UCS was preoccupied not with learning, but with producing, marketing, and selling its products. The success of the first phase enabled people to better appreciate the value gained from reflecting on and learning from their experience.

I suggested applying the concept of the learning organization to the product development process—an area in which high-technology companies often experience management and organizational problems. In November, I conducted focus groups with each of the four engineering teams, the objective of which was to identify factors related to high versus low project success at UCS. I anticipated that a variety of recommendations and specific actions would emerge from reflection on how the most successful products had been developed and managed. I also wrote a feedback report summarizing the focus group discussions.

The CEO strongly supported the learning organization focus and discussed it at the next executive staff meeting. I met individually with the vice-president for research and development and the vice-president of operations, to discuss the upcoming process and to gain their support. I held a similar group meeting with four engineering project managers who would participate in the upcoming focus groups with their engineering team members. They, in turn, discussed the focus groups at their weekly team meetings. The project managers summarized views about the learning organization and implications for improving future project management and product development. Once I was satisfied that these groups understood and supported the learning organization process, I held a series of focus groups.

Focus Group: Process and Methodology

A total of 19 engineering personnel attended the four sessions; three to seven people attended each, which lasted one-and-one-half to two hours. Every participant knew about the initial change focus from the CEO's quarterly meeting, so I began each session by reviewing the organizational improvement process that had taken place. Additional support came from a variety of sources, including meetings held by project managers; an organizational improvement task force; and the vice-president of research and development and the vice-president of operations. I explained the learning organization concept as follows:

> The framework for this organizational improvement consulting project is "the learning organization"—the capacity of an organization to gain

insight from its own experience and to modify the way it functions according to such insight. One key factor related to learning from one's experiences, that is, what's working well and what's getting in the way, is to provide opportunities for reflection and discussion. Just as a football team meets on Monday morning to reflect on Sunday's game by watching videotape, focus group discussions can serve a similar function. In this regard, the consultant plays a facilitative role to engage a group in reflecting on their perceptions and experiences of selected organizational events, activities, projects, and so forth. Just as a football team focuses on better coordination and execution for next week's game in light of what they learned from watching and discussing the game video, companies can benefit from providing key individuals and groups with similar past-learning–future-implementation discussions.

This paragraph also appeared in a feedback report that I gave to all participants after analyzing data from the focus groups.

I then gave the participants two large index cards. One card was titled, "Learning From Past Successes: Lessons for Future Projects"; the other, "Learning From Past Failures: Lessons for Future Projects." Participants used these cards to brainstorm for 15–20 minutes before the focus group discussion to maximize diversity of individual perspectives. Participants discussed their views and experiences during the remainder of the session. This approach to recording and sharing information provided the foundation for a new orientation to understanding organizational events for engineering project teams as well as for cross-functional teams and task forces. I also provided an easy-to-use process that facilitated learning from actual past successes and failures.

I used flip charts to summarize the extensive discussion during each focus group. I collected all the index cards without names to preserve anonymity and encourage candid responses, and I did a content analysis of the results to identify key factors associated with high and low project success.

We discussed a total of three successful and unsuccessful product development projects during each of the four sessions. Below, I present highlights from one of the sessions to illustrate the kind of data generated and its impact on team and organizational learning.

Factors Related to the Success of the ABX Project

All four focus groups acknowledged that the ABX project was very successful from a variety of vantage points. A content analysis identified seven factors that contributed to project success: 1) priority focus,

2) key skills and continual involvement/commitment, 3) project management focus, 4) communication/decision-making climate, 5) key input from clinical application sites, 6) cross-functional coordination, and 7) senior management's focus. In the next section, I amplify three of these seven factors and summarized their implications for team and organizational learning.

Project Management Focus

In successful projects, managers performed excellent big-picture project planning. In the past, they focused on smaller project pieces with scattered priorities and with little project direction. One manager was particularly flexible and modified the schedule as new problems arose. His style was consistently praised and he was described as creating a climate of enthusiasm and feelings of ownership among the engineering personnel. He held his arms snugly, but not tightly, around the whole project.

Communication/Decision-Making Climate

Key technical specialists periodically gathered to discuss relevant issues. People stated that it was the first time it was appropriate for them to admit that they had problems, but did not know the answers. Brainstorming occurred, problems were solved, and directions were given to proceed. Major decisions were made through group consensus.

Senior Management's Focus

As a result of prior projects, managers learned not to push the ABX project too fast or to make unrealistic promises to users or the investment community about product release. Senior management allowed engineering to set the schedule, which in the past had been driven by sales or marketing promises to customers. Engineering insisted that every user be trained. There was an open door communication policy for the entire project. Senior management empowered project members and fostered an innovative climate by assigning a less structured project—development of a catheter that was smaller than the ABX but that did not have its problems, such as flushing.

The Impact of the Process on Team and Organizational Learning

The most significant impact the process had on organizational learning was to create a new mental model for understanding organizational events and for action-taking—the past style of senior management began to change. The implicit, companywide mental model,

"Here's what's wrong" was evolving to "Here's how we see the situation—how does this get you thinking about things?" Prior to this process, there was little opportunity for real input from personnel below the executive level. Afterward, executives began to seek the perspectives of diverse personnel.

The linear thinking and top-down decision-making style began to change. In the past there had been a tendency to view organizational events as isolated phenomena, to focus on symptoms of complex problems, or to focus only on parts of a complex problem. Now, discussion focused more on the variety of factors that were related to problems and to the impacts that these factors had on each other.

To illustrate, some executives began holding monthly discussions about the product development process. The meetings were attended by a sample of cross-functional project personnel. During these meetings, executives served as role models for the learning organization they were trying to create. For example, rather than begin the meeting by presenting their views of issues or problems with product development, they began by inviting the technical staff to discuss *their* views. They also probed for information: "I was not aware of that; tell us more. Why do you think that happened? What might be some actions for us to take to improve the situation and get at the real problem?"

In another example, the vice-president of research and development had his engineering staff discuss key factors related to project success and failure with each of their project teams. Subsequently, project teams discussed these factors when analyzing requirements at future project planning sessions. In essence, future project development began with a series of meetings focused on "learning from past project success and past problems." Index cards and flip charts were used to capture the perspectives of individual team members. Some examples of these perspectives included project assessment and planning for key technical skills; the establishment of clearly defined project goals, time deadlines and priorities, action items, and accountability; and determining critical cross-functional coordination, adequate market/user product definition, and requirements for product testing.

Managers at the supervisory, middle, and executive levels used this approach over the following months to plan, coordinate, and evaluate product development. People at UCS began to use the assessment-planning-implementation model to analyze project problems and successes. Overall, the process created a paradigm shift in the manner in which organizational events were perceived, discussed, and acted upon.

In addition, executives began taking a more active role in the organizational change process. In mid-February, two vice-presidents requested that I begin a similar learning organization process focused on quality issues. This marked the first time that any UCS personnel initiated an organizational change process. The prior learning organization focus provided a strong foundation to support the subsequent design and implementation of TQM based on a companywide, cross-functional perspective.

In a meeting with the CEO during June 1995, I was pleased to hear that the company is continuing to use the assessment-planning-implementation model and, most important, has total ownership of the process. The executive team has integrated the learning organization focus into "how work gets done though people at UCS."

Questions for Discussion

1. Discuss how the specific focus of any learning organization intervention depends on a variety of situational factors.
2. What unique characteristics of Ultrasound Coronary Systems affected the learning organization focus described in the case?
3. The consultant decided to introduce the learning organization focus as the second OD intervention. Do you agree with his rationale, or would you have begun the initial OD process with a focus on the learning organization? Explain your rationale.

The Author

Michael Albert is a professor of management at San Francisco State University, teaching courses in advanced management, organizational behavior, and organization development. He is the author of *Effective Management: Readings, Cases and Experiences* and a co-author of *Management: Individual and Organizational Effectiveness*. Both books were published into third editions by Harper & Row. He also has written numerous articles in the area of human resource development and corporate culture, and has provided consulting services to several organizations in these areas. He can be contacted at the following address: 15 Sotelo Avenue, San Francisco, CA 94116.

A System for Managing Job Expertise: On-the-Job Training

AMEV Nederland Insurance Company

I.M. Broere and J.A. De Jong

Line management of an insurance company initiated, developed, and carried out an on-the-job training for client administrators to support an extension of their responsibilities. This case shows how training led to a system in which learning is integrated with daily work, a system that links the cycles of externalization (developing new expertise) and internalization (disseminating existing expertise).

Background

The need for the training arose when AMEV consolidated its four different collection departments into one. The basic idea was that, in the event of a problem, clients could be served by any employee in the district-block. This implied that the client-administrators had to become "all-around" employees.

The line-management initiated, developed, and implemented the on-the-job training (OJT) to support this extension of responsibilities. The particular design of the training turned out to be a major step toward creating a learning organization.

Traditional organizational structures are designed to indicate two primary characteristics: hierarchy and specialization. Hierarchy serves to separate planning and control from actual work performance, which limits the amount of problem solving that front-line employees are required to do. Specialization implies assigning individuals a limited number of tasks to be performed and limits their scope of concern

This case was prepared to serve as a basis for discussion rather than to illustrate either effective or ineffective administrative and management practices.

with the total work process. Traditional organizational structures, therefore, minimize the amount of thinking and learning done by many workers.

Learning organizations intend to do just the opposite. The culture of such environments recognizes the role that front-line employees can play in tailoring service and production to meet customers' needs and in making optimal use of material and human resources. In traditional organizations, learning is an individualized, top-down, limited-scope process mainly structured by job-specific training programs. In a learning organization, the act of learning is considered a team-based, bottom-up, broad-scope process that is embedded in a continuous innovation effort.

Engeström (1991) discusses two complementary forms of work-related learning: internalization and externalization. Internalization is concerned with the induction of new hires and with training in general. It has to do with disseminating expertise. Externalization has to do with the development of new responses to a changing external environment. It has to do with developing expertise. When the new responses are sufficiently consolidated, internalization will again become the dominant form of learning. A great deal of literature about on-the-job learning and learning organizations (e.g., Marsick, 1987; Marsick and Watkins, 1990; Watkins and Marsick, 1993) basically addresses externalization. A large part of the literature about OJT is focused only on internalization. Engeström places both the learning organization and OJT in a wider context—that of the continuous evolution of activity systems and the continuous alternation of externalization and internalization.

This discussion of the AMEV case shows how one department of a large insurance company makes the transition from a traditional organization with specialized sections to a more client-oriented learning organization by managing the cyclical process of externalization and internalization.

AMEV's Collection Department

AMEV Nederland (2,450 employees) provides insurance, finance, investment, and savings services. Until 1985, collection activities were divided among four departments. In September 1985, a large reorganization took place. The aim of the reorganization was to increase the quality of service by introducing more efficient customer communication and increasing overall company recognition. The separate collecting departments were integrated into the central administration management, and district blocks were formed. Under this new structure, teams of client-administrators carry out collection activities for their designated districts in The Netherlands.

Since the reorganization, it is the client-administrator's task "to carry out all activities belonging to the responsibilities of the district block or the department." The client-administrator deals with collections, defaults, and AMEV monthly accounts. "Monthly accounts" offer clients an opportunity to defer payment of the insurance premiums. Each month one-twelfth of the total premium is debited.

The collections, as well as the reminders and defaults procedures, are largely computerized. Every client-administrator has a computer terminal connected to several data bases. These contain information about clients, debtors, and contracts. Only when a client fails to pay the premium within the fixed term does the client-administrator's job begin. A district block receives daily a certain quantity of mail, which has to be dealt with as quickly and as accurately as possible. The mail is distributed among the employees of the district block. The contact with the client is made by telephone or by mail.

The training for client-administrators takes about one year. There are two introductory modules: Basic Knowledge of Central Administration and Service-Oriented Thinking and Acting. In the three modules called Collection, Default, and AMEV Monthly Account, all professional knowledge is described in the form of tasks and procedures. These modules are covered on the job. The two communicative-skill modules—Written Communication With Clients and Telephone Calls With Problematic Clients—are presented off the job by the AMEV training department. Finally, there are some technical background modules, which are presented as reference manuals.

Shared Expertise

The consolidation of four departments implied that client-administrators were to receive expanded job responsibilities. All client-administrators had to become able to help any client on any matter concerning collection. Client-administrators, however, were familiar only with the activities formerly carried out by their respective departments. In other words, all client-administrators employed by AMEV needed training. As a result, the line-management didn't only change the organization, but also created a system to capture and share expertise.

In order to exchange expertise, employees within each department were selected to provide oral reports of their previous work to their colleagues in other departments. These "instructors" received a one-day train-the-trainer seminar to prepare them for this task. In order to document the expertise needed in the new department, project groups were established, each being assigned to describe the procedures for one of the main tasks. These project groups were composed of experienced employees, and group managers usually coordinated the efforts. The activities of the project groups resulted in extensive written instructional books that now serve as training materials as well as reference guides to daily practices and procedures.

From the first day of the reorganization, the client-administrators worked together in a district block. After deepening their knowledge of the activities that were formerly carried out in their own departments, the employees were cross-trained in the activities of other departments. This cross-training was supplemented with the written instructions provided by the project groups. The group managers were then responsible for determining what knowledge and skills each employee had acquired. A job training plan was developed and used to document such information.

Apart from the modules on professional knowledge, courses were to be developed in the field of "service-oriented thinking and acting." All client-administrators participated in exploratory meetings, during which an inventory was made of the bottlenecks experienced in this field. On the basis of this inventory, the AMEV training department implemented two off-the-job training modules on communications skills.

No special budgets exist for on-the-job training. Over the last few years, employees have spent an average of 5 percent of their work time in training—both on and off the job.

Internalization of Expertise

The following describes the way on-the-job training for newly hired client-administrators currently is being handled. The district block managers bear direct responsibility for the training of the new client-administrators. They select the tutor and complete the evaluation when an employee finishes a module. No tutor training is provided, and there are no written guidelines for tutoring. The tutors have considerable freedom in the execution of their task. Different tutors use different didactic methods and self-made materials.

On an employee's first work day, he or she is introduced to the tutor and training begins. The tutor is an all-around client-administrator who works in the same district block as the newly assigned employee. Although the tutors consider the training to be part of their function, it does constitute additional work. In the initial phase of on-the-job training, this sometimes caused stress. It was concluded that time had to be made available for training. In practice this means that tutors have fewer activities to carry out when they are training than when they are not.

The on-the-job training begins with the daily correspondence received by the collecting department. Each district block receives a certain quantity of mail, which is distributed among the client-administrators. At the beginning of the training, the tutor works with the new employee in handling the collection letters. Most tutors provide intensive support at this stage. After some time, the new employees start working independently and the tutor functions more or less as an adviser.

When the tutor and the new employee conclude that enough knowledge of collection has been acquired, the second part of the training starts. From that moment, the tutor also selects letters concerning nonpayment and gives explanation when necessary. The same procedure is followed when the new employee starts with the third part—the AMEV monthly account.

Each district block has a circulating telephone system. That is, incoming calls circulate over the telephones within one district block. Initially, new employees listen to the conversations of their tutors. After a few weeks, the telephone of the trainee is connected, and the tutor becomes the proactive listener, intervening or offering assistance when necessary. The communicative aspect, which in this case is crucial, is treated in the off-the-job training module offered by the AMEV training department.

During the on-the-job training phase in the collecting department, new employees are given no additional assignments. The new employees contribute to the daily activities from their first working day. Their share of responsibilities increases in direct proportion with their knowledge, skills, and proficiency. New employees generally are trained to be all-around client-administrators within 12 to 18 months.

Updating Instructions: Externalization of Expertise

The written instructions initially compiled by the project teams are used not only for training purposes but also as reference books for situations not covered by routine procedures and as new-hire orientation manuals. Consequently, regular updating of those instructions is mandatory. This task is carried out by project teams that are viewed as successors to those originally formed during the restructuring.

Each permanent project team consists on average of three people and has its own mission for keeping instructions current (e.g., updating the "default" instructions). For special update tasks, temporary project teams are created. Employees are motivated to innovate. If they have an idea about changing standard letters, forms, or work procedures, a temporary project team may be formed to work out the proposed change.

Effects on the Organization

The client-administrator's way of functioning is a result of all the different activities that originate from the reorganization: On-the-job training is only a part of this. A new kind of management has been introduced as well, and a combination of factors has led to, among other things, the following results:

- a more flexible workforce
- quicker new-hire assimilation and job proficiency
- immediate use of new knowledge
- fewer errors and higher quality
- increased employee involvement and overall job satisfaction
- fewer internal and external complaints
- higher employee qualifications.

Although the data on which this case is based were collected more than two years ago, the on-the-job training process for new client-administrators remains the same. The new department has since integrated with another department, however, and the restructuring has followed the original process closely. The managers who were responsible for the original new client department also have helped to lead other departments through their reorganization by using the same recipe.

Conclusions

The on-the-job training at AMEV is a viable proposition. Apart from the function it served during and shortly after the reorganization of the collection department, its current aim—training new employees in a short period to be all-around client-administrators—also is being realized. The training has created a system in which learning is integrated with daily work activities. And it has led to a system in which internalization and externalization are integrated on a continual base.

Two success factors can be deduced from the case study. First, many collections employees contributed to the development of the on-the-job training. In fact, the project groups that wrote the job/task instructions comprised original, seasoned, departmental employees. In this way, a platform for the training was created. Because the project groups still are revising the training, the client-administrators continue to support the training efforts.

Second, employees in the collection department are actively involved in the on-the-job training of new hires. If strain should arise between training and service, the training is in principle given preference. Thus, training is a continuous process that is interrupted rarely. In addition, the collection department's employee involvement is evident through visible displays of their interest and motivation.

In hindsight, one may say a learning process has been initiated that far surpasses the mastery of the broader tasks of the client-administrators. According to Wexley and Latham (1991), "there is more potential in on-site training approaches than anywhere else in the training and development area." The AMEV case shows that this is true in an unexpected way: The whole department reaps the benefits. The organization as a whole has become involved in the continuous process of developing and sharing expertise. And isn't that what the concept of the learning organization is all about?

Questions for Discussion

1. What are the key success factors in this case?
2. What was the motive for developing the on-the-job training program? Is the motive unique to this company?
3. What lessons can companies faced with a similar challenge draw from this case?
4. Learning organizations find procedures for collective adaptation and growth. How has this worked out at the AMEV collecting department?

The Authors

Martine Broere completed a master's program in educational studies at Utrecht University, Utrecht, the Netherlands. She performed a case study at AMEV Nederland Insurance Company. She is a research associate at the CIBB, a Dutch national institute for the advancement of vocational and workplace training. Broere can be contacted at the following address: Quadrant Communications, Hengeveldstraat 29, Utrecht, The Netherlands.

Jan A. De Jong is an associate professor in human resource development at the Department of Educational Science of Utrecht University. He worked as a researcher, teacher, and university professor. His research focuses on on-the-job learning, both in the context of vocational training and the context of training and development in work organizations. In cooperation with other Utrecht researchers and doctoral students, he has described many varieties of on-the-job training programs in Dutch organizations.

References

Engeström, Y. (1991). Developmental work research: A paradigm in practice. *Quarterly Newsletter of the Laboratory of Comparative Human Cognition,* 13.

Marsick, V., ed. (1987). *Learning in the workplace.* London: Croom Helm.

Marsick, V., and Watkins, K. (1990). *Informal and incidental learning in the workplace.* London and New York: Routledge.

Watkins, K., and Marsick, V. (1993). *Sculpting the learning organization: Lessons in the art and science of systemic change.* San Francisco: Jossey-Bass.

Wexley, K., and Latham, G. (1991). *Developing and training human resources in organizations.* 2d ed. New York: Harper Collins.

Building a Learning Pyramid

A British multinational corporation

Alan Mumford

A consultant describes his work with an executive team that used the creation of Personal Development Plans to foster individual, one-to-one, and group learning. The case lays out a learning pyramid model and describes what is involved in each stage.

Overview

The learning organization can be conceived of as a goal, a value system, a collection of disciplines or practices, or all three. My definition is most strongly related to the third of these: "The learning organization is one that creates an environment where the behaviors and practices involved in continuous development are actively encouraged" (Mumford, 1995). I argue that the relevant "behaviors and practices" need to be adopted at four levels.

I propose that effective learning must be created and encouraged at the levels of individual, one-to-one, and group learning if the fourth level, organizational learning, is to become operational, rather than aspirational. Each level can be seen as a sequential step, and those steps can be envisaged as a learning pyramid as shown in Figure 1. Each level can also be examined in terms of quantity of learning that takes place and likelihood that learning will occur.

Nothing of quality and significance can happen effectively at subsequent levels unless individuals learn. The number of individuals who learn at the base of the pyramid suggests that the greatest amount of learning takes place at this level. The next level, one-to-one relationships, accounts for much learning but is often not fully recognized, used, or

This case was prepared to serve as a basis for discussion rather than to illustrate either effective or ineffective administrative and management practices.

Figure 1. The learning pyramid.

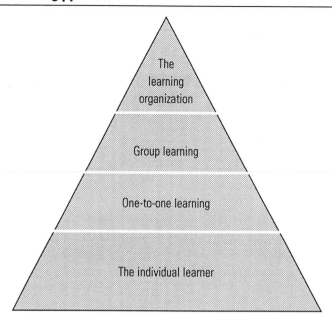

achieved. Effort is expended instead on formal management development practices such as appraisal, coaching, or mentoring. While useful, these practices reflect only a small amount of the learning that can be achieved in effective one-to-one learning (Mumford, 1993; 1995). The third level, learning within groups, is likewise not well-recognized or utilized. It poses more problems than one-to-one relationships because of the difficulties that can arise through interaction among group members. With some exceptions (Watkins and Marsick, 1993), very little has been written about learning in groups at work, as distinct from learning in specially created groups or courses. Finally we reach the top of the pyramid, the learning organization as a total achievement. This is the peak in terms of significance, but has the least likelihood of being attained.

The metaphor of the learning pyramid illustrates that: 1) an organization must climb up the pyramid, and must cover each step before reaching the top; and 2) climbing gets more difficult as one proceeds toward the top.

Background to the Case

The organization involved in this case was a division of a subsidiary, with a turnover of £400 million (approximately $600 million), and a staff of around 4,000 people, within a very large multinational company. My initial contact as a consultant was with the management development advisor, who reported to the company personnel director. I was then invited to meet the divisional director, Tony. Tony had supported the idea of personal development plans (PDPs) for his middle managers. Tony now wanted to extend PDPs to himself and his direct reports, but wanted to enlist the help of a high-quality external advisor who was used to working at the director level. I was invited to carry out a project that would

- enable each participant to produce a PDP and discuss it with Tony (Tony would discuss his with his chief executive)
- survey the participants about the competencies they had drafted and agreed to a few months earlier
- generate a general report covering issues of significance for the development of the "team," that is, Tony and his direct reports.

At least two participants either were not convinced of the value of the project, or actually worried about what it might bring out. These concerns, however, were not raised directly with Tony, and the project started with participation from Tony and all nine members of his team.

I did not introduce the concept of the learning pyramid, as it had not yet been designed as a model. I did subsequently include a comment in my report on the relevance to the learning organization of PDPs and further activity on "developing self and others." Tony and the personnel director were much more interested in the benefits of PDPs and other related activities. In general, clients are more interested in specific answers to their questions than in models, even though we as consultants might use these models to guide our practice.

The Individual Learner

Tony was (deliberately) the first to talk with me, using a prepared list of topics for discussion. The discussion yielded three results, two of them sought and one accidental. As I had hoped, Tony was very happy with the discussion and even more convinced of its value. I collected the information necessary to draft Tony's PDP. Finally, at the last minute, Tony asked that my discussions with the other participants include the question, "Is Tony open to your ideas?"

During individual PDP discussions, I inquired into the appropriateness of agreed-upon competencies and solicited specific feedback on Tony's acceptance of ideas. I approached personal development by analyzing an individual's strengths and areas for improvement, as tested against the existing competencies. We reviewed previous experiences of personal development and possibilities for future development. All participants, including those who had been uneasy, seemed pleased even though they were not sure how Tony would react to the plans. I subsequently produced a draft PDP for each individual to approve or amend, and then to send on to Tony for discussion and action planning—steps that took place without my involvement.

Each participant also completed two instruments designed to provide information on the individual as a learner. The first instrument, the Learning Styles Questionnaire (LSQ) (Honey and Mumford, 1992) assesses an individual's preferences about the ways in which she or he may learn. The Learning Diagnostic Questionnaire (LDQ) (Honey and Mumford, 1990) looks at three issues—an individual's learning skills, an individual's attitudes and emotions about learning, and the environment in which he or she works. These instruments help learners to better understand their own learning processes, a step which I consider crucial to effective personal development. The LSQ and LDQ helped me assess the alternatives for development that I eventually included in the draft of each participant's PDP.

Recommendations in the PDPs were not confined to formal courses. They included, for example, learning from existing work activities, from additional activities that could be created with a specific learning objective, and from opportunities for learning other than through courses. This kind of development helps to define whether an organization is really a learning organization, or whether it is merely effective in traditional forms of development.

One-to-One Learning Relationships

The existing appraisal process, as is often the case, had not proved effective for discussion of development needs. The PDP process addressed this deficiency because of its structure, its intention, and the provision for detailed discussion between individual managers and Tony. Tony, the managers themselves, and the internal advisor to the program independently confirmed the value of these discussions for enhancing learning and development.

Group Learning
Learning Through Information and Team Discussion

My original discussion with individuals provided the stimulus for learning in the group, because members were asked to look at their effectiveness as a team, as well as their interaction with Tony. At this point, however, they were individually collecting their views about the group. In that sense, they were learning about the group, rather than learning as a group. At that stage, their individual understandings were not shared, except perhaps informally.

Afterward, I circulated my general report on the issues raised in the individual discussions. The report identified the following issues: 1) competencies; 2) initiating and managing change; 3) innovation in product development; 4) a definition of what was meant by "world class" and how the company might achieve this; 5) team effectiveness; 6) developing self and others, a process which began with the PDPs, but which had not yet been completed; and 7) Tony's openness to ideas. The report was discussed at a meeting with Tony that I did not attend. During this discussion, more group learning occurred. For example, members found that the competencies to which they had agreed were broadly acceptable, but needed augmentation. The group also learned from their individual responses to the question of how effective they were as a team. The main response was "could be better." What the group learned here was probably that they all held this view, because it had never been discussed in a management meeting.

The group examined their responses to Tony's question as to whether or not he was seen as being open to ideas. The majority reported that Tony was open to ideas and was a good communicator, but they also said that they held back from presenting some of their ideas to Tony. Interestingly, only one of the participants admitted that he himself held something back; others said they saw other people holding back although they themselves did not.

Follow-Up Workshops

The report showed that several team members wanted some kind of structured event dealing with teamwork, change, and developing themselves and others. Tony said that he liked the idea of workshops on all three issues. He preferred to start with a workshop on "developing myself and others," to be followed by a workshop on innovation and change. Tony subsequently reported that his management team also supported this strategy.

The first workshop, Developing Myself and Others, covered the following: 1) the meaning of development, 2) myself as a learner, 3) influences on learning, 4) reviewing my personal development plan, 5) using work opportunities for learning, 6) links to company management development processes, 7) the manager as developer, 8) understanding others' development needs, and 9) helping others to learn.

The following highlights from the workshop capture themes relevant to the learning organization.

Individual results on the LSQ and LDQ had been included in the PDPs and had been summarized in a table for discussion at the workshop. The individual results, however, were not circulated to everyone. In preparing for the workshop, I asked all participants for their approval to share these results. One member strongly objected. At the workshop, I again raised this question. Several people felt that it was inappropriate to publicly share results, and I agreed. Tony said that he respected the reason that the information would not be shared publicly but that he also was prepared to take the lead by presenting his own results—which he did—saying, "so amongst other things you will understand some of my reactions during this workshop." I commented that the concerns that had just been raised mirrored those identified in my report.

After this uneasy start, trust and exchange gradually increased, in part through the exercises (initially conducted in pairs), as well as through subsequent group discussions. At the end of the workshop, I suggested that the process they had just completed demonstrated the need for further exchange, and I showed how this could be done in a helpful rather than hurtful manner.

The workshop was successful. Participants shared their PDPs in pairs (Tony with me), and in most cases, were able to add to them. Most of the managers said that they wanted to extend the process of PDPs to their own management hierarchy. Some, but not all, said they were enthusiastic about using concepts from the workshop with their managers, such as the task cycle, the learning cycle, and learning styles. Tony said he would introduce a review, centered on the learning cycle, at each of his management meetings. Finally, two groups decided to undertake projects (e.g., How do we become world class?) that would facilitate their learning as well as focus on task accomplishment.

Subsequent Review

I visited Tony 10 months after the workshop to discuss progress. Tony reported as follows:

- He was "not sure" if his employees were more open with him, but felt that they talked more openly in meetings.
- He had not been able to satisfactorily take up his own PDP with his boss for a variety of reasons, but he had acted on all the points within his personal control.
- He had held further discussions with all individuals about their own PDPs, using his own one-page summary.

- He pursued particular items from the PDPs at different times, but integrated action on the PDP, for example, in appraisal meetings.
- He had introduced the regular learning review at his management meeting and was using the learning cycle as a reminder of how to look at things (the Honey and Mumford version of the learning cycle is Experience—Review—Conclude—Plan).
- He had introduced an item called "stolen with pride." He asked at his meetings what each individual had learned from other people and, especially, from outside the organization. He rewarded the learning exhibited.
- He had postponed preparation for the workshop on teams because of changes in the organization.

Issues in Building the Pyramid
Individual Learning

Everyone, including those who had prior reservations, felt that the PDPs and the workshop had improved their capacity as learners. A weakness, however, was that I did not build in a structured review process through which subsequent action on the PDPs could be measured over a longer period.

One-to-One Relationships

Most participants, including those who had expressed doubt beforehand, felt that the PDPs enhanced effective discussions with Tony. Several managers commented that, in addition to learning about their own learning style preferences, they now understood better their own subordinates' learning style preferences.

Learning in the Group

The participants saw the value in learning from real work experiences and, as a result, paid careful attention to learning how to learn. For example, one manager identified real work experiences to aid in subordinates' development, and another replicated the workshop with his management team. Finally, another manager saw the value of this approach for identifying different learning styles.

Line-Management Ownership

The line manager was responsible for getting help for the issues that the project addressed, initiating personal development plans, and arranging workshops. He or she tapped internal and external resources for help. This ensured that learning was more meaningful than it would have been if sponsored by human resource or management development specialists.

Extension Beyond the Division

We had hoped that our success would lead others in the company to take up the same process. Tony, the divisional director, was interested in serving as a "product champion," but thought that he was already seen as "different" and did not want to take on something that would reinforce that perception. Personnel decided to take up the PDP process, augmented by group discussion, both to benefit themselves and to test further the process with a view to "selling it" to other divisions.

The Learning Organization and the Learning Pyramid

The concept of the learning organization was neither a part of the original plan nor a major feature of the Developing Myself and Others workshop, even though I discussed it with the group at the end of the activity. I decided not to push the concept earlier and harder because I believe that focusing on particular behaviors and practices first is the best way to engage managers in more effective learning. In addition, Tony was more interested in solving particular problems than in discussing concepts. Concepts are primarily of interest to those who are theorists in learning styles. In retrospect, I now regret that I did not give more time to the definition of the learning organization, because many managers in the group were theorists. My learning pyramid could be used as a basis for discussion and, in fact, was developed as a result of reviewing the experience gained through this project. The model enables participants to recognize what is involved at each stage in the climb up the pyramid.

Questions for Discussion

1. The author adds the one-to-one level to the learning organization concept. Do you think this differentiation is helpful?
2. How might the model of the learning pyramid assist managers in recognizing the actions they need to take?
3. What are the benefits and problems of using diagnostic instruments, such as learning styles, in this context?

The Author

Alan Mumford's experience in management development has included periods with John Laing & Sons, IPC Magazines, International Computers Ltd., and the Chloride Group. In 1983 he was appointed professor of management development at International Management Centres, where he is now visiting professor. His main work is on improving management performance, especially through effective learning processes, with senior managers, directors, and developers in a variety of organizations, including Ford of Europe, Pilkington, Brooke Bond, and Unison (the U.K.'s largest trade union). He has worked with organizations in Australia, South Africa, and the United States. His publications include *The Manual of Learning Styles*, 3d ed., 1992; *The Manual of Learning Opportunities*, 1989; *Developing Top Managers*, Gower, 1988; *Management Development: Strategies for Action*, IPM, 2d ed., 1993; *How Managers Can Develop Managers*, Gower, 1993; and *Learning at the Top*, McGraw-Hill, 1995. He can be contacted at the following address: Linden Cottage, 37 Nightingale Lane, London SW12 8SY.

References

Honey, P., and Mumford, A. (1990). Learning diagnostic questionnaire. In P. Honey (Ed.), *Manual of Learning Opportunities* (Section 2), Maidenhead, U.K.: Peter Honey.

Honey, P., and Mumford, A. (1992). Learning styles questionnaire facilitator guide. In P. Honey (Ed.), *Organization design & development.* (3d ed.), Maidenhead, U.K.: Peter Honey.

Mumford, A. (1993). *How managers develop managers.* Aldershot, U.K.: Gower.

Mumford, A. (1995). *Learning at the top.* Maidenhead, U.K.: McGraw-Hill.

Watkins, K., and Marsick, V. (1993). *Sculpting the learning organization: Lesson in the art and science of systemic change.* San Francisco: Jossey-Bass.

Personal Transformation and Organizational Learning

Fretwell Downing U.K.

Mike Pedler and Kath Aspinwall

The authors show how organizational learning grows through the interaction of individuals in a small specialist software company. They develop the idea of learning relationships and illustrate this idea by showing how the learning of two individuals interacts over time and influences business decisions.

Creating a learning organization is at the top of many companies' agendas today. Yet the fostering of learning relationships in the company and the linking of individual and organizational learning are easier to talk about than to practice. Fragmentation, disconnectedness, and a lack of synergistic thinking are prevalent in today's organizations.

People who learn something significant and relevant to their work usually want to pass it on. Often the willingness is there, but the confidence is lacking. We think, "If only my boss had attended this course . . . had had this experience... understood this idea." In a seminar led by Roger Harrison, a man from the motor trade said, "If I go back and tell my boss we've been talking about love in organizations, he'll be horrified." We can well imagine. And that goes for many new ideas. How can we organize ourselves in ways that encourage innovation and collaborative learning?

In this chapter, we examine the case of Richard Plumb, managing director of Fretwell Downing, a specialist software company in the United Kingdom. The story is told in three episodes. In the first, the

This case was prepared to serve as a basis for discussion rather than to illustrate either effective or ineffective administrative and management practices.

company's need to change becomes apparent, and Richard decides he must take "time out" for his own development. In the second, he seeks to spread the learning habit and to integrate what he has learned in developing a different sort of business. In the third episode, Richard uses the metaphors of the learning company and the virtual organization to steer the business. At this stage, the fundamental changes in particular people and in the company as a whole become clear. At the end of each episode is a brief commentary. Finally we summarize some critical assumptions, lessons learned, and important success factors in this case.

At the heart of this case are questions about the creation of the learning company (Pedler, Burgoyne, and Boydell, 1991). How can we learn to organize in ways which facilitate personal development and at the same time enable the company to develop and transform itself as a whole? As the Fretwell Downing story unfolds, the dual processes of individual and business development interact in a reciprocal and mutually reinforcing way.

Before moving on to the case, we'll explore this linkage.

Linking Individual and Organizational Learning

Fisher and Torbert (1994) have suggested that there can be no organizational transformation without the personal transformation of those involved. The key is in the coordination of individual and organizational learning.

To understand how to make this link, we must study what goes on between people in the company. Many people assume that learning is something that individuals do. This focus on the isolated individual rather than upon learning relationships obscures the possibilities for learning in groups, networks, organizations, and other collectivities.

Whether the focus is on individual or collective learning, the phenomenon can be described as a cycle of experience, action, reflection, and making meaning. As Revans (1982) has pointed out, this involves going out into the world to take action and gain experience, then coming back to reflect and make meaning.

In this chapter we use the notion of reciprocity to link individual and organization at Fretwell Downing and to see how learning relationships can be developed in the company.

Fretwell Downing Computing U.K.

The company began as a family-owned catering management business, serving among others the traditional employers of Sheffield—the

Master Cutlers. Richard Plumb spent part of his early career managing the catering at the Cutler's Hall. The company's business of managing catering systems led to diversification, and in 1983 Richard shifted the focus of the company to computing. In 1989 Richard became managing director (MD) of Fretwell Downing Computing at a time when there was increasing pressure to make considerable changes. Richard decided that, having learned all he could within the company, he must look outside. He decided to take part in an executive master's of business administration (M.B.A.) program.

Today the company is a specialist software organization employing about 100 people. The original interest in catering systems was redirected, first into other information systems, such as library systems for the education market, and then into wider collaborations and joint ventures. Despite its size, Fretwell Downing has some "big company" characteristics—the nature of the product and the market require a wide perspective and a worldwide orientation.

This case covers the period from 1989 to 1994. With the development of the business from catering management to information systems to software design to collaborative working, we see a parallel personal transformation in Richard, from professional catering manager, to strategist, and finally to company developer.

Episode 1: Time Out

The story in this first episode is told in two side-by-side columns to illustrate this parallel development. In both columns, Richard is sharing his story: In the left column, he recounts his personal transformation; in the right, he reflects on the transformation of the company. Richard refers to "Anthony"—Anthony Fretwell Downing, the chairman and co-owner of the company.

Richard

I have been through various career changes with the company—the most major one was when I switched from the catering company to the computer company in 1983. I had to live by my wits and learn from everyone else—it was terrific. And then in 1989 I took over as MD.

Fretwell Downing

At the time, the company needed to change. It had grown rapidly on the back of one particular market sector—educa-

Richard

I got to a point where I couldn't learn what I needed from anyone around me. I needed to look outside the company, and through Mike, a friend and lecturer at the university, I heard about the executive M.B.A. I was intrigued.

I suggested that I do an M.B.A. and, although there was some surprise initially, there was no real resistance. What it gave me most was space outside the company. To be honest, 1990 was a very tough first year.

Fretwell Downing

tion administration systems for continuing education colleges. The whole company was centered around that activity.

Until then there hadn't been time for any formal training programs. It was either learning on the job or we recruited people with the right skills. On the computer side, we brought in some very bright Cambridge graduates who seeded the research and development team—their presence became known as the "Cambridge Syndrome" and is still part of the folklore. In those early days, the company was led by technology. Management training was not on the agenda at all, and even technical training was seen as an expense rather than an investment.

The company had grown quickly. We had been through a phase of believing that our top technical people would automatically be good managers; as a result, we promoted many of them to positions in which they were totally incompetent. Anthony and I battled and debated hard at this time, trying to achieve a better balance for the company. He represented the technical "heart," and I the marketing perspective.

Richard

So what did the M.B.A. give me? It was like a holiday, being able to stop for three days each month to focus on one topic. I happened to join an extremely good class; there were 11 or 12 of us. What it gave me was reassurance and self-confidence. I was already a reasonably confident person, but it was important to get the reinforcement at a time when I was trying to give day-to-day leadership to the company.

The M.B.A. program provided reassurance and confidence not only through textbooks but also through spending time with other people in similar positions. The class included directors, technical managers, and marketers—a great combination. I am a competitive person, and it felt good to test myself—to be given marks.

Fretwell Downing

It was a hodgepodge of a company, pulled between technology, products, and markets. My instinct was to simplify, and we explored the idea of strategic business units. At one point, we decided that we should split the already small company into three completely autonomous companies—education, catering, and libraries. We ran into a cash flow problem and brought in a financial director who, as another nonfamily director, was for me almost as important as the M.B.A. He provided balance and a lot of experience. It was ideal.

The appraisal system provides feedback for the staff, but we tend not to use it on ourselves. I'm seriously thinking of introducing both peer and upward appraisals, perhaps on a confidential basis. I believe they would have a positive effect.

Richard	**Fretwell Downing**
Each monthly assignment was focused on my experiences at the company. I found them stimulating.	
	During these two years, there was constant feedback to people on the board or in the company.

Episode 1: Reflective Questions and Commentary

Three comments can be made here. First, Richard's learning and that of others in the company, especially Anthony's, are closely related. People learn with and from each other, and what comes about in a company is a mixture of many people's ideas, emotions, and motivations.

Second, there is the "coincidence" of Richard's M.B.A. and the company's need to change. There is a great opportunity for personal learning at a company that is searching for a new direction and struggling to balance an old expertise with a new perspective. Going out for learning is of key importance. Richard recognizes that he can no longer learn anything "fundamental" inside the company. He takes this time-out in another company of learners, a temporary organization of people from different businesses and backgrounds. This setting provides novelty and a greater variety of ideas and experience. Because he brings his learning back to Fretwell Downing, however, his new ideas are linked closely to the work there.

This is the in-and-out flow referred to earlier—going out into the world to take action and gain experience, returning back to reflect and make meaning, and then going out to test this learning in action. In this story, the contrasting worlds are represented alternately by the company and the M.B.A. program, by Richard and the company, and by Richard and Anthony. What matters is the contrast, even the contest, in the relationship and the dialogue within the pairs.

Third, we can note the difficulties and the struggles involved in learning, in moving forward. Richard feels he must move on (to the M.B.A. program); Fretwell Downing has to move beyond what it knows—its mastery of the one market, its scientific and technical expertise; and yet there is a desire to stay put. Schön (1971) has termed this "dynamic conservatism," in which people "fight like mad to stay the same" and old competencies become the enemy of new learning.

Episode 2: Back at Work

In episode 2, Richard integrates what he learned from his M.B.A. program, including soft systems analysis, and discovers the learning of many other people. At the same time, the company is undergoing significant changes. Richard takes over from Anthony and also assumes general management responsibility for the largest of the business units. He does a soft systems analysis up to the point of drawing a rich picture, interviews the staff, explains the process to them, and then repeats their views and perceptions of each other back to them.

Other people also bring in new questions and ideas, and there are other strong influences for change. Julie, the training and quality manager, and Liz, Richard's assistant at the time (and who subsequently became group marketing manager, having also completed an M.B.A.), provide valuable perspectives on the company. More people-oriented views than the board's, such as those of women and of middle managers, are voiced. The learning opportunities start to spread. Whereas previously there was not a specific training budget, Jim, who joined the company from the Health Service, wanted to know how much there was to spend. As a response to a general upsurge in personal training requests at a time of great change, the Learning Company Programme is introduced. The focus of the training is more on company-organized learning than on personal learning.

One of the pressures of running a small company is learning how to cope with young people who want to develop. Richard says, "There is a fear that if you invest in people they are going to leave or they are going to want more money, but that has definitely not been our experience. People have wanted to learn. We sponsor M.B.A.s where we can see good career potential, but there are an awful lot of other types of learning, not higher or lower, where people are doing it for personal fulfillment and motivation."

The boundary between the company and the wider world fades. The company achieves much growth through networking. It is the same size in terms of people but much larger in technical and marketing terms because of links made with other organizations—for example, collaborative partnerships for research and development projects. A global market now becomes available through networking with the Oracle company, which is taking Fretwell Downing's library product to the world. The company evolves from having a very constrained, local focus to being a "virtual organization" with access to the world. This is what Richard calls "the learning company"—the network, the virtual company.

Four comments on the second episode can be made here. Taking time out is a critical aspect of learning, but only when this "outside" experience is brought back in for dialogue and making new meaning. In some organizations, time-outs have been fashionable but ineffective; no one really expects anything to happen back at work.

Second, some grit in the dialogue is needed to maintain this learning edge. According to Pascale (1990), an organization's ability to cope with competition and turbulence outside is a direct consequence of the ability to generate, manage, and learn from an appropriate level of conflict on the inside. This is especially true when what is needed is something transformational rather than incremental. If a company is going to change habitual ways of acting, it cannot start unless someone finds the courage to challenge or disagree. In this case, Fretwell Downing found a challenge to the board's "business" orientation, and achieved a "people" perspective. Fortunately for the company as a whole, Julie and Liz were willing to make their views known.

Third, how is individual learning welcomed back into the company? As MD, Richard was in a position to urge new practice, and he was well placed in other ways because the company needed to change and to get new ideas from the outside. In a different situation, however, innovative people may be seriously disillusioned if their new ideas are not welcomed.

Fourth, there is a clear need for a variety of learning. The MBA option is only for the few. Yet, if it is overvalued by a company, elitism may result, and other employees may feel that *their* new ideas are not welcomed.

Episode 3: Transformation

Both Richard and the company experience changes fundamental enough to be termed transformations. Crucial to these transformations are issues of relationship—between Richard and Anthony and between the company and its trading partners. A crucial change concerns Richard's relationship with Anthony. Anthony came into the company from a teaching career when his father became ill. He then ran the catering management company and subsequently built the computer company. But Richard felt that Anthony was blocking efforts to initiate training. At that time, the cultural norm was that you did not need training other than what you learned on the job.

After Richard went to the M.B.A. program, Anthony's position changed. He has since become the chairman of the University Management School. He now points to Richard and the other M.B.A.s in the company as examples of learning transformation. The relationship between Anthony and Richard was once like that of a father and a son, but now they are on the same level.

Anthony had to go out to let the company go forward. He sees working at the University Management School as equivalent to Richard's achieving his M.B.A., and the two men occasionally compare notes. "The effect on the company is incredible," says Richard.

This sense of development has spread into other relationships. Richard notes, "In the last three years, we have done a lot of learning and brought down a lot of barriers. The company was fairly arrogant, and it is now going into very meaningful partnerships with both educational and business partners. And we are clearly seeing the benefits of that approach."

Learning becomes central to the company's way of life. Richard co-presents on day-long question-and-answer sessions for small groups. At the end of each session, people are asked what they liked or what surprised them about the presentation. The company had established a core competency of digging itself out of holes, but the new learning company reminds people of the need to get better at laying the tarmac flat to start with. Becoming a learning company means achieving the ability to change on the basis of what has already happened and to adapt in such a way that negative things do not happen again.

Two results of Richard's M.B.A. program are that he has acquired a new language of organizing and that he has reacquired the habit of reading. The significance of his learning in terms of concepts and language is illustrated by the way he thinks about and constructs the company (Figure 1).

Richard's ability to think about the development of Fretwell Downing Computing in this way marks the end of this particular story.

Summary

The Fretwell Downing story demonstrates how the processes of individual and business development can interact in a reciprocal and mutually reinforcing way. Fisher and Torbert's (1994) assertion that there can be no organizational transformation without personal transformation at least demands serious consideration.

Several assumptions on the part of Richard Plumb, the managing director of Fretwell Downing, were important in this case. Chief among these were the following:

- that the company needed radical, not incremental, change
- that he needed to get outside the company to learn something new.

Another important assumption was that complete succession— the usual process of removing one person from a position and

Figure 1. The transformation of Fretwell Downing.

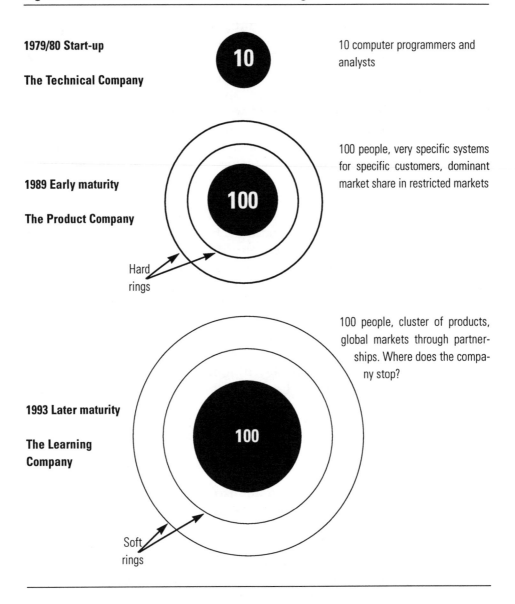

1979/80 Start-up

The Technical Company

10 computer programmers and analysts

1989 Early maturity

The Product Company

100 people, very specific systems for specific customers, dominant market share in restricted markets

Hard rings

1993 Later maturity

The Learning Company

100 people, cluster of products, global markets through partnerships. Where does the company stop?

Soft rings

putting in someone else—was not necessary at Fretwell Downing. One of the critical factors that made possible the successful integration of Richard's new learning within the company was his relationship with Anthony, the company chairman and co-owner. Richard and Anthony were able to debate, argue with, and influence each other. Had this not happened, the move to strategic business units, for example, might have been mandatory.

This kind of relationship at the top helps to create in the company wider dialogue whereby constructive conflict is legitimized. This freedom to raise questions and challenges is essential to real learning. The power of learning is seen in the development of Richard's conceptual thinking about the company and the language he uses to describe it. Without such personal development, his perspective on the company's evolution from a technical organization to a learning or virtual organization would not have been possible.

The relationship between personal and organizational transformation is particularly important in the small firm because of the typically dominant influence of the owner or manager. The centrality of this person means that the company relies heavily on the thinking at the top. Additionally, the learning style and preferences of this person may set a pattern for those of the company as a whole. The lesson for small business owners is that, if they want their companies and the people in them to develop, they themselves must be visibly learning, developing, and breaking patterns.

Small companies can have a learning advantage. Such companies, especially when young, often find that learning spreads quickly and easily. Further, a small company can move forward as a unit more easily than a large one. As a company gets bigger and older, especially if it achieves preeminence in a particular business, learning becomes more difficult.

Questions for Discussion

1. How good is your organization at welcoming and integrating learning from individuals and making it available to others in the company?
2. How do people learn in your company?
3. Is learning valued?
4. Are all people—whatever their jobs—expected to learn?
5. Are there lots of ways of learning or just a few?
6. Is there evidence that people with seniority are developing?
7. Does your company learn from other organizations?
8. Are people encouraged to experiment?

The Authors

Mike Pedler is a writer, researcher, and consultant and a partner in the Learning Company Project. With his colleagues Tom Boydell and John Burgoyne, he has published a number of best-selling books, including *The Learning Company: A Strategy for Sustainable Development* and *A Manager's Guide to Self-Development*—now in its third edition, both with McGraw-Hill. His other books include *Action Learning in Practice,* Gower, 2d ed., 1991, and *Managing Yourself,* HarperCollins, 2d ed., 1994 (with Tom Boydell). He can be contacted at the following address: Rivelin Cottage, Hollow Meadows, Sheffield S6 6GH UK.

Kath Aspinwall is Senior Lecturer at Sheffield Hallam University, where she specializes in the personal and professional development of people in organizations. She has written a number of books, including *Learning to Change,* Falmer Press, and *Managing Evaluation in Education,* Routledge. With Mike Pedler she has just published *"Perfect plc?": The Purpose and Practice of Organisational Learning,* McGraw-Hill, 1996.

References

Fisher, D., and Torbert, W. (1994). *Personal and organisational transformations.* Maidenhead, U.K.: McGraw-Hill.

Pascale, R. (1990). *Managing on the edge: How successful companies use conflict to stay ahead.* Harmondsworth, U.K.: Penguin.

Pedler, M., Burgoyne, J., and Boydell, T. (1991). *The learning company: A strategy for sustainable development.* London: McGraw-Hill.

Revans, R. (1982). *The origins and growth of action learning.* Bromley, U.K.: Chartwell-Bratt.

Schön, D. (1971). *Beyond the stable state.* New York: Random House.

Section 4:
Team and Action Learning Programs and the Learning Organization

Earning While Learning

Volvo Truck Corporation

Judy O'Neil, Eva Arnell, and Ernie Turner

A large truck company launched an executive development program that not only developed the capacity of individuals to learn but also fostered organizational change through the use of project-based action learning. This case describes the five-year initiative and the impact it has had on the company through intended and unintended results.

Background

In the late eighties, the Volvo Truck Corporation (VTC) found itself facing the same issues challenging companies around the world. In order to continue to succeed, it needed to deal with the significant changes that were taking place around it and that threatened to leave it behind. The formula that had brought it success in the past—one that stressed production, manufacturing excellence, and rapid decision making—now needed to be reconsidered in light of the recognition of new competition, the environment, and ethical issues. There was also a realization that the stress on manufacturing excellence may have created a culture that did not stress behaviors that would enable VTC to be a customer-oriented organization.

Added to these external changes was the fact that VTC was going through a rapid global expansion through both acquisitions and new alliances. VTC was becoming part of a global community of interrelated economic, political, cultural, and ecological interests. Its employees, suppliers, and customers began to differ widely with respect to languages, time zones, business practices, values, and cultures. At the same time, VTC reorganized into a more decentralized structure. The

This case was prepared to serve as a basis for discussion rather than to illustrate either effective or ineffective administrative and management practices.

VTC recognized that, to continue to compete successfully, it needed leaders and managers who not only would be able to manage in this rapidly changing environment, but who had the skills to thrive on the challenges and differences that VTC was facing.

At this time, VTC focused on management development in fairly traditional ways. Recognizing that what had worked in the past would not be sufficient in the future, the executive management team of VTC requested that an approach to leadership development be found that would help produce managers who could create and reinforce the unified, global culture needed in VTC. Existing within VTC was the Personnel and Leadership Development Consul, a steering board for competency development issues. This board requested that Eva Arnell, who was in charge of the training department and leadership development, take on the task of developing this new, overall approach to leadership development.

One of the approaches that Arnell had used in the past for leadership development was less traditional than some others. A few executives were sent each year to the MiL Institute in Lund (Sweden) to participate in a different kind of development program. MiL Institute is a nonprofit, independent foundation that designs and implements executive and management development programs in close cooperation with its member companies. The VTC had been a member company in MiL's network for about 10 years. At its founding in 1977, MiL developed a learning and leadership philosophy for change and development that was later labeled Action Reflection Learning (ARL).[1] MiL provides various forums for exchanging experiences and innovations for both executive and organizational development. These experiences had helped these VTC executives to view themselves, and their work, in different ways than was the norm in other more traditional management development programs.

As a result of VTC's membership in the MiL network, Arnell had the opportunity for deep involvement in the development of programs and the concept of ARL. Based on this experience, Arnell recognized the potential of ARL not only for executive development, but also for organizational change and development. Recognizing that systemic thinking and the capacity to learn and change were going to be needed for global success, Arnell saw ARL as a means to enable VTC to work toward becoming a learning organization.

---

[1]Action Reflection Learning is a trademark of Leadership for International Management, Limited (LIM), and is used with permission.

Organizational Profile

Volvo Truck Corporation is one of the leading companies in the truck business. The VTC has about 22,000 employees working in more than 70 countries. It is a part of the Volvo Concern. There are Volvo Truck companies in Scandinavia, Europe, and North and South America, with expansion planned in the emerging markets of Eastern Europe and Asia. The VTC develops and manufactures medium and heavy trucks and components for the driveline (powertrain).

The VTC head office and executive management team are located in Sweden along with production, product development, product planning, purchasing, marketing, and executive staff units. The Volvo Truck Component companies producing the driveline are also located in Sweden. These functions are spread throughout the country, making Sweden the only country that has a variety of corporate locations. The VTC is an international company with a Swedish base. Its strong Swedish cultural heritage can make employees from other countries feel separated from the corporate culture and head office and can work against efforts to become a global organization.

Key Players

From 1989 until the first program began in 1990, Arnell worked within VTC to position the ARL initiative and to get the support of key people within the organization. Through determination and faith, she was able to sustain the momentum of the concept during that time. Finally, she was able to get the first program launched by building on the concept of including project assignments that would earn money while enabling learning to take place.

One of the key people that Arnell influenced was Kjell Svensson, the director and vice-president of personnel. Svensson was a member of the management team, and it was very important that he become a supporter of the initiative early on. In the first presentation to him about the program design, he had expected to hear that the entire group of 200 senior managers would participate in the first year. When he heard that there would be only 20 participants, he remarked that "the need was for 200." Arnell responded by asking if the need was for "quantity or quality." After thinking about the implications of her question, he decided to buy into the idea.

Past and present members of the executive management team have been involved in the development of the initiative and have become key supporters and players in the program. As players they serve as members of the program advisory board, attend and present at the program, dialogue with the participants, and make the final selection of project hosts. In this way they ensure that the right projects, with key managers as hosts, are in place to help move VTC toward becoming a global learning organization.

Description of the Initiative

The first step taken to cultivate this new leadership development initiative was to identify VTC's strategic business objectives, its leadership philosophies, the underlying change-management concepts that would be used to build a common culture. A target group of managers also needed to participate in the initiative, and internal and external resources that would be needed. Arnell began this identification process by individually interviewing all members of the executive management team. These interviews identified how these leaders currently viewed VTC, how they would describe VTC by the end of the 1990s, and what gaps existed between the VTC of today and what it needed to be by the end of the 1990s. This information was analyzed and discussed by the executive management team so that they could decide on the program's objectives and key areas for development.

The first Volvo Truck Management (VTM) Program was held in 1990. The conceptual underpinning for the initiative was ARL. Well over 500 ARL projects have been run within the MiL Institute since the late 1970s (MiL, 1994). This philosophy was later carried to the United States by MiL's sister organization, Leadership in International Management, Ltd. (LIM). The VTM Program is now a global, three-way effort of the VTC, MiL, and LIM, which share in the design and staffing of the program.

In the VTM program, an ARL team comprises diverse participants who have no inherent expertise in the problem that is being presented. As described in the brochure:

> The participants selected for the program are the key people for our future global success. The participant group in each program reflects the multicultural and multinational character of VTC. Proactive participants are the most vital resource, and participants are involved in the design process during the program.

An important focus of the ARL method is on helping participants to learn through dialogue, critical reflection, and reframing of the strategic problems faced by the team (ARL Inquiry, 1995). Using the help of a project team advisor (PTA) and their teammates, participants begin to look at themselves and their organization differently. In the case of VTC, participants begin to think outside of their current culture and norms and to understand what it means for the organization to become a global learning organization.

VTC has one program per year. A brochure describes the rationale and purpose of each program, gives the schedule, and provides pictures and write-ups of participants and program staff. In describing the purpose, the brochure states:

> To compete successfully, VTC must have global managers and leaders who understand these differences and can work cross-culturally, cross-functionally, and cross-regionally in high-performing teams. We need managers who thrive in an environment that is increasingly uncertain, where objectives are frequently unclear, and where organizational relationships are often complex. We need leaders who know themselves and are wise and courageous enough to lead VTC into the future, who can think globally yet act locally, who will question the status quo, and who welcome the challenge of change.

To accomplish this goal, each program engages 16–20 participants. Programs run for a total of 25 days. The days are divided into four weeks and split between residential seminars and project work. Participants are divided into four project teams of four to five people each. They work with projects that are of strategic importance to VTC, but are outside the normal scope of their respective professional skills. There is one advisor for each project team. Each project is presented by a high-level executive who serves as a project host. Past projects include the following:

- When, how, and why should VTC use supplier partnerships?
- How can we reduce commercial lead time?
- How can we improve dealer profitability?
- What can we learn by benchmarking truck assembly operations?
- What is required for every manager to be a communications manager?
- What can we do about standstills (unplanned stops of the truck on the road)?

The three primary threads of the program are 1) cross-cultural understanding, 2) leadership, and 3) personal development and teamwork.

Because each week's program takes place in a different part of the globe, cross-cultural communication is actively promoted. By being "on location," participants are able to see what is going on in the company from both a business and a cultural perspective. Cultural differences have become a key learning element of the program.

VTC leadership is the thread that runs through the whole program. Kjell Svensson, the personnel director, attends at least three of the four weeks of each program so that he can have a dialogue with participants about what they're learning about leadership and what implications their learning has for the VTC leadership culture. A 360-degree feedback instrument developed specifically for the program by the participants, the Leader Managers' Survey Instrument helps participants assess their strengths in this area. The participants use the survey results for their personal and professional development and assess their own contributions to VTC as a system.

Personal development and cross-cultural/cross-functional teamwork make up the third thread running through the program. Both are key building blocks to fundamental organizational development. Individual "Passion Contracts" are developed in each program. Through the support and follow-up of these contracts by the PTA and the team, each participant is able to use his or her experience and learning to develop and change personally and as a leader.

Intended and Unintended Consequences

Among the intended consequences of any ARL program are individual, team, and organizational learning through the solution of an important strategic problem or project. Often an additional consequence is either increased savings or profit for the organization as a result of the solution to the problem. The learning that takes place is sometimes a result of the critical examination of individual and organizational norms, ideas, and assumptions. This type of learning is referred to as "double-loop" learning by Chris Argyris (Argyris, 1982). This learning is often manifested in the solutions that come from the work of the teams. Rather than simply solving the problem presented to them by the project host, teams will instead become involved in problem framing or reframing. As participants begin to surface and examine their own and the organization's norms and assumptions that created and framed the original problem, they begin to question those assumptions and look at the problem from a new perspective.

One example of the process of problem reframing, as opposed to problem solving, is exemplified by one of the projects in the first program. VTC was in the process of developing a new product that eventually became a "truck of the year." One of the project teams in the program was assigned to look at how the process was being managed and make some recommendations that would improve the "project management." The team studied the process and interviewed stakeholders.

Through the questioning and reflection process inherent in an ARL program, participants began to realize that instead of focusing on how to improve the present project management process, they needed to think about what the concept of engineering needed to look like in the future. They looked at the strength of the cross-functional/cross-cultural process that they were using within their ARL team and the underlying assumptions that drove that process. They began to apply it to the way engineering was being done at VTC. The end result was not a recommendation of how to improve the current method of project management, as the problem was originally framed. Instead the team recommended implementing the concept of simultaneous engineering.

This example also illustrates how the learning that came about as a result of the project team has ended up influencing the learning of the organization as a whole. After seeing the results of that project team, the CEO promoted the use of cross-functional teamwork throughout the company. What was once an idea to help create a learning environment within the program has now become a revolutionary way for business to be done throughout the company.

Another example of reframing a problem was illustrated by a team that was asked to find a common definition of a "standstill"—that is, a truck's unplanned stopping—and then figure out how to handle it. It would seem that the concept should be a pretty simple one and would not take several months to figure out, but as the team started to study the subject, the scope of the project changed from just a definition to looking at the problem from a more systemic perspective. By identifying the reasons for standstills, the team could then go through the service organization and warranty part of the business to the design and engineering departments. They came to realize that, through a lack of systemic communication, valuable information regarding manufacturing issues and servicing cycles was not reaching the right people in a timely fashion. Given the importance of servicing to a customer, what had started as a fairly straightforward question about standstills evolved into questions about relationships between customers, dealers, service centers, distributors, and manufacturers and ended up improving communications throughout the chain.

The project team met with their host in the third week of their program and a rather heated conversation regarding the project ensued. At that point the host was saying, "That's more than I want you to do. I just want to get a better system for accounting for standstills." The team said, "Anybody can do that. The people in your organization can do that. We need to look at this from more of a systemic perspective." The team finally won, and some of the ensuing results were significant. One of its data-gathering meetings was with a customer who said that because he wasn't getting the kind of help he needed in dealing with standstills, he intended to go to another company. Here was a group of high-level managers sitting with a customer telling them he was leaving their company, and at that point in the project, they had no answer for him. What they did was go back to the CEO, who responded by visiting the customer himself. The work of the team eventually helped develop a faster, more efficient way of identifying problems that caused standstills and getting information about those problems back to the appropriate source.

Two other examples that demonstrate both intended and unintended consequences that contributed to the growth of VTC as a learning organization came from the project teams that addressed the questions "What can we learn by benchmarking truck assembly operations?" and "What is required for every manager to be a communications manager?" In the case of the benchmarking project, not only did the project team learn the best practices within the company and share that information to shorten assembly time and create savings, but it also paved the way for a growing worldwide network that is capable of sharing and sustaining learning on an ongoing basis.

In investigating how VTC managers could become effective communications managers, the project team traced issues back to the process through which managers were introduced into their first management positions. The team realized that the emphasis and discussion were primarily on areas of responsibility and salary. There was very little dialogue around their actual roles as leaders and their obligation to their subordinates' development as well as their own. As a result of the team's project work, VTC established a management contract. Through this contract, which is revised and signed each year, VTC has moved to institutionalize the dialogue between managers on all levels about their goals and the development of their personnel and the organization.

Strategies for Assessment

The VTM program uses formal evaluations at the end of each week, as well as an overall assessment at the end of each program. The feedback from these evaluations is used on an ongoing basis to develop and improve the VTM program.

During the spring of 1995, VTC also began the formal process of evaluating the more systemic outcomes of the VTM program by looking at individual long-term effects and organizational change. The process being used is that of reflective-dialogue interviews with former participants, their supervisors, subordinates, and peers, and other managers in VTC throughout the world. The concept of reflective-dialogue interviews was developed for this evaluation process in order to reflect the concepts espoused in the ARL VTM program. The results of these interviews will be used to help plan and design additional development within the company.

Lessons Learned

Over the five years of the VTM program, VTC has engaged nearly 100 managers from 16 different countries in the completion of 20 strategic projects. Upon evaluation of the effects at the individual, team, organizational, and global levels, the following results were found.

Individual Level

On the individual level, the managers exhibited

- a more explicit understanding of themselves and how their assumptions and beliefs influence how they view the world
- more openness to change
- more open, proactive behavior and communication
- a better understanding of the importance of others' perspectives resulting in taking time to listen, reflect, engage in dialogue, and integrate diverse perspectives into decision making and actions
- an increase in initiation and support of risk-taking activities
- improved time management skills.

Team Level

The changes exhibited on the team level included

- greater emphasis on teamwork and team building
- more delegation of responsibilities
- greater empowerment of employees
- improved skills in running meetings
- increased use of cross-functional teams
- increased ability to work in an international environment on international teams.

Organizational and Global Levels

The changes that took place on the organizational and global levels included

- an expanded global network
- a common communication platform through a culture of reflection and dialogue

- a better understanding of the global business environment
- a change from "spontaneity" to preplanning
- a greater emphasis on evaluating work processes
- more open and honest performance evaluations
- a greater understanding of other cultures.

Key Success Factors

There are certain factors that need to be in place for the VTM program to be effective as a major change initiative. These include
- top leadership that supports and acts in accord with the vision and values
- a truly tailor-made design, built around an interaction between program staff, company, and participants, that includes a balance of reflection and dialogue, lectures, and interventions
- support of authentic behavior in line with participants' values and beliefs, and engagement of participants' hearts, heads, and guts
- preparation of participants before the start of the program, and the support of each participant's supervisor and home organization during the program
- project work and follow-up on real tasks of importance to the company that are outside the expertise area of the participants
- PTAs and a program staff experienced in working with ARL who can serve as role models by "walking their talk."

Conclusions

At this point, the story of the VTM Program continues into 1996. It is viewed by executives in the company as an excellent way to learn how to learn and create breakthroughs for change. Some executives who have served as project hosts have returned as participants and vice versa, so they see it as a valuable use of their time. The program is also viewed as a way to serve the company productively through working on important strategic issues and helping it become a global company and a learning organization. The participants provide the best ending to this chapter of the story. These quotes come from the reflective-dialogue interviews.

> "The most fulfilling and gratifying thing I have done as an employee of Volvo."
> "A small group of people can have a large influence on the whole group if they live the VTM philosophy."
> "VTM provides me with a global view of Volvo that I find invaluable in making work-related decisions."
> "VTM is the light in the sky of Volvo's future."

Questions for Discussion

1. Action reflection learning is a management development and change method that involves learning from experience. How does this method compare with other kinds of management development methods? What advantages does it have over other methods like classroom work or case studies? What disadvantages does it present?

2. VTC emphasizes the need to develop skills that enable managers to surface and examine their assumptions as a way to learn. This is referred to as "double-loop learning." Single-loop learning is similar to making midcourse corrections while implementing routine procedures. Can you think of examples of both "single-loop" and "double-loop" learning in your learning organization?

The Authors

Judy O'Neil is currently a managing partner of Northeast Training Services and an associate with LIM, Ltd. She is a doctoral candidate in adult education at Teachers College, Columbia University; an adjunct assistant professor at Teachers College and Eastern Connecticut State University; and co-director of the ASTD Learning Organization Network. She is on educational leave from AT&T, where she had more than 20 years experience in education and human resource management. She can be contacted at the following.address: 22 Surf Avenue, Warwick, RI 02889-6121.

Eva Arnell is director of management development and internationalization at Volvo Truck Corporation and has developed and directed the company's Executive Development Program for Global Leaders. She also has worked as a training manager and personnel director. Eva works part-time at MiL Institute in Lund, Sweden. She has been involved with MiL since 1983 and has been responsible for international activities since January 1994. She has specialized in the field of internationalization, looking at organization, leadership, and competence development. Eva received her B.A. in business economics, personnel, and organization at the University of Gothenburg, Sweden, in 1975.

Ernie Turner is a senior partner of LIM and a partner of Teamwork International. With LIM, Ernie designs and staffs executive development programs for international companies. With Teamwork International, Ernie helps teams to become aligned and high-performing. Client companies with which Ernie has worked include AT&T, Apple Computer, Coca-Cola, Grace Cocoa, Hilmont, and Volvo Truck.

References

ARL Inquiry. (1995). Life on the seesaw: Results in an Action Reflection Learning program. *Proceedings of the 36th Annual Adult Education Research Conference.* Edmonton, Alberta, Canada, pp. 1–6.

Argyris, C. (1982; Autumn). The executive mind and double-loop learning. *Organizational dynamics, 5–22.*

MiL International Newsletter. (1994, December). Dalby, Sweden: Management Instititute of Lund.

VTM Program Brochure. (Unpublished company document). Gothenburg, Sweden: Volvo Truck Corporation.

Learning Your Way to a Global Organization

Grace Cocoa

Christopher B. Dennis, Lars Cederholm, and Lyle Yorks

A multinational cocoa and industrial chocolate company is learning its way toward becoming a global organization using project-based action learning. This case shows how managers experience this kind of learning and how they use learning to foster change in the organization's culture.

Action Reflection Learning: The Primary Vehicle for Change

At the center of the organization change process at Grace Cocoa is an approach to management development called Action Reflection Learning (ARL),[1] a time-tested variant of action learning. This approach was derived from the work of Reginald Revans (1982, 1984), who developed the idea of action learning "sets" (small groups that work on solving real problems through repeated cycles of action and reflection). The reflection helps participants integrate what is learned into a *personal* management theory.

Independent of Revans, the Management Institute of Lund (MiL) in Sweden developed its own form of action learning in which managers work in teams on projects in companies or businesses other than their own. Equal emphasis is given to using the team as a vehicle for learning and to working on the project. As indicated by the name, more emphasis is placed on learning to learn through reflection than is found in many other variations of action learning. The ARL model was brought to the United States by Leadership in International

---

This case was prepared to serve as a basis for discussion rather than to illustrate either effective or ineffective administrative and management practices.

[1]Action Reflection Learning is a trademark of Leadership for International Management, Limited (LIM), and is used with permission.

Management, Ltd. (LIM). ARL was the central delivery system for implementing the change strategy at Grace Cocoa.

Context for the Learning Intervention

Grace Cocoa's roots go back to 1964, when W.R. Grace & Co. purchased Ambrosia Chocolate in the United States and Cacao DeZaan in Holland. In 1988, Grace Cocoa was formed through a joint venture with Berisford Cocoa, creating the world's largest industrial processor. In 1991, W.R. Grace took full ownership of Grace Cocoa. In 1992, a limited partnership was formed with private investors (Grace owns 79 percent of the stock). Today Grace Cocoa has operations in 14 locations, in 10 countries around the world, and is the only company in the industry with an operating presence on five continents. Business development continues worldwide with special emphasis in South America, in China, and on the West Coast of Africa.

In the early nineties political activities in cocoa-growing countries, as well as an oversupply of cocoa beans and cocoa powder, led to lower prices and margin pressures. Additionally, a subsidy of 10 million marks received from the German government in support of Grace Cocoa's East German operation was discontinued in 1991 following reunification.

To compound the negative situation, corporate management of W.R. Grace & Co. introduced a far-reaching restructuring plan that would tighten the focus of Grace's diverse business operations and establish six core product lines centered around chemicals or healthcare. All other operations were declared "non-core" and were to be divested. Immediately customers contacted Grace Cocoa, concerned about the company's future and its ability to supply them consistently with critical ingredients in the event of divestment. Internally, Grace Cocoa personnel began to question whether the commitment to build Grace Cocoa by integrating its operations would hold true or whether the new developments would result in a piece-by-piece divestment.

The initial impact of the decision to sell Grace Cocoa was to widen a gulf that already existed between the operating units. The companies making up Grace Cocoa were proud organizations with their own brand names; they were steeped in their own traditions and organizational cultures. This gulf can be seen in an incident that occurred in 1990–1991. Ambrosia was building the largest chocolate manufacturing plant in the United States. Although people in Cacao DeZaan possessed leading-edge knowledge and expertise on constructing certain aspects of cocoa and chocolate processing facilities, Pedro Mata, the president of Grace Cocoa, recalls, "They [Ambrosia] never called the

Dutch to tap into our in-house resources and transfer technology for our collective benefit" (interview, March 31, 1995). Now, with the sale of the company looming, the three division presidents—Wim van Bergen of World Press, Dominique de Lattre of Chocolate Europe, and John Timson of Chocolate Americas—were managing units comprised of potential customers and/or competitors.

Top management from W.R. Grace & Co. and Grace Cocoa recognized the value of keeping Grace Cocoa together. To ease the uncertainty, announcements stating the intent to sell Grace Cocoa as a whole were made both internally and externally. Nevertheless, customers and many within the organization remained concerned.

Pedro Mata believed that the company's future success depended on its becoming an integrated global organization with a single profit and loss statement mentality. If Mata were to realize his vision, he would have to have the strong-willed division presidents committed to this strategy of globalization. He did not believe he could force such commitment. The cultures and identities of the operating companies were too deep and too strong.

Initiating Change

In 1990, Pedro Mata hired Christopher B. Dennis as Grace Cocoa's vice-president of human resources and organizational development and as a member of the executive committee, with the charge of devising the ways and means to bring the organization together. It proved to be a tough assignment. Distrust, coupled with Grace Cocoa's long history of autonomy and a perceived lack of cultural awareness held by the American headquarters function, generated apprehension and an unwillingness to work together. His early attempts to get involved were resisted. In reflecting on his experience for this case, he recalled, "It was frustrating but not unexpected. There was a level of credibility that needed to be established, as well as a sense of trust." Holding to his "pull" approach, Mata encouraged Dennis, "You can get frustrated, but not discouraged. Keep trying to do what you want, but I cannot impose you on them."

The key question to be answered was, What kind of intervention would allow Dennis to make real progress toward the organization's transformation into one company with one culture? As a first step, in April 1991, Dennis, with the help of Marvin Weisbord, organized a four-and-one-half-day search conference involving the top 50 managers from across the company.

The conference went reasonably well. Small, functional mixed groups worked together to identify directions and priorities for globalization. A tangible outcome was a marketing/communication task force that began to organize joint presentations at key industry trade shows in the United States and Europe and that established itself as an internal communications network. Yet other task forces that grew out of the conference lost momentum and died. It was clear that a more extensive intervention was necessary. Although the tangible results were few, the search conference may have been important in seeding the vision of Grace Cocoa as a global industrial cocoa and chocolate company. Recalling some of the skits that were put on as part of the conference, Mata recalled:

> I still remember them. They acted out a receptionist on the phone. "Hello, Cacao DeZaan. You need chocolate? I'm sorry, we can't help you." "Hello, Ambrosia Chocolate. You need cocoa powder? You called the wrong place." Boom. They would hang up the phone. Then, jumping ahead to the future. "Hello, Grace Cocoa. You need cocoa powder? Let me help you."

In all, it was a solid step in Grace Cocoa's evolution in the areas of vision, structure, and culture, but what was lacking was follow-up. More was needed.

Dennis's next effort, with the growing support of the executive committee, was the creation of a companywide organization development task force. Consisting of Dennis, Dominique de Lattre, and four upper level managers from the three divisions, the task force systematically gathered data on 120 organizational indicators through a customized corporate culture survey. The data suggested that many people in the organization believed that the company was suboptimizing and that a significant management skill gap existed in the organization. In reporting its findings, the task force focused on seven dimensions that were most prominent in the data—the need to develop 1) a global perspective, 2) interpersonal communication, 3) teamwork, 4) trust, 5) conflict management, 6) leadership, and 7) innovation and change. The executive committee agreed some kind of action should be taken.

Dennis could have proposed a traditional management development program organized around courses with guest speakers, case studies, and skill-building exercises. Or he could have initiated team-building efforts in parts of the organization, a method that was being tried with very few visible results. Neither approach, he believed, would lead to the kind of transformative change required. Following

Kilmann (1989), he thought that influencing the culture of the organization required a transformative change in how people understood their roles in the organization.

At this point, Dennis met Lars Cederholm, a senior LIM partner, and decided that ARL was the intervention needed in the organization. He introduced Cederholm to Mata, who also bought into the approach as powerful and business-oriented. Mata recalls making the decision: "I didn't understand all the language, but what they were proposing made sense. Bring people together several times. Build relationships and trust and work on real problems. All of these things made sense to me. After a half-hour, I said, 'I trust you guys. Let's do it.'"

Putting on a program would require the approval of the other members of the executive committee, who would have to send their key people to the program and actively support it as sponsors of projects. It was a gutsy decision. DeZaan had just reduced its workforce by a third, and van Bergen was concerned about whether he could justify spending the money for the program. Mata counseled, "Now is when you need it."

The decision to go ahead with ARL was made during a meeting of the committee in Singapore in June 1993. Dennis, with the support of Mata and Stephen Rhinesmith, a consultant on globalization who works with W.R. Grace and Grace Cocoa, sold other members of the executive committee on investing in ARL rather than on other approaches. Working on projects that the company should be working on anyway—and creating the opportunity to realize future financial payoffs for these efforts—made sense.

The Grace Cocoa Leadership Forum

Over the course of two years, three ARL programs were designed to address the needs uncovered in the corporate culture survey. Each program would consist of 20 participants drawn from the upper management ranks and representative of the worldwide organization. A program would consist of four six-day meetings, spaced approximately five to six weeks apart. Each six-day meeting was to be held in a different part of the world where Grace Cocoa had an operation. This would, as part of the program, permit visits to these facilities and would also provide cross-cultural exposure beyond the experience of many of the participants.

During the first week of each program, participants would be divided into four teams, with each team assigned a strategic project to work on. Each project would have a sponsor(s) or "client(s)" from the executive committee. The criteria for projects were that they be strategic in focus, systemic in implications, and relevant for application around the world.

As a first step, the teams would contract with their clients and organize themselves around the task. In subsequent weeks and during the periods in between, they would work on their projects. At the end of the last week of the program, the teams would present their recommendations to their clients. Although only part of the time during any of the four weeks would be devoted to project work, experience in project teams was central to the design of the leadership forum. The rest of the time would involve learning from one another and the program staff in the total community. There would also be visits from outside experts to discuss timely issues.

Dennis would serve as the program director, make presentations within the meetings, and provide the key connection between the program and the executive committee. Susan Tocco, a member of his staff, would be the program assistant. Senior LIM partners Lars Cederholm and Ernie Turner would be project team advisors (PTAs), each working with two teams. The overall effort would be called the Grace Cocoa leadership forum, with "Working the Global Network" as its theme.

Each of the four weeks of the leadership forum had a focus based on the seven dimensions highlighted by the organization development task force. The first week's focus was globalization; the second week's was communications and people; the third week's was teamwork, trust, and conflict management; and the fourth week's was leadership, innovation, and change.

Each team was helped in its learning by a project team advisor (PTA) who carefully contracted with the project teams around the PTA role. In general, the PTA observed a significant segment of a project team's meeting, then structured a brief period of reflection on how members felt about both their own participation and how effectively the group was performing. After listening to the reflection, the PTA might make some descriptive observations and suggest some ways in which group members might handle certain process situations. During team meetings, the PTA might interject an observation into the group such as, "I am aware of the fact that there has been no mention of leadership," or "Has a decision been made not to address the timing issue?"

As the forum progressed, the PTAs would occasionally, and by design, become more active, helping teams facilitate their projects and use new skills and tools. The primary role of the PTA is facilitating learning—helping participants to learn from their experience and helping them to learn *how to learn* from their experience. At times, the PTA moves from process issues and contracts for task participation—a difficult shift that requires specific skills.

The learning dynamics are complicated and, at times, intense. The PTAs must be very aware of the dynamics of the teams and of the total program community. They must be aware of what is going on in the larger organizational system, because the events of the larger system influence the dynamics of the program and vice versa.

Experiencing the Program

When the participants in the first leadership forum walked into the meeting room on the first evening of the program, they were "nervous and very tight," according to Dennis. That October night in Fairfield, Connecticut, had begun with a reception, dinner and an informal talk by Pedro Mata. As they convened after dinner, the participants all sat together with members of their own operating units. The chairs were arranged in a large circle. There were no conference tables. Cederholm remembers that "there was a lot of anxiety and anticipation in the meeting room."

Six months later, after meetings in Noordwijk, The Netherlands, and Milwaukee, Wisconsin, the teams presented their project recommendations to their clients and the rest of the executive committee in Lausanne, Switzerland.

The four projects for this first forum were as follows:
- What additional products/ingredients can we add to our distribution/manufacturing systems to sell food systems, and what volumes and margins can be achieved?
- How can we meet the unsatisfied needs of our customers and supplies?
- How can we better serve our customers through more creative ways of simplifying our logistics and lowering freight costs?
- What should we be doing as a united Grace Cocoa to achieve total quality and continuous improvement with regard to our employees, our products, and our services?

Some of the returns from these projects were tangible and immediate. For example, the logistics project was able to make recommendations that represented a 100 percent return on the investment in the program. Other returns, such as the establishment of an ongoing task force on customer value, were less tangible but in the longer term perhaps even more valuable. Mata comments that "that doesn't show up as savings, but it is at the core of all that we do and will pay us back a million times over."

It became clear to the executive committee that many of these key managers felt that the future of the company lay in becoming truly global, and that they did not believe the organization was moving quickly enough in that direction. Though not everyone who had participated in the forum experienced such a change of viewpoint, most participants did.

An executive committee meeting was held following the final day of Forum I in Switzerland. The presentations by the project teams had made a significant impression. During their meeting the executive committee members solidified their commitment to go forward as a global team. This was a watershed moment in the history of the committee. The barriers between the companies had fallen. Where before there was a tendency to protect the turf of one's operating units, now there was an eagerness to cooperate across units. Translating this commitment into reality would require a continuing process of learning on the part of the executive committee and the rest of the organization.

As this case is being written in April 1995, the organization is in the middle of the third leadership forum. In all, 58 senior-level managers from around the world have participated. Each leadership forum triggers a change in the dynamics of the organization, and subsequent groups bring something new to the program.

Data gathered through observation, conversations among participants, and interviews throughout the company demonstrate considerable learning on the part of participants around the seven issues identified in the 1992 corporate culture survey. Five of these issues— teamwork, trust, conflict management, leadership, and communication—form a cluster of interdependent behaviors that develop synchronously, most often through team learning.

Each leadership forum also has its watershed moments that mark the learning that is taking place within the forum as a total community. Every leadership forum evolves into a microorganization with its own formal and informal structure that is shaped by the personalities and needs of participants, the design of the program, what happens in the projects, and the larger context of the company. Periodically, events that take on a life of their own in the informal network of the forum surface as grist for learning in the community as a whole.

Research on the leadership forum shows a pervasive pattern of learning and development that moves from struggling with one's own relationship to the program and how much one is willing to risk being open to the experience, to learning within the project teams, to learning within the larger community of the leadership forum, to struggling with how to transfer the learning back to the workplace.

From Leadership Forum to Learning Organization

The impact of the forum on the larger organization is complex and still evolving. Interviews with people throughout the world organization, participants and nonparticipants alike, reveal that the forum has accomplished its goal of establishing a global network of managers who are now comfortable and more proficient at working across traditional boundaries. More important, they are learning to work differently.

For example, one of the European units recently had a problem with meeting production specifications for a certain powder and approached one of the American plants for help in processing it. As one of the members of the forum put it, "Two years ago we would have said no, it's not our problem. Now we said sure, if we can help we will." While in Europe, another forum participant from the United States observed a manufacturing process that would help his plant and eventually sent his maintenance manager to visit and transfer the technology. A manager in Singapore who was not a participant in the forum said, "I see a difference. We had a meeting with a group of the Americans last night. They were interested in learning from us... listening. Before they would have been disinterested." The change in perspective is summed up well by one senior manager who said, "The biggest impact on me was the change in scope in my thinking... seeing the business globally."

Dominique de Lattre credits this global network with facilitating change at the executive committee level. He says, "Leadership forum people have forced the executive committee to look at things differently and pushed the members to evolve." In February 1995, the executive committee announced that the company would restructure from a divisional organization to a globally functional one. The executive committee would become an executive team. Elements of the new organization came out of the recommendations of various project teams, including a team on global synergies.

In terms of management style, the leadership forum does not have the same impact on every participant. The change is more or less dramatic, although subordinates of most participants report that their managers tend to be more open and more willing to listen. The greatest change occurs when there are several managers in a location who have been through the forum and who work together.

The leadership forum has generated spin-offs that extend learning into the organization. A clear example of this is found in the

Chocolate Americas Division (CAD). In the fall of 1994, the division vice-presidents began talking about how to make the annual division meeting more useful to the top 50 or so managers in the division who attend. In the past, the managers shared the latest information on product lines and business segments via presentations, but little action, dialogue, or learning occurred. The vice-presidents approached John Timson with the proposal that the annual meeting be conducted like the leadership forum. Timson and the vice-presidents would identify key projects central to improving the performance of the division. Timson agreed and invited Cederholm, Turner, and Dennis to facilitate the meeting. Project teams were formed to work throughout the year on issues basic to the business. During interviews held in one of the CAD plants the following week, every manager who attended identified this meeting as one of the major benefits growing out of the forum.

In another example, the impact of the first leadership forum on Wim van Bergen was so strong that he immediately called Hans van Dooren, his director of human resources in The Netherlands, directing him to put on hold any plans for traditional management training. He wanted to implement an approach similar to the leadership forum in DeZaan. The local Netherlands program has involved more people in the leadership forum's learning methods and contributed to collaboration across functional boundaries.

Another spin-off grew out of the quality team project in Leadership Forum I. One of its recommendations was the development of team-building skills in people throughout the organization. As a consequence, a team-building skills workshop involving 27 participants from around the world was held in The Netherlands during the fall of 1994. The participants were younger and from lower levels in the organization than those taking part in the leadership forum. The team-building skills workshop was three days long and was modeled on the forum.

The role of senior management has been critical. Unlike many executive teams, they wanted exposure to the process. This was accomplished through the use of reflection by Cederholm and Turner during executive team meetings. Additionally, the organization has noticed that when the forum meets, members of the executive team are often present in their role as clients. For example, Brian Kenny, the chief financial officer and member of the executive team, makes himself available to the project team for which he is a client at virtually every leadership forum meeting. Such modeling of the principles of the leadership forum is very powerful. One person related the following story during an interview.

I was attending a meeting that was going to be very tense and difficult. It was about an issue that people in differing parts of the organization held strong views. Prior to the meeting, my manager [Dominique de Lattre] came into the room. He said, "I am not a participant in this meeting, but I want you to know it is a very important meeting." He asked us to take a minute before we got started to write down what we were thinking. We then went around the table and each of us commented our thoughts without discussion. The meeting went very well. After the meeting he came back and had us reflect on it. I thought to myself, What is this? But the meeting had been very productive.

We have chronicled changes in the organization that are consistent with the goals of the leadership forum. An intervention of this type, however, produces a number of complex responses, and the story would not be complete without highlighting some of the challenges that still face the organization and its ongoing change effort.

Many people in the organization experience few, if any, direct results from the leadership forum unless they are participants, become involved in one of the spin-offs, or have managers who strive to utilize some of the methods in interactions with subordinates. Many employees do not link changes in the organization to the leadership forum, and some wonder where the payoff is for all the expense and effort. Also, implementation of the projects is complex and can take time. Even participants can get frustrated with the pace of change.

Although many people in the organization observe a difference in how participants manage, changes in style are not always readily visible. This is partially because the forum does not change people in some dramatic way. Rather, it changes them in terms of their capacity to learn. Not everyone is comfortable transferring the skills they have learned into work contexts when they are the only people with these skills. One person in Holland observed that

> behavior of people has changed. Out of three [participants in the forum], one didn't change at all. The other two became more open... tried to delegate more to the environment... give more responsibility to the environment only slightly, but it is a process that has to build.

Conclusion

The picture that emerges is that of an organization that is making a deep and sustained effort to change its culture. This effort has already influenced the organization at the global level in terms of how its business is conducted. When what is happening in Grace Cocoa today is contrasted with the organizational context of two years ago, considerable change can be seen. As one person put it, "Two years ago, Grace Cocoa was a name, not an organization."

Grace Cocoa is an organization that is learning its way through the challenges confronting it. Within Grace Cocoa, there is a pervasive pattern of learning and development. Interviews with participants in the leadership forum provide evidence of their having gained considerable personal insight and competencies around working globally, teamwork, communication, leadership, innovation, and change. The process, however, is not one that "fixes people"; some participants do not seem to gain these abilities from the forum. The leadership forum represents a significant organizational intervention, building a strong capacity within Grace Cocoa to respond globally with flexibility and creativity.

Questions for Discussion

1. How does action reflection learning integrate principles of adult learning theory and organization development to produce the kinds of changes described in the chapter?
2. In what ways does the approach to organizational change described above differ from other models of trying to transform organizations that are being widely used today?
3. What contextual factors do you think are important in helping to create a successful intervention in Grace Cocoa?

The Authors

Christopher B. Dennis is vice-president of human resources and organization development for Grace Cocoa. Prior to joining Grace Cocoa he was vice-president of human resources for W.R. Grace & Co.'s research division. From 1970 to 1973, Dennis was personnel manager for Cryovac. He has extensive experience in facilitating organizational development and change. Dennis holds a B.A. in psychology from Wichita State University and an M.S. in human resources and organization development from The American University. He can be contacted at the following address: Grace Cocoa, Inc., 300 First Stamford Place, Stamford, CT 06902.

Lars Cederholm is a senior partner of the Institute for Leadership in International Management (LIM) and president of Cross-culture Teambuilding Inc. From 1972 to 1978 he was president of Scandinavian Touring in Malmoe, Sweden, and from 1968 to 1972 vice-president of sales for AB ONOS, Tollarp, Sweden. He has done extensive organization development work globally and serves on the faculty of the University of Moscow. Cederholm has an M.B.A. from the University of Lund, Sweden, and an M.A. in organizational psychology from Columbia University, and has done postgraduate study in organizations and systems development at the Gestalt Institute, Cleveland.

Lyle Yorks is chair of the Department of Business Administration and professor of management at Eastern Connecticut State University. He also serves on the executive development faculties at Louisiana State University and the University of Tennessee, Knoxville. He regularly serves as a consultant for companies worldwide. Before coming to E.C.S.U., he was a senior vice-president of Drake Beam and Associates in New York City. He is the author of several books, and his articles have been published in *The Academy of Management Review, The California Management Review, The Sloan Management Review,* and many other professional journals. He holds master of arts degrees from Vanderbilt and Columbia Universities and an Ed.D. from Columbia University.

References

Kilmann, R. (1989). *Managing beyond the quick fix: A completely integrated program for creating and maintaining organizational success.* San Francisco: Jossey-Bass.

Revans, R. (1982). *The origin and growth of action learning.* Lund, Sweden: Studentlitteratur.

Revans, R. (1984). *The sequence of managerial achievement.* Bradford, U.K.: MCB University Press.

Implementing the Learning Organization: A Collaboration Between Business and Education

Ford Motor Company

Laura L. Bierema and David M. Berdish

Guided by a vision of the learning organization, an automotive components division that embraced TQM partnered with a community college to develop learning capacity in employees. This case features the learning model they built and examples of the way in which these ideas were taught. It also describes the intentional extension of these ideas to the community in which the company and college are located.

Partners in Learning

This case presents an ongoing study of learning organization implementation at the Electrical and Fuel Handling Division (EFHD) of Ford Motor Company in collaboration with Washtenaw Community College (WCC). This unique business/education partnership between EFHD and WCC is an innovative approach to designing human resource development (HRD) initiatives. The case features EFHD's learning model as an example of merging theory and practice to design creative maps and tools for implementing learning organizations.

EFHD: A Business Transformation

The EFHD is part of the automotive components industry, one of the largest industries in the world. The EFHD supplies starters, alternators, wiper motors, injectors, fuel pumps, and throttle bodies to Ford

This case was prepared to serve as a basis for discussion rather than to illustrate either effective or ineffective administrative and management practices.

and other automobile manufacturers. Chartered in 1988, EFHD originally managed facilities in Michigan and Indiana. Today, EFHD is a global business with 6,135 employees at facilities in Michigan, Indiana, Ireland, Great Britain, Hungary, China, Japan, and Mexico. The majority of the plants are unionized. Sales and profits in 1994 showed an unprecedented and dramatic turnaround for the business. The EFHD gives much of the credit for its resurgence to its efforts to become a learning organization.

The EFHD is transforming itself from a traditional bureaucratic, hierarchical organization to one that is more responsive and systemic. It is using learning organization principles to facilitate this transformation. For instance, EFHD pared its management hierarchy down to only five layers from the division general manager to the general salaried and production associate levels.

The EFHD began its learning organization initiative in 1992 with the formation of the product launch success team (PLST), chartered to create high-performance launch processes of new and current product lines. Simultaneously, the executive management, or division operating committee (DOC), began its efforts to create a culture based on team learning and shared vision.

WCC: A Period of Transition

Located in Ann Arbor, Michigan, WCC serves more than 10,000 students in the county. The college was founded in 1964 and has enjoyed significant growth since that time. Nestled between two major state universities and a variety of private educational institutions, WCC exists in a competitive, but supportive, educational environment. The environment is characterized by students who depend on acquiring employable skills; a community that expects strong school-to-work programs and an affordable, diverse curriculum; and businesses that expect an emphasis on quality, teamwork, and systems thinking. To meet these challenges, WCC has embarked on a significant organizational improvement and change initiative. It is now trying to grow beyond the bureaucracy and stratification that resulted from its quick growth. WCC's mission is to ensure the success of students, staff, and community.

A Strategic Imperative

In its quest to become a best-in-class, high-performance organization, EFHD designed plans to improve work and interpersonal processes based on Peter Senge's book *The Fifth Discipline* (1990). Part of EFHD's vision states, "As a learning organization, we will generate a high level of customer satisfaction by providing subsystems, products, and services with best-in-class quality and best-in-class costs." The goal of EFHD is to achieve maximum organizational performance.

The EFHD's strategic initiative proposes "to be an organization that fosters the five disciplines of the learning organization; specifically, systems thinking, personal mastery, shared vision, team learning, and mental models."

Knowledge gives many U.S. companies leverage in competitive markets where total quality management (TQM) is embraced and applied to analyzing problems and their causes. Quality tools such as problem-solving models, root-cause analyses, or statistical-process-control charts are revered as infallible management instruments. These analytical, linear tools are an important part of the TQM movement. Yet, for EFHD, these tools were inadequate to meet the goal of creating a learning organization able to understand and transform the organization's system.

The EFHD's goal of creating a learning organization was based on strengthening "soft skills" through developing true openness and understanding of assumptions that govern behaviors and beliefs about the organization and its members. There was also a focus on cultivating open and honest communication among all employees. Of course, EFHD needed to pursue these goals while embracing continuous improvement.

In response to the need for new tools that would support its learning organization goals and values, EFHD designed an organizational learning model. The purpose of the model was to increase understanding of the systemic processes that would influence EFHD's future.

The Cast

The impetus to make EFHD a learning organization came from Bob Womac, EFHD's general manager. He appointed David Berdish, process leadership manager, to lead the initiative. Inspiration and support were provided in 1992 by Jeff Quick, general manufacturing manager, until his untimely death in 1994. Other key DOC members and plant and area managers contributed to the vision and success of several learning teams. Laura Bierema, faculty member at WCC, worked with Berdish to create and facilitate the EFHD-WCC learning course.

In January 1993, EFHD sought WCC's help to devise a learning process that would support EFHD's strategic objective of becoming a learning organization. A mutually beneficial partnership evolved between EFHD and WCC. Both organizations are committed to helping one another become learning organizations and responsible community members.

Participants in the learning include EFHD employees and their spouses, community college employees, and other representatives from the community, including EFHD suppliers. The course is open to a diverse population with the goal of benefiting from multiple perspectives and experiences. The participants range in age from 24 to 60. Seniority with the company spans from one to 40 years. Participants represent a diverse mix of gender, minority status, and rank in the company. United Auto Workers (UAW) members, officials, and management representatives attend the sessions and practice together. One learning session involved a globally diverse group, and was so effective that, in the future, the course demographics will be international.

The Model, Process, and Application

In this section the EFHD learning model will be introduced, and the ways in which it is used in the context of the five disciplines will be highlighted.

EFHD Learning Model—Theoretical Overview

The learning model, now used in all EFHD learning projects, was developed by the product launch success team. In a large organization, it is difficult to share lessons learned. Because of time constraints and constant personnel changes, procedures are rarely written, and this results in repeated errors. The EFHD organizational learning model emphasizes shared learning by developing and documenting processes, policies, and stories.

The objectives of the team learning projects include 1) to create or reengineer a process critical for EFHD maximum performance; 2) to share the learning via documentation and process maps; and 3) to practice the five disciplines to encourage empowerment, dialogue, and community. The process incorporates techniques that clarify observations and assumptions and provide opportunities to apply process reengineering and focused improvement methods.

The learning model (figure 1) follows these steps: It provides processes for capturing learning, the purpose of the model. The next step is active reflection about work-related problems and visions through a process of dialogue. Once the learners generate issues, they determine critical clusters of issues that are similar. Finally, actions and decisions can be generated from the critical clusters. All this information is recorded and owned by the team. The final step in the process is to determine success and repeat the cycle. The circular model represents a continuous loop of learning that can begin at any point.

Figure 1. Electrical and fuel handling division learning process.

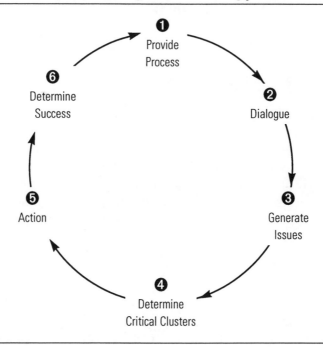

Framework, Duration, and Design

The EFHD-WCC learning course, emphasizing both theory and practice, embraces the values underlying systems and adult-learning theory. The course is designed to promote learning rather than to transmit knowledge. It is facilitated by learning partners rather than expert teachers. Careful attention is paid to creating a process that both respects the adult learner and celebrates the diversity of the participants. Every aspect of design is grounded in creating an interactive, collaborative, and supportive environment for learning.

The purpose of the learning organization course is to create awareness, commitment, and involvement in the learning organization process. The learning objectives include introducing the EFHD learning model, cultivating a team environment, promoting collective sharing and community learning, surfacing mental models, stimulating new thinking, and practicing the tools of the learning organization. The course is approximately 60 hours long, facilitated over five consecutive, intensive days.

The course includes both theory and practice, devoting four hours each to the disciplines of personal mastery, shared vision, team learning, and mental models. Twelve hours are spent on the theory and practice related to systems thinking. Sixteen hours are devoted to tools application. Twelve hours are used for dialogue, and finally, four hours focus on the leadership skills needed to implement the process.

The EFHD Learning Model Applied

Ideally, the model is practiced after the learners have covered each of the five disciplines from both theoretical and practical standpoints in the course. Examples are used to illustrate how the model works in the context of the five disciplines. While examples of the five disciplines are used in this section to show how they interface with the EFHD model, it should be noted that the five disciplines apply throughout the model, often simultaneously. We presume that different stages of the EFHD model draw on different disciplines. We also believe that understanding and practice of the five disciplines is imperative to effective use of the EFHD model.

Issues Generation

The learning process is begun by generating issues through dialogue and reflection using the hexagon tool. This instrument is based on the idea icons (Idon Magnetics, Ltd., 1992). Hexagons help teams to bring assumptions, perceptions, opinions, and emotions about work issues to the surface. Such "soft" data are considered as critical as "hard" data in team projects. This step in the model demands that the discipline of personal mastery, or individual awareness of values and commitment to them, be well-developed and applied. Awareness of mental models, or assumptions and beliefs, is also imperative because participants must be open to ideas other than their own.

The hexagon process requires at least one facilitator. The steps are as follows. The team engages in dialogue. The facilitator captures the essence of the conversation's meaning on magnetized hexagons. The hexagons are color-coded to represent the emotional intensity of the dialogue (for instance, red represents opinion, green symbolizes action). The process is not a verbatim capturing of the dialogue, but rather a snapshot of the conversation that serves to remind the team of what was shared as it moves through the model.

For example, during an early EFHD learning session, an engineering manager said he could not understand why the machinery always operated on Saturday without breaking down. The underlying meaning, or mental model, behind his statement was that he believed that some of the line operators tolerated machine breakdowns Monday through Friday because they coveted overtime pay on Saturdays. A union employee—one of the operators—was angered by the implication and insinuated that the problem would disappear if management stopped using inexperienced engineers and buying inferior material and machinery.

Clustering

The next step in the model is clustering, which is similar to affinity diagramming (Brassard, 1989). It involves giving each team member several of the hexagons that were generated during the dialogue. Each team member is responsible (with the rest of the team) for clustering his or her hexagons by critical issue. The end result will be five to ten clusters of issues.

The disciplines that are particularly important at this step of the model include continued demonstration of personal mastery and a commitment to creating shared vision with the team. Participants also are cognizant of team learning as a process and open to engaging in it as a means of creating a shared vision and surfacing mental models.

To continue the story about why the machines never broke down on Saturdays, the scene became very emotional. Feelings surfaced and were talked about. Such dialogue was not characteristic of traditional business meetings. The players realized that, although they did not know each other as individuals, they were strongly related to one another in the company system, and indeed shared the same vision of EFHD success.

Once critical clusters are established and named, the names are transferred to an erasable board or flip chart. Then the team assesses the relationships each issue has with the other clusters. For instance, each cluster would be evaluated based on its state of having an effect on, or being affected by, the other key clusters (or variables) in the system. This tool gives a snapshot of the system and shows a picture of leverage points in the system. Understanding and applying the discipline of systems thinking is important at this point. Returning to the example of the Saturday machine operation situation, the systems analysis pointed to a lack of consistent procedures and the need for cross-functional collaboration and cooperation.

This elementary systems analysis illustrates that the system is complex. System members are part of a dynamic organism of interrelationships and patterns (Ackoff, 1993). Individuals are not merely positions in an office or on an organizational chart. People cannot hide inside functional chimneys, without seeing that their behaviors and actions truly influence the future of the organization. The ability to see in wholes and understand the structure of a complex scenario is the discipline of systems thinking. These insights were important lessons for EFHD.

Action Generation

Once the causal loops are drawn and the key leverage points are identified, actions are brainstormed based on each cluster at this step of the learning model. Beginning with the most critical cluster (that which has the most arrows coming in and out of it), the team imagines that anything is possible and creates action lists. In the final step, team members commit to actions they will take to move their vision forward. At this point in the model, the Saturday breakdown team not only resolved the problem, but also created a maintenance process that became a Ford benchmark.

Results

The EFHD has remarkable stories to share about creating a learning organization. The learning initiative has generated unprecedented performance and growth for EFHD. The EFHD's financial results generated a dramatic turnaround for the division from 1992 to 1994. The company continues to perform well. Participation in the process has grown from 38 employees in 1992 to more than 700 today. There are approximately 25 team learning projects involving all functional areas and levels, including executive management, administration, engineering, production, UAW leadership, and UAW hourly employees. The learning projects focus on product launch success, material cost reduction, customer relationships, supplier relationships, supplier performance, total productive manufacturing, equipment specifications, plant scheduling, culture on the plant floor, and the incorporation of learning organization principles into the product development process.

The EFHD encourages all employees to attain a personal vision. This aspect of personal mastery is a major goal of organizational learning; as EFHD strives to provide a safe place for people to grow and attain their personal visions, the organization grows and attains its vision. This requires a culture that encourages continuous learning. At EFHD, the DOC is developing a leadership model that emphasizes a culture of trust, creativity, and communication, and behavior that requires coaching skills rather than command-and-control attitudes. Awareness of organizational learning is increased by communications such as dialogue sessions, electronic mail, and videos.

Case study research is being conducted on the implementation process at EFHD. Preliminary results of implementing the learning organization indicate that it improves individual and collective capacity to reflect, to see connections within work and the community, to exercise courage, and to apply the concepts. The findings also suggest that this type of learning process yields meaningful results both individually and collectively. Many participants reported improved personal relationships, greater community involvement, and better interpersonal relationships at work. The strength of this HRD model is that participants have transferred the learning to both their work and their personal lives. The link to company strategy is clear, and employees have courageously embraced the ideas and tools of the learning organization. Employees of EFHD are thinking in a new way, and are achieving impressive results.

The product launch success team surfaced several assumptions about the purchase and maintenance of equipment, production process, work ethic, and administrative support that would never have been discussed in traditional business meetings or even during a root-cause analysis. Understanding assumptions, perceptions, validity of data, and the nature of language is the discipline of mental models. The product launch success team created an involvement roster that lists which personnel should be involved at each step of the launch process. The roster also lists equipment specifications that were written collectively by engineers, manufacturers, purchasers, hourly employees, and vendors and includes a spare-parts consignment policy that saves EFHD $700,000 a year. Documentation also includes informal stories of good and bad experiences and a resource list of EFHD personnel who can help with learning organization issues. The ability to share experience is the discipline of team learning and a cornerstone of the learning model. Since embarking on the learning organization process in 1992, EFHD's product launch success teams have shifted from consistently launching new products over budget, under quality, and late to product launches that are under budget, on time, and with quality at or better than objectives. Additionally, EFHD has developed stronger technological capability.

The total productive maintenance team uses team building, common understanding, creative tension, and generative action to create its own quality operating system. This team achieved its quality, cost, and timing objectives. The disciplines of mental models, shared vision, and team learning are particularly prevalent at this point.

Results of the EFHD learning organization initiative are gaining momentum, and there has already been significant progress in several areas. The 1993 employee survey showed that 48 percent of EFHD salaried employees sensed a positive change in the culture at EFHD. Other group projects include a commitment team that is working on building relationships in the workplace by stressing cross-functional involvement in equipment maintenance, and a group of engineering and production personnel working together with the objective of developing core competencies on the plant floor. All of these efforts require the discipline of shared vision in order to achieve success. The EFHD has enjoyed remarkable success with the learning organization. Now it is focusing on taking this message to the community.

Building Community Vision

The EFHD's commitment to learning extends far beyond the company. The EFHD offers both expertise and involvement to the community as it pursues community vision. Driven by a belief that personal growth spawns community growth, EFHD "loans" employees to community groups to engage in visioning exercises. The process strengthens EFHD's employee and organizational ties with the community. WCC faculty and staff contribute to the community visioning efforts as well.

Based on a belief that community is a shared change or exchange, much of the initial work and vision for a learning community came out of an organization called the Washtenaw Education Work Consortium (WEWC). This organization's vision is to "achieve a globally competitive and employable workforce." The mission is to "foster collaboration among business, education, labor, and government." The goals of the WEWC include establishing a forum for exchange of information and ideas, linking educational programs to workforce needs, and facilitating community awareness and involvement. The WEWC has been an important ally with both EFHD and WCC in the learning organization initiative.

The WEWC participates in dialogue and community learning projects. Some school-to-work programs are now using organizational learning tools. For instance, Saline Schools in Washtenaw County—chosen as the model school system in the United States—uses organizational learning as part of a school improvement process. The Michigan Small Business Development Center (SBDC) in Washtenaw County uses the model as part of its leadership certification for entrepreneurs. There has been a proposal to expand this model across state SBDCs. Washtenaw County government also is working to become a learning organization, as is Phillips Components Company, a local hospital, and several small businesses. Several EFHD suppliers also are participating in EFHD learning projects and are using the learning model.

In large organizations it is difficult to share learning. It is even more difficult in a community. To facilitate sharing, a community learning day was sponsored by WCC in 1995. The meeting brought together a diverse range of community groups to engage in dialogue about learning projects. Plans are already under way for a 1996 community learning celebration.

Conclusion

The learning organization process challenges employees and communities to use their collective intelligence, ability to learn, and creativity to transform existing systems. It helps people connect with each other, their work, and their community. It is not a program, but rather a new process for understanding and learning together. The EFHD, WCC, and other organizations engaged in the learning organization process believe that, by using the tools and adopting the values of the learning organization, they will be able to compete and prevail in ever more complex and dynamic markets and systems.

Questions for Discussion

1. What are the advantages and disadvantages of creating a learning community? Of forging business-education partnerships?
2. How does creating a learning organization differ from implementing traditional total quality management initiatives?
3. What is the role of strategy in creating a learning organization?
4. What constituencies should be involved in creating a learning organization? a learning community?

The Authors

Laura Bierema is a faculty member of the Business Management and Institute for Workforce Development at Washtenaw Community College in Ann Arbor, Michigan. She has a B.A. and an M.L.I.R. from Michigan State University, and an Ed.D. in adult education from the University of Georgia. She is a former executive in the automotive industry. She can be contacted at the following address: Washtenaw Community College, Faculty-Business Management and Business/Industry Center, P.O. Box D-1, Ann Arbor, MI 48106-0978.

David Berdish is manager of process leadership for the Electrical and Fuel Handling Division of Ford Motor Company. He has a B.A.

from the University of Michigan and an M.S. from Virginia Commonwealth University.

References

Ackoff, R. (1993). *From mechanistic to social systemic thinking.* Discussion conducted at the Systems Thinking in Action Conference, Boston, MA.

Brassard, M. (1989). *The memory jogger plus+: Featuring the seven management and planning tools.* Meuthen, MA: GOAL/QPC.

Idon Magnetics, Ltd. (1992). *Thinking with hexagons: User manual.* Pitlochry Perthshire, Scotland: Idon Magnetics, Ltd.

Senge, P. (1990). *The fifth discipline: The art and practice of the learning organization.* New York: Doubleday.

Building General Managers Globally

Coca-Cola Company

Mike Grissom

Like Grace Cocoa, Coca-Cola has found that creating action learning teams to address real problems in a global business environment is an effective way to train managers to work at a more global level. Using a combination of intensive instruction in leadership and management followed by project work in potential or underdeveloped global markets, individuals learn to manage while learning about working in new cultures.

J.J.'s Story

Once upon a time, a man named J.J. worked as a manager for a multinational beverage company. He considered himself a good worker and enjoyed his job. One day his boss called him into his office and told J.J. that he would attend the best training program ever developed by Coca-Cola. So this is where we find our character sitting in a modern office building, heading for a new world. What he would find he did not know, but he was full of joy, for he was sure that it would be good.

He flew to Atlanta and found himself surrounded by 14 classmates from all over the world. How could he ever have dreamed that he would be studying with others from places he had never been—places like the Philippines and Korea—and working on a team with people from Egypt, Kenya, and Bulgaria? And what would he say in meetings with the "lords" of the company? J.J. realized that he was but a drop of water in the ocean, but an idea entered his mind. If one drop could gather other drops, he could convince them to become a wave and make a large impact.

This case was prepared to serve as a basis for discussion rather than to illustrate either effective or ineffective administrative and management practices.

When J.J. went to another country, he worked together with people. He learned patience from his colleagues, and pride by watching others accomplish great things. He was ready for anything. At least that's what he thought. Time went quickly, and J.J. returned to his office. The first two days passed in a happy blur, but by the third day he became unhappily confused. On the one hand, he was able to apply every learning that he had been taught. Wasn't he a better communicator and negotiator? Didn't he feel that he could review plans and execute them better? On the other hand, he could not find words to tell others all the things that he had learned. There were always other things and higher priorities; there was always Coca-Cola.

Then the time came to go back where it all began. J.J. packed his suitcase and met again with his old friends. He looked in their eyes and heard their words and read between the lines. J.J. started to see the light at the end of the tunnel. He realized that he himself was the biggest obstacle to spreading his work and knowledge and realizing his goals. He realized that knowing this was a step toward overcoming it. He realized that only leaders who transcend themselves will flourish.

This is the story of one individual who participated in Coca-Cola's Leadership for Marketplace Excellence (LME), an eight-week program that combines classroom learning, field experience, and follow-up. All the midlevel executives who participated felt that the program had influenced them the same way it had influenced J.J. Would J.J. and others have gained the knowledge, experience, and inspiration necessary to drive Coca-Cola in the global marketplace without LME? Perhaps in a decade or two, but most certainly not in time to meet the global marketplace challenges facing the company today.

The guiding principle of action learning—that people learn the most when working on unfamiliar tasks in unfamiliar relationships—is at work in Coca-Cola's LME. The program emphasizes both content and process to develop general business managers for the future.

Company Overview and Program Background

The Coca-Cola Company's business planning process requires individual plans from each international division. It became apparent to the senior management of the international business sector that the development of future international business leaders was critical to the achievement of their objectives as a global company. One of the most critical developmental needs was broadening the international and business knowledge of functional midlevel managers. Management Planning and Development (MP&D) was charged with the responsibility for designing and implementing a solution. This solution was to become the LME program.

The program started with the development of a competency profile that defined the key skills, abilities, and attributes necessary for success as a general manager in the system. Following are some of the competencies included the following:

- business awareness—demonstrates an understanding of the company's business
- business planning—develops plans that anticipate short- and long-term business demands
- financial know-how—uses pertinent financial information to manage profitability
- high-performance leadership—invests in human resources to accomplish goals.

The second step was the development of a conceptual model for the program. This model had to meet the following criteria:

- offer participants an integrated business education that would allow them to acquire the competencies from the general manager profile
- be specific to the Coca-Cola system
- provide immediate application of the learnings through real-world, real-time experiences
- ensure reinforcement of the learnings.

The design team felt that a blend of classroom methods and project assignments would accelerate the learning process, reduce risk of failure for the participants, and generally be more acceptable to the organization. The conceptual model of three phases—the first in the classroom, the second in the field, and the third a regrouping of the class for follow-up—was presented and accepted by senior management (see Figure 1).

The third step was to contract with a team of instructional designers who worked with internal content experts to develop the classroom portions of the program. Simultaneously, the internal design team defined the requirements for a successful project and began to build commitment from field management. In early 1993, 15 midlevel, high-potential managers from all over the world attended the first LME program.

Phase I: Business Management Curriculum

This phase consists of a four-week, cross-functional approach focusing on three central content and skill areas inherent in Coca-Cola's business: marketplace review, business planning, and marketplace exe-

Figure 1. Program model.

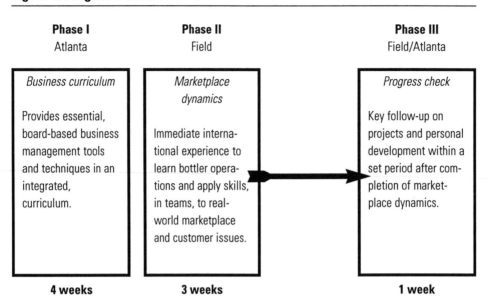

Phase I Atlanta	Phase II Field	Phase III Field/Atlanta
Business curriculum Provides essential, board-based business management tools and techniques in an integrated, curriculum.	*Marketplace dynamics* Immediate international experience to learn bottler operations and apply skills, in teams, to real-world marketplace and customer issues.	*Progress check* Key follow-up on projects and personal development within a set period after completion of marketplace dynamics.
4 weeks	**3 weeks**	**1 week**

Total program length: 8 weeks

cution. Because general managers in the Coca-Cola business system must be able to analyze a given situation, go through a business planning progress, and perform a marketplace execution, the objective is to provide tools and training to develop this mindset.

Through the data collection process, the LME planning team discovered that certain tools were essential. Finance skills, presented in the context of managing for profitability, are important. Negotiation and influence are essential because general managers need to negotiate internally and externally. Diagnostic measurements provide a baseline on which to discuss individuals' leadership styles, and feedback is molded into the entire LME process. The leadership component focuses on the area of performance management and coaching.

Coca-Cola is a presentation-oriented organization, and participants practice these skills on a formal and informal basis. While working on a specific project, the facilitator may focus attention on a presentation given in this context. This provides participants the chance to stop during a presentation and question what they have learned. People practice presentations and develop the action learning component to apply to other situations.

The LME planning team determined that a key distinction between international and domestic managers is the former's willingness to accept an international position and adapt to another culture. Experts address cultural differences and discuss how business is done differently throughout the world. Managers at Coca-Cola who have worked internationally give firsthand accounts of their assignments and encounters with other cultures. This ties the academic knowledge to real-world experience and provides a framework within which the participants may learn from their peers.

For the first week and a half, Phase I is conducted on an individual learner basis. While this has the appearance of traditional expert-led training, participants are informed that they are an important part of the learning process. In the first few days, groups of two to three people form learning partner groups to discuss key learnings, formulate questions, and define crucial issues. This fosters responsibility for others' learning, as well as for one's own. The experts can impart knowledge but cannot substitute for the experience and knowledge gained from sharing among colleagues.

An example of how this philosophy is structured is Coca-Cola's Idea Mart. One person presents a problem on a flip chart, and the rest study the issue and write suggestions on how to solve it. Multiple flip charts may be used, with the entire class circulating from one to the next, offering insights and engaging in discussions about the issue. This creates a sense of openness and trust, vital to strengthening the teams as they prepare to tackle issues in the marketplace.

Phase II: Marketplace Dynamics

Phase II begins immediately after participants complete the four-week business management curriculum phase. Projects are determined by local management who define needs in their respective areas. Program staff work with the local sponsors in developing a project worksheet that defines the project at the highest level and identifies goals and objectives. Because action learning is driven by key questions, local executives identify these questions: What are the underlying business issues? What needs led to the project? What focus does the project have in the market? Who are the customers? Who are the shareholders likely to be influenced by the outcome?

All projects must be focused on the marketplace. LME planners decided that projects more operational than strategic in nature present the best opportunity to apply what participants learned in Phase I. These projects tend to have immediate turnaround potential and usually are very effective. Examples of projects include

- development of strategic plans and programs to strengthen trade channel management
- preparation of a launch plan for a new product
- conducting a feasibility study to determine the relevance of fountain service
- preparation of an alternative beverage (noncarbonated drink) strategy
- identification of local market channels and preparation of channel strategies.

It is imperative to build strong relationships on the local level to overcome resistance to this process. Feelings of distrust tend to arise if local executives do not understand the objective of the project. Practitioners designing global action learning programs need to consider the importance of establishing these relationships to realize successful implementation.

Halfway through Phase I, participants are told what country they will visit and who the members of their team will be. Up to this point, they do not know anything about the project they will tackle. The facilitator introduces the briefing form and leads initial sessions in which the team gathers and begins to formulate assumptions about the project. These sessions generally present more questions than answers, and team members begin to become comfortable with the ambiguity inherent in the process. The two-page briefing form is often new to people at Coca-Cola, who are used to dealing with exhaustive information and data. Teams have to wrestle with forming a plan of action and compiling a list of people who will assist them in their field projects.

During this preparation time, people who have been assigned to particular countries will coach teams and help identify issues, cultural differences, and key people. The goal of this preparation is to separate the known from the unknown in order to formulate a plan of action. This process continues in the field. When teams first arrive in the host country, they meet with regional executive managers, bottlers, and customers to review business plans describing the marketplace and bottler operations. This helps to ground the team, identify those questions needing answers, and define the scope of the project. At the end of the first week, the teams have formulated a work plan, reviewed it with local management, and received feedback. During the second week, the teams work against that plan to execute the project. Local management, the project briefing form, and LME preparation provide parameters for the project, but the final plan of action is developed by the teams. There are no set rules or procedures.

This is when the power of the team emerges. It becomes clear that no one person has all the answers, and people need to rely on others to implement the plan successfully. Various disciplines are represented, and each functional area contributes to realizing the goal, with the assumption that people with different functional expertise working together leads to better business.

The remaining time is spent implementing the work plan, applying business learnings, presenting findings to local management, and developing crucial leadership skills. The benefits for participants and the company are enormous. Teams work to increase market share in emerging global markets, and individuals gain the competencies to continue the growth of Coca-Cola's business worldwide.

Phase III: Ending It Where It Began

This case ends where it began, with J.J. and his colleagues gathering together eight months later for follow up and debriefing. J.J.'s reactions are common after an intense training program. People leave the training situation, return to their jobs, and slowly lose their learnings under the steady flow of day-to-day business as usual. Without intervention at this point, the program could be seen as a waste of financial and time resources. Phase III allows participants to gather together to discuss the challenges of moving their business units forward, overcoming the barriers of isolation, and internalizing the learnings in order to make real culture change. Time and distance allow participants to reflect on their experience and learnings.

During Phase III, project sponsors report on the results of the teams' efforts. Because the projects are operational and focused, eight to ten months allows enough time to gauge their influence on business. These reports are the true indicators of success. Team recommendations have increased market share and have pointed Coca-Cola in the right direction to succeed in the international marketplace. The progress of LME is central to the progress of Coca-Cola.

Currently, Coca-Cola is running two LME programs annually, training those who will lead Coca-Cola into the next century. Creating leaders for change one person and one team at a time, Coca-Cola plans to be ready to tap emerging markets throughout the world.

Questions for Discussion

1. How is this program an example of a strategic organizational intervention?
2. Based on your current level of understanding about the program, what changes would you suggest to strengthen it?

3. What would you do as program manager to prepare participants and facilitators for the Phase II field project?
4. What are the key cultural and leadership learnings one could expect from participation in this program?
5. What are the key success indicators management should review to determine the success of this program?

The Author

Mike Grissom is an independent consultant in Atlanta, Georgia, specializing in organization and management development. Before becoming an independent consultant, he had 14 years of corporate experience with two *Fortune* 10 companies, working in strategy formulation, organizational planning and development, management selection, management assessment, and management development. Mike began his corporate career in 1981 at Philip Morris USA, where he held positions of increasing responsibility in executive development and employee relations operations. He managed the start-up of a management and organization development unit for a division of 4,500 associates, creating a strategic direction, staffing the unit, and directing program development and implementation. In 1990 he received the President's Award for high achievement. In 1991 Mike joined the Coca-Cola Company, where he was responsible for the worldwide executive development system including executive resources planning, executive assessment, and executive development. He was responsible for the creation of the unit's strategy that emphasized linking business strategy with executive development. Mike directed several innovative initiatives, including a leading-edge program to develop international business leaders. In addition, he supported country-specific efforts to identify and develop leaders for South Africa, China, Japan, and other countries. Mike received his B.A. degree at the University of Richmond, his master's degree in counseling at Virginia Commonwealth University, and his Ed.D. in educational leadership at the College of William and Mary. He is a frequent guest speaker. He is active in numerous civic and professional organizations including the Society for Industrial and Organizational Psychology (SIOP) and the Human Resources Planning Society (HRPS). He can be contacted at the following address: 510 Ladyhank Lane, Alpharetta, GA 30202.

Community Learning Organizations

Middle and Southwest Georgia Communities

Allen B. Moore and Rusty Brooks

This chapter features communities that function like learning organizations. The case explores strategies used by two informal community groups to develop visions, make them tangible, and involve key stakeholders in their design and implementation.

Defining the Learning Organization Within Communities

We work with a wide variety of community groups and organizations. Some have a history of meeting and working together, such as a community board for the local library, the town council, or the county commission. Others are "zero history" (Moore and Feldt, 1993) groups that have not met before but have been called together to discuss issues, concerns, or some community problem. An example of a zero history group might be the participants invited to a meeting about starting a "clean and beautiful" organization in a county or region. Individuals might know a few of the other group participants, but it is unlikely that everyone knows all of the people attending the meeting.

A community learning organization, in our view, is a group (existing or zero history) that agrees to work on a shared concern or problem for more than a few meetings. The group meets, works on a shared vision, identifies concerns, prioritizes their interests, designs an action plan, implements strategies to resolve problems, and reports back to the group about the success or need for redesigning strategies for problem resolution. The reporting-back process includes time to discuss results of their efforts in decision making and problem solving and to redirect their efforts if necessary. The time required to accomplish all the above activities

This case was prepared to serve as a basis for discussion rather than to illustrate either effective or ineffective administrative and management practices.

varies with each group. Very few groups, however, can accomplish these steps in less than six months and some require one to two years if they continue to update their vision and revise their action plans to address new issues and concerns. Members of community groups that we would classify as learning organizations are willing to do the following:

- share information
- discuss local issues (e.g., crime, solid waste disposal, economic development strategies)
- solve problems and make decisions
- participate in, and take responsibility for, getting at least some part of all major tasks completed
- ask for help from others when needed
- find time in their busy schedules to meet and discuss results (either positive or negative) with members of the community.

We identify two additional action planning factors that we consider to be important to the success of learning organizations. First is the capacity and willingness to create a vision that is shared with the larger group or broader community. Second is a future-oriented, rather than retrospective, outlook.

These two factors are embedded in the Watkins and Marsick (1993) Learning Organization Action Imperatives Model. These concepts are also very close to the results reported by Collins and Porras in *Built to Last* (1994), which catalogs many factors related to organizations that have lasted more than 50 years. Two factors they identify as important are 1) creating a climate conducive to growth and development by providing time and opportunities to continue learning and 2) having a vision for the organization that is shared by its employees.

The Community Learning Organization

Community learning organizations (CLOs) that we organize or observe in our work with the Institute of Community and Area Development (ICAD) at the University of Georgia are informally organized, and their purpose is usually to solve problems or make decisions about community issues. The two communities we discuss in this case, Middle Georgia Community (MGC) and Southwest Georgia Community (SGC), reflect the informal organizational pattern in that neither formed a traditional organization with articles of incorporation, by-laws, or elected officers. Instead, both communities formed learning organizations to solve their problems. Each community experienced different levels of success and provided different lessons about community learning organizations.

For our purposes, MGC was less successful as a community learning organization than SGC. As we outline the development and agendas of each organization, we will identify factors that contributed to both success and frustration.

Case One: The Middle Georgia Community

Who Was Involved
The MGC called together six to eight community members to discuss ways they could improve the appearance of their downtown shopping area and promote economic development activities by bringing in new businesses to occupy vacant buildings. In MGC these discussions were presented to various other community groups, including the clean and beautiful commission, county commissioners, and the city council for confirmation and advice.

Process Followed by the CLO
Both communities used formal and informal organizations to communicate about dilemmas and community issues. For example, MGC used chamber of commerce meetings, clean and beautiful commission meetings, recreation committee meetings, and meetings with elected officials to identify and discuss the need for working on community issues. Issues that were raised included cleaning up downtown sidewalks, developing a walking tour of homes, and recruiting new businesses to the community.

Informal networks also were used to recruit residents to help paint a community mural in an alley. The teacher and students of a local art class took on the responsibility of painting the "canvas" (backs of stores on the main street). The class designed the initial sketches for the mural, a Creek Indian illustration, and began painting the anchor part. Additional community participants helped paint the historic buildings and events that completed the mural.

Models and Techniques Used by the CLO
The MGC attended a four-day community economic development meeting in May 1992 at the University of Georgia to get ideas and to identify statewide resources. At this session, the MGC and other communities began to explore and expand their visions of change. Before leaving the meeting, MGC developed an action plan. Their charge was to return home and share the action plan with other members of the community and to add ideas or projects to the plan. Within six months

of the meeting, the group had initiated or completed all of the items on their two-year action plan.

A retreat was held for MGC in March 1993, facilitated by representatives of a statewide utility company. At the retreat, the MGC discussed completed projects, such as recruiting businesses to the downtown, developing a video to attract retirees to the community, getting commitments from local and nearby agencies to help in the renovation of the train depot for chamber of commerce office space, repainting historic signs in the downtown area, and implementing the "clean up downtown" plan with the newly formed clean and beautiful commission. Additional ideas were identified by the group at the retreat and were included in their revised action plan. For example, the group planned to secure a fast-food franchise for the downtown area, offer a second mural for merchants on another block of the downtown, complete train depot renovations, locate housing or a small hotel for the MGC, work on cleaning up entrances and exits to the community, promote an annual community festival, and expand the membership of MGC.

Changes Effected by the CLO

Both communities developed action plans from visioning sessions. In the case of MGC, the original small group developed a vision from what the individual members understood to be shared concerns in the community. Their visions expanded to ideas and then to the projects earlier identified. These were but a few of the ideas that the CLO raised, discussed, and prioritized for implementation over a 12-month period. When a team of community developers from the university visited the community three months after the initial development of the MGC action plan, all of the projects were underway and most of the projects were finished. Six months after the visit, another agency helped the community learning organization (now 15 to 18 people) to update their action plans and begin another round of changes, improvements, and developments.

Lessons Learned

Because MGC could not get active participation from more than the initial six to eight participants, it resorted to keeping other groups, such as elected officials, informed of events and projects. The chamber executive director of MGC made special visits to explain what the group was doing, and the group received recognition and approval for its actions. Although there was informal support for learning organization planning, actions, and results, the leaders of the CLO in MGC "burned out" after two years of doing all of the work themselves. Some projects, such as the train depot and another alley mural, remain uncompleted.

Case Two: The Southwest Georgia Community

By contrast, the SGC wanted to extend its track record of improving the quality of life of the community by looking into the future and planning for growth and development. The SGC produced a "community vision" of what it wanted to see happen in its town and community.

Who Was Involved

In both communities, a core group of six to ten people began the initial discussion of disorienting dilemmas (Mezirow, 1978) or the need for community change. The SGC learning organization membership quickly expanded to include 23 people who were employed in the local area as farmers, small business owners, chamber of commerce members (including the chamber's executive director), local elected officials, representatives from nearby community colleges and technical institutes, and representatives from the financial community.

Also, there was frequent communication between the learning organization and the existing community boards and work groups that had an interest in the future direction of the SGC. The learning organization has stayed together informally and worked on a variety of action planning ideas. The SGC, like MGC, presented ideas and projects to multiple boards and groups in the community to seek support, confirmation, and help in implementing community plans.

Process Followed by the CLO

The SGC has had a history of community development accomplishments. In the mid-1980s, a group of residents wanted to develop a park facility for the community. At that time a small, informal learning organization was formed. The group worked with university faculty and students to design a recreation facility for the community. Community members covered the expenses of the university group to visit, measure land area and streams, make sketches, and return with a suggested plan for development. The SGC took on the task of locating volunteers, contracting work, and getting ideas from the community. They developed a recreation facility for organized sports and walking trails along streams and into swamps.

The original community learning organization expanded in the 1990s. The group has envisioned, described, designed, prioritized, implemented, and updated community projects that have increased the quality of life of residents and generated new jobs in the city, county, and region. The SGC meets about six times per year and more often when needed.

Models and Techniques Used by the CLO

The SGC members also attended the University of Georgia community economic development meeting in May 1992. They came to share their "vision" of what they wanted to accomplish. Their vision was an artist's watercolor of the downtown depicting street lighting, landscaping around the courthouse, and a renovated historic hotel on the town square. Upon returning to SGC, representatives presented their ideas and resources to the local learning organization. Ideas that were added to the action planning vision included the following:

• expanding community recreation facilities and park
• promoting the community play as part of the Cultural Olympiad at the 1996 Olympics
• securing funds to renovate the historic hotel, and hiring local craftsmen and women to do the renovations
• getting estimates on street lighting and seeking "subscriptions," sponsorship of one light per family
• recruiting additional businesses to the community
• establishing a formal relationship between the nearby community college and the town for education and training services
• brainstorming ways to secure funding for the design of an international telecommunications center for the community.

Changes Effected by the CLO

Periodic follow-up sessions, conducted by the University of Georgia, served to recognize, and stimulate implementation of, SGC's action plan. To date, the first phase of the downtown landscaping has been completed. An initial goal of 18 installed light poles was exceeded by 10, and they have been installed at a total cost of $1,000 for each pole. The renovated hotel was dedicated in September 1994, with more than 700 people attending the opening ceremonies. The community play has moved into permanent quarters near the downtown square; it has been designated the official state play and is part of the Cultural Olympiad for the 1996 Olympics. A building has been located near downtown to house the international telecommunications center, and discussions have been held with state and local officials about including the statewide distance learning system in this center.

Lessons Learned

The SGC has been able to maintain participation of 20 to 25 people over five to six years. All of the visioning sessions have included broad-based support from the community. After five years, all of the buildings, street improvements, sidewalk changes, and landscaping in the original vision have been implemented and promoted to the public. At vision update meetings, the group has reviewed the original illustration and connected new ideas to the old vision.

The SGC has maintained or expanded its membership by encouraging members to bring a friend (sometimes called a cosponsor, helper, or partner) to meetings to promote and share the results of working on "visioned" projects. Additional projects that have required new skills and new members have been implemented, and existing learning organization members have been successful at recruiting these residents. The SGC periodically recognizes its own accomplishments and continues to add new "visioned" ideas that have bubbled up from the group. The learning agenda is constantly changing.

Conclusion

Community learning organizations are usually informal. We do not know of a community learning group that has called itself by such a name. We are aware, however, of communities that have formed focus groups, economic development groups, forward development groups, maintaining-the-quality-of-community-life groups, and so forth. The groups have, in fact, become learning organizations. They have tended to discuss, bring in experts for presentations, develop action plans, and implement projects related to economic development, environmental protection and the like. Both MGC and SGC formed informal learning organizations. In other words, they did not adopt a charter, or by-laws, or become incorporated, but they did discuss issues and design strategies to solve their respective problems.

Groups do indeed learn. In both communities, individuals in the learning organizations gained new knowledge and insight into issues and community problems. They explored options for solving their dilemmas and designed strategies to implement these solutions. Getting each group to take the time to reflect on what it did, why it did or did not work, and to suggest new action plans is a relatively easy task. Individuals are interested in results. They want to know what happened: What happened with the community festival? Where did the time or money come from to paint and put up the downtown walking tour? Who was able to get the junk cars moved from along the highway?

No single strategy seems to work all the time with every community or learning organization. What does seem to be successful is for the group to take time to explore issues, dilemmas, and situations, and then to facilitate these discussions into a process for understanding and taking responsibility for action. Another important factor is allowing time for the group to study, discuss, reflect, and clearly understand issues or problems before suggesting possible solutions or alternatives.

Hard work and action plans seem to be the formula for forming and maintaining learning organizations. Learning and continued participation depend on the members' ability to see a dilemma or situation, suggest possible options, do the work, and discuss the results.

Questions for Discussion

1. What are the educational and training advantages of a CLO versus a more traditionally organized adult education group? What are the disadvantages?
2. Does the extent to which a community is rural or urban influence the potential for success of CLOs for educational or training purposes?

The Authors

Allen B. Moore is an associate professor jointly staffed with the Institute of Community and Area Development (ICAD) and the Department of Adult Education at the University of Georgia, Athens. He teaches and directs graduate student research in the department of adult education. In his ICAD position he assists community groups in problem solving and decision making related to community economic development activities. He is the coauthor of two books—one with James Feldt, entitled *Facilitating Community and Decision Making Groups* (1993), and the other with Rusty Brooks, entitled *Transforming Communities: Empowering for Change* (1995). He codirects, with Rusty Brooks, the Community Economic Development Program—a county team-based approach to community and economic development for rural areas in Georgia. Moore may be contacted at the following address: Institute of Community and Area Development, University of Georgia, 1234 South Lumpkin Street, Athens, GA 30602.

Rusty Brooks is an associate professor at the University of Georgia. His appointment is in the Institute of Community and Area Development, where he works primarily on community economic development, action planning, and decision conferencing for public and private sector organizations. He earned a B.A. and an M.C.J. from the University of Alabama and a Ph.D. in sociology from the University of Georgia. He has authored more than 100 community-level studies in Georgia and has helped to develop strategic plans for clients such as the Georgia Power Company, numerous chambers of commerce, the Council of Economic Development Organizations, the Atlanta Regional Commission, the Southeastern Regional Directors Institute, and the Georgia Department of Transportation. He served on the Rural Advisory Committee for the Southern Growth Policies Board study, "After the Factories." He also served on the 1983 United States Department of Agriculture task force that developed *Rural Development: A Commitment to Change.* He recently served on the Southern Rural Development Center Committee on Infrastructure Investment, which in 1990 produced the monograph, *Innovative Infrastructure Financing and Delivery Systems.* He also has published his work in *Southern Rural Sociology, Small Town, Journal of the Community Development Society, Broiler Industry Review, Extension Review, The Rural Sociologist, The Southern Journal of Agricultural Economics,* and *The Journal of Agribusiness.* He is a past president of the Southern Rural Sociological Association and a former book review editor for the Journal of the Community Development Society, and has served on major committees for the Rural Sociological Society.

References

Cole, M. (1990). Cultural psychology: A once and future discipline. In *1989 Nebraska Symposium on Motivation: Cross-Cultural Respective.* Lincoln: University of Nebraska Press.

Collins, J. and Porras J. (1994). *Built to last.* New York: HarperCollins.

Mezirow, J. (1978). *Education for perspective transformation: Women's re-entry programs in community colleges.* New York: Center for Adult Education, Teachers College, Columbia University.

Moore, A., and Feldt, J. (1993). *Facilitating community and decision-making groups.* Malabar: Krieger.

Watkins, K., and Marsick, V. (1993). *Sculpting the learning organization: Lessons in the art and science of systemic change.* San Francisco: Jossey-Bass.

Section 5:
Organizational Restructuring as Prelude to the Learning Organization

A New Vision for Government: Learning in the Public Service

Alberta Labour

Jennifer Bowerman and Robin Ford

A well-established provincial government agency adopted a new vision, Quality Service Through Partnerships, that spurred restructuring, the engagement of new leadership, teamwork, identification of key competencies, and a move toward creating and using business plans for greater accountability. This case shows how learning served as the glue that helped people and the organization move toward innovation and change.

The Past

In the past, the public service in Canada was not renowned for its commitment to change and renewal. Instead, it was associated with tradition and bureaucratic hierarchy. The problem with bureaucratic systems was that as they grew, the needs of the system predominated over the needs of the people whose interests they were supposed to represent. The words, "I'm here from the government; I'm here to help," were not comforting to most people because they reflected the interventionist and regulatory culture of the public service. When problems arose in this culture, they were traditionally resolved by providing more money and more people at the taxpayers' expense.

For many people, a job with the Canadian government was defined as a job for life. Employees were paid to do specific jobs, their roles carefully defined by rigid classification systems and heavily controlled hierarchies. If employees were good and did not challenge their superiors, they could anticipate a promotion. Many of their activities

This case was prepared to serve as a basis for discussion rather than to illustrate either effective or ineffective administrative and management practices.

were almost unconsciously designed to protect and expand this existing system.

Forces for Change

Beginning in 1991, some major forces for change began to occur in Alberta, Canada:

1. Albertans have a resistance to overgovernance; almost imperceptibly, a movement began against government overregulation.
2. Provincial and federal debt problems became a part of the national and provincial consciousness, and there was a strong awareness that government expenditures had to be cut.
3. Some of the organizational and learning initiatives that were being adopted by the private sector, in its effort to be more competitive in the new global economy, began to have an effect on the government structure. In the face of fiscal crisis and massive organizational change, some politicians saw an opportunity to reinvent and restructure their departments.

Alberta Labour: The Case for Change

Alberta Labour was one of the oldest departments in the Alberta Public Service. Seven hundred employees enforced technical safety and workplace regulations through a system of hands-on investigations and inspections. Each technical discipline was organized into its own branch, with its own corresponding bureaucratic hierarchy. Sometimes there were as many as seven levels of hierarchy in one branch, which might consist of no more than 50 people. Headquartered in Edmonton, the department operated like most other government departments. Activities in the field were controlled by the head office; classification and payroll activities were controlled by the activities of the Public Service Union and the centralized Personnel Administration Office.

In 1991, a new minister and deputy saw an opportunity to implement major changes in this department. Motivated not only by fiscal constraints but also by a new and exciting vision of what government could be, Alberta Labour underwent a major transformation that has touched the life of every employee.

The Prerequisites: Vision and Leadership

Alberta Labour adopted a vision, a new view of what the public service could be. A noticeably absent consideration in the traditional system had been the client. A client-centered focus, therefore, had radical implications. The new vision that was eventually adopted—Quality

Service Through Partnerships—was the beginning of the learning curve for the organization and its employees. Working with clients to implement the required kinds of safety systems and developing new partnerships to maximize effectiveness were new roles for government.

To organize and implement change of the magnitude of that in Alberta Labour required new, innovative leadership. Traditional civil service leaders tend to be too mired in past practices and old stories to model or drive the new vision sufficiently. A combination of individuals from outside and inside government were brought together to form the backbone of the new senior management team. They were hired because they understood the concepts of client-focused operation, frontline empowerment to serve clients more effectively, and partnerships with clients. They understood the magnitude of the changes that had to occur and their role in directing them. They included two new assistant deputy ministers with experience from the private sector, an innovative executive director of finance and administration, and a director of personnel. It is interesting to note that the director of personnel had absolutely no background or experience in the field of personnel management.

This senior leadership team made a very conscious decision not to rely heavily on consultants in this change experience, because overreliance on consultants in the change process can deprive an organization of the learning experience that results from doing things the hard way. They had a strong belief that personal learning would be of vital importance if this change were to be sustained. Consultants were used only when the leadership team felt that objective external involvement would be helpful. For example, the team believed that external consultants could bring an objectivity to team training that would benefit staff in the introduction of the team concept.

Implementing the Plan

The first major task was to break down the bureaucracy and the barriers that existed between staff members and between disciplines. Although people might have worked for many years in the same department, in the same building, and maybe even on the same floor, the only contact that many staff had with each other was in the elevators. Computers were slowly being introduced, but on a discipline-by-discipline basis, and their use was essentially reactive, for the recording of statistics.

The following structural changes were implemented overnight. The technical branches, which previously had been separate, were amalgamated and blended into a new division called Client Services, reflecting the new vision and the purpose of their work. The province was reorganized into four decentralized regions, each headed by a regional coordinator. All staff were organized into teams, each headed by a team leader (this position rotated among team members). Team training started almost immediately; there were well over 100 teams now—some single-discipline, others multidiscipline, depending on numbers and location in the regions. A new systems plan was implemented; the increased use of computers and electronic mail allowed for a very different and much more extensive communications system, which helped to break down many of the barriers.

While these changes were occurring, competency profiling for all the disciplines was initiated. A team of consultants whose expertise was in developing curricula worked closely with the new director of personnel and various discipline teams throughout the organization to develop comprehensive competency profiles. The purpose was to implement a new classification system based on broadbanding, and to pay for skills.

Another major change occurred in the area of finance and budgeting. In the old days, financial management and control had always been viewed as a managerial concern. Line staff had little knowledge or sense of the economic effect of their own activities on the larger picture. The new vision, however, required a business-planning approach. Alberta Labour was the first government department in the province to develop a business plan. By 1993, when the third one was written, such plans had become mandatory for all government departments. Using the business plan to provide direction, staff teams participated in a process of results-based budgeting. The focus was on the results each team hoped to achieve in the coming year, the activities necessary to generate those results, and the performance measures that determined whether or not the planned results were achieved.

The struggle to understand results-based budgeting has been one of the most difficult lessons for staff, because it puts the focus of work fairly and squarely on the results that the work is supposed to achieve. Doing the job means achieving the results; the resources are merely means to an end. Each team now has its own expenditure officer, and teams grapple daily with questions such as how best to spend training dollars or travel dollars to achieve projected results.

Learning: The Glue

A major investment in learning was required to cement all these structural changes in the minds and activities of the staff. Indeed, vital components of the mission, vision, and value statements of the department, presented to all teams by the assistant deputy ministers, are the values placed on staff through learning and the recognition that the department is a learning organization. To give explicit recognition to this, a small training group was initiated in 1993 in the middle of a major cost-cutting exercise. The aim of this group was to align training and learning initiatives with the department's goal of competency acquisition.

The final curriculum development session was facilitated with the senior management team when the team had identified those competencies required by staff to take the department into the future, as defined by the business plan. Training Services then compiled all competency profiles into a major curriculum calendar in which common present, common future, and discipline-unique competencies were clearly defined. When possible, training and learning opportunities for these competencies were identified, and training requirements were prioritized according to need, cost, and availability.

Internal training focused on building team dialogue skills wherever possible, and the whole team was encouraged to come to internal training sessions. Many of the competencies are interrelated and serve a human resource function as well as a function for the work performed with clients. For example, a course titled Results Setting, which was delivered to over 400 people in one year, was designed to assist with the results-based budgeting system, the encouragement of team dialogue and participation, and the implementation of a new team-based performance-management system. In the minds of staff, the new performance-management system is one of the main solidifiers of the changes in the department.

The other major solidifier is a team-based approach to assessment, and the vision of an assessment as an opportunity for learning. This is delicate work, and use of appropriate language is vital. There is a recognition that supporting skills, such as conflict resolution and anger management, are necessary, as is the development of skilled coaches and mentors to assist in the process.

Much individual and personal learning also has occurred through involvement in cross-discipline and project teams. The "dissolution" of the old head office meant that many functions of the former managers and technical specialists could now be carried out by staff from across the province, operating in discipline coordinating teams. As a result, much of the specialized knowledge formerly "siloed" and available to only a few people is now spread around the organization and is accessible not only to other staff but also to clients.

Project teams also have been very successful in developing expertise. The use of such teams has encouraged staff to involve themselves in the creation of the very change in which they are participating. One example is the creation of "third options," one of the cornerstones of the department's business plan and an integral component of its vision.

Contrasting greatly with the program-cutting or quick-privatization options usually selected by governments in their attempts to cut costs, third options are carefully considered ways of doing work differently, based on facilitation and partnerships. They involve working with communities and industries in a shared approach to such issues as safety regulation. Their establishment allows for department costs to be cut because functions formerly carried out by department staff are now carried out by private-sector partners. Usually, however, these new partners require qualified staff, and this becomes an employment option for staff who would otherwise be displaced by downsizing. Staff who remain in the department fulfill the residual roles of monitoring public policy and auditing the new partnerships to ensure that they fulfill their new mandates.

The most recently launched third option is the Alberta Boilers Safety Association. This nonprofit organization, funded through fees paid by users of the service, is responsible for most of the inspection and design functions of pressure vessels in the province. These functions were previously carried out by the department at the expense of the general taxpayer. The new Boilers Safety Association has provided employment for almost 90 percent of the inspection and design staff previously employed by the department. The few employees who remain in the department are responsible for ensuring that the association operates in accordance with the governmental requirements for public policy.

Organizational Learning: How Have We Done?

Because of the department's commitment to its business plan, and the results-based budgeting process, there is a constant preoccupation with the results. Questions frequently asked, however, are, "To what extent has the regular departmental employee been brought into the changes? Has the department succeeded in developing a committed workforce dedicated to achieving its vision?" Any answer has to be considered carefully.

The fact is that when the new leadership started to implement the changes and teams, many staff shook their heads. They could not envision the future. There was a sense that if only the deputy would go away, then things could get back to normal. Four years later, it is now generally understood that "normal" is gone forever. Changes in the rest of government and enormous layoffs in other departments have made staff realize some of the advantages of the department's approach. The carefully crafted business plan, including third options, is very attractive when contrasted with straight layoffs.

The new approaches also have forced staff to contend with a significant amount of unlearning. Approximately 100 staff members have made voluntary severance agreements. Many have been "pink slipped" or demoted. Pink slips result from the recognition that the old classification system is no longer relevant to the realities of the new world. Despite this rational explanation, some staff have difficulty coping with their new status. They are required to learn new competencies while living with the awareness that their former competencies have little place in the future of the organization. The old system is gone, yet the centralized forces that represented stability in the old system are still present. The public service union, for example, still espouses the view that multiskilling and competencies are merely employer ploys for blind downsizing, and the union has openly discouraged departmental staff from participating in the new competency-based classification system.

Despite such obstacles, and the human resistance to change, there are some strong indicators of success. The second annual general meeting was recently held, with over 500 staff in attendance. Several awards, planned by a cross-departmental project team, were given at the meeting to recognize achievements publicly. Sometimes success is measured in small increments. An external trainer commented to a staff member on how wonderful it was to be back in the Department of Labour, where staff were always so keen and open to learning. Another departmental employee, who was planning on moving to another country, was overheard saying that she could not believe the incredible learning opportunities she had been given before leaving.

Individual learning plans are now an integral part of employee performance, and in recognition of this, there are frequent requests for advice on how to start. To this end, a new human resource information system is being implemented. Designed to capture position and individual competencies, it will provide employees with a clear picture of what they already know and what they need to know to pursue their learning plans.

There is clearly an acceptance on the part of staff that life has changed. The change has been viewed by some people as an opportunity and has generated enormous excitement; others have viewed it as something to watch and occasionally to resist. A sense of stress and displacement is bound to occur when changes of this magnitude are implemented, particularly in institutions as traditionally stable as government. It is healthy to recognize this inevitability, but even healthier to move on immediately with the change initiative.

In four years, this department changed its systems of management, compensation, and classification as well as its way of interacting with its clients. Further, the department developed a planned approach to learning in order to achieve its results. These changes are merely the beginning steps toward becoming a more accountable, and much more valuable, public service of the future.

Questions for Discussion

1. There is often a debate about how fast change, particularly of this magnitude, should be introduced in an organization. Do you think it would have been better to introduce the team concept more slowly?
2. Long-term employees tend to feel a sense of entitlement about their jobs that makes it difficult for them to handle rapid change. What can be done to help ease tensions and promote the kind of learning that is necessary for the new vision to succeed, particularly in light of the fact that the organization is in its fourth year of ongoing change?
3. The case describes how external consultants were used minimally in implementing the changes. What are the advantages and disadvantages of using consultants in the change process? How can consultants enhance learning?
4. What can be done to continue the process of learning and to ensure that the organization does not fall back into its old ways of knowing?
5. The case describes a total approach to change, one that includes all components in the organization. Is it possible to produce similar results by just patching the existing system?

The Authors

Jennifer Bowerman is a training consultant with Alberta Labour. Her career with Alberta Labour has included five years with the Human Rights Commission as an education officer, 10 years with Employment Standards, and two years as a regional director. She has a bachelor of science with honours from London University, and a master of arts from the University of Saskatchewan. She is currently working on her certificate in adult education. Bowerman can be contacted at the following address: Alberta Labour, Room 702, 10808-99 Avenue, Edmonton, Alberta, Canada T5K 0G5.

Robin Ford was appointed deputy minister of labour in October 1990. Before that he served as deputy minister of Alberta Consumer and Corporate Affairs and as an assistant deputy minister with Alberta Municipal Affairs. Ford has a master of arts degree with honours in social sciences from Oxford University and earned a postgraduate degree in adult education in London, England.

Creating a Customer-Driven Organization Using Future Search

Environmental Protection Agency

Mary Burner Lippitt

A consultant describes how the Human Resources Department of a large federal government agency used a Future Search Conference to involve its multiple customers and stakeholders in a nonlinear, concurrent change effort. The case lays out steps taken in planning, implementing, and following up on this large group intervention strategy.

Background

Given the mandates to reorganize, increase manager-to-staff ratio, reduce staff, merge units, introduce new strategies, and become a customer-driven organization, the Environmental Protection Agency (EPA) found that it must embark on a new method for managing change. Rather than use the traditional hierarchical approach to reorganization, EPA decided to implement a new strategy that stressed educating the workforce, encouraging employees to seize business opportunities, and creating customer service-based teams.

The agency's leadership was faced with several tough questions, and the challenge of answering them was made even more formidable by a tight time frame. Among the questions this agency's leadership faced were the following:

- How can EPA adapt to its new mandate to reinvent and reengineer?
- How can its newly created teams learn about the changing customer requirements and needs in this agency?

This case was prepared to serve as a basis for discussion rather than to illustrate either effective or ineffective administrative and management practices.

- How can EPA employees be encouraged to actively and creatively seize opportunities, develop new competencies and skills, and maintain a cooperative and flexible approach to both work and the agency's customers?

This case illustrates how a learning strategy facilitates organizational change. It also demonstrates how to involve others in change. This strategy engaged all levels of employees by discussing why the change was necessary, and it included multiple customers and stakeholders to ensure that current and evolving needs were known. It also used a nonlinear, or concurrent, strategy when various activities were occurring simultaneously.

Overview

In August 1994, EPA appointed a director of human resources (HR) and charged him with the responsibility of merging four new units within the HR department and improving customer service. In addition to these two internal changes, President Clinton's "reinventing government" initiative mandated changing the management-to-staff ratio from 1:5 to a goal of 1:11 and reducing the total number of management levels. Facing these dramatic shifts, the director developed a change strategy that involved customers and employees in large-scale change techniques. This choice of strategies was fueled by his conviction that the whole organization needed to understand what types of services were required, how to work smarter with both people and technology, and how to respond to a changing environment.

EPA consisted of approximately 18,500 employees at headquarters and regions across the country. The HR department's mission was to assist the staff in fulfilling the organization's goals. The approximately 190 people in HR had historically been guided by the Office of Personnel Management (OPM) and its federal personnel manual. Because OPM and the manual were also in the process of radical change, the HR department needed to develop a new road map balancing service and supervision.

As shown in Figure 1, the journey through organizational change evolved as needs arose and as suggestions were made. It started with a proposed "strawman planning document" and a steering committee to guide the process. Two conferences were held to identify customer needs and to determine future directions for the organization. To develop an organizational structure at the macro level, a design conference also was held. Detailed structural design plans were provided by volunteer teams for each proposed new organizational segment. Plans for shifting to the new structure were developed concurrently by a transition team. Throughout the process, an aggressive plan for two-way communication was in place. Members of the detailed design team and the transition team were encouraged to contact the director with questions or resource requests. Employees also were encouraged to communicate through e-mail, all-employee meetings, and skip-level meetings. Change came through involvement, communication, learning, and creativity.

Figure 1. EPA human resource department redesign chronology.

Date	Action	Person/Group responsible
August 1994	New director hired HR consultants planning group formed	Director
September	Strawman planning document created recommending a future search process and an external advisor for director	HR planning group
	Customer and HR volunteers for steering committee recruited	Director
	External advisor retained	Director
	Steering committee created	Director
October	Steering committee meeting held • Review committee mission, charter, and planning group's "strawman" proposal • Consultant presentation on future search	Director and consultant
	Steering committee meeting held • Develop conference themes • Identify potential participants	Steering committee
	Conference planning, communication, and data collection subteam formed	Steering committee

Figure 1 (continued). EPA human resource department redesign chronology.

Date	Action	Person/Group responsible
December	First future search session conducted	Conference planning consultants and steering committee
	Second future search session conducted	Consultants and volunteers
	Meeting results summarized and reviewed by steering committee	Consultants and volunteers
	Consultant develop design conference	Steering committee, director, and consultant
January 1995	Design conference develops two alternative organization structures	Conference planning consultants and steering committee
	Steering committee submits single proposal to director and appoints detailed design teams and transition team	Steering committee, director, and consultants
February	Design team meetings held Subunit structures developed Unit staffing level needs determined Proposed structure test with work flow analysis	Design team
	Detailed design team leaders meeting held and "gaps committee" established	Detailed design team Team leaders
	Implementation plan developed	Transition team and consultant
	Proposed substructure presented to steering committee	Detailed design team leaders

Planning for Change

Because the director was confident that new ideas would surface as more people became knowledgeable about the process, he pursued a nonlinear change strategy. He wanted customers and employees at all levels of the organization to be involved and informed about change at each stage of the process.

To initiate the change effort, the director formed a planning group, made up of internal HR development consultants, that would outline options to comprise a strawman planning document for the proposed steering committee. The methodology recommended by the planning group was to use a "future search" process. This process, popularized by Marvin Weisbord (1995), stresses the need for an organization's stakeholders (customers, employees, stockholders, volunteers, suppliers, etc.) to interact and develop a common understanding of the organization's desired future. The planning group also recommended that an external advisor be selected to assist the director and that teams be created to help plan and implement the change effort.

Volunteers for the steering committee were recruited from all organizational levels. The director held individual meetings with customer units to inform them of the process and to encourage customer involvement. Information on steering committee goals was distributed. After two weeks, the director selected 16 volunteers, including customers and employees. The role of the steering committee was to oversee and implement the entire change effort. Fifty percent of the steering committee was made up of the agency's customer base.

At the first steering committee meeting, the committee's mission and charter, as well as the planning group's strawman proposal, were discussed. Members were intrigued with the concept of large-scale conferences on the change effort but wanted additional information before endorsing this unique strategy. External consultants were brought in to present an overview of the process and to discuss potential outcomes. They explained that the future search process might include 72–81 people and that half of those must be customers and stakeholders. This limitation permits people to interact with one another in multiple table groupings. The steering committee recommended holding two future search conferences to involve as many HR employees as possible. The consultants also recommended the use of a design conference based on the work of Dick Axelrod (1992) to develop a preliminary organization structure from the findings of the future search.

With guidance from external consultants Mary Lippitt and Gil Stiel, the steering committee met to develop plans for the future search conference, to identify potential participants, and to confirm expected outcomes. In addition, they created subgroups to select attendees and assist in conference planning, communication, and data collection processes.

Selecting attendees for the conferences was key for two reasons. First, to ensure that decisions made would reflect organizational reality, the conference had to be a microcosm of the organization. Second, because participant identification is one of the longest processes in conference planning, it had to be tackled early. All the participants in the future search process would be volunteers; more than 40 percent of HR employees volunteered to participate in future search conferences.

Conferences

Traditionally, the future search conference is a 16-hour event spread over three days, with evenings used for reflection and integration. Because of organizational needs, the time was extended to 20 hours over three days to increase the quantity and quality of information that the EPA would receive.

The conference developed a common understanding of the participants' organizational reality, past and present. In fact, conflicting priorities and needs surfaced during this exploration. Some customers wanted greater flexibility, others more supervision. The diversity of customer expectations turned out to be a key learning experience for many HR employees.

Largely because of everyone's willingness to assist and knowledge that a consensual decision-making process would protect minority viewpoints, the group began to feel a sense of community. Conflict over priorities, processes, and programs gave way to solutions such as more delegation, increased automation, and clearer customer contact points or one-stop shopping for service.

Comments from the participants on completing the future search process indicated their increased awareness and understanding of the organization's current situation and future goals. Stakeholders and customers reported an increased understanding not only of the difficulties HR staff face in meeting numerous customer requests, but also of the complexities involved in responding adequately to those requests. Findings from the two future search conferences were shared with the entire organization via e-mail, written documentation, and staff meetings.

While participants agreed on common future themes, recommendations that were not unanimous also were captured and communicated. These nonconsensual themes included more delegation of authority to line supervisors for review functions, establishment of a formal workforce planning process, and formation of common goals within the HR and line offices. Several of these ideas were incorporated in the substructure design.

After the future search conferences, the steering committee met to consider the results. Volunteers compiled findings from the two conferences and found that, although each conference had different participants, the recommendations and priorities of each were similar. Eight themes surfaced: strategic workforce planning and development, automation, consulting services linked to the "bottom line," valuing of diversity, flexible policies and guidance, customer partnerships, working in teams, and effective oversight. The director summarized his observations and invited people to volunteer for the next step—the design conference to develop a new structure based on the findings of the future search. More than half of the future search participants volunteered.

The goals of the design conference were to examine creative organizational structures to meet customer needs, to recommend a preliminary design or designs, and to identify issues associated with the implementation process. The steering committee asked the consultants to customize the design conference to fulfill these expectations.

A two-day format was suggested and accepted by the steering committee. During the design conference, participants reviewed the eight future search themes, examined historical options for organizational design, and developed creative alternative organizational structures that emphasized each of the eight identified themes. They also designed a new integrated structure and discussed implementation issues.

Designing the Structure

Two designs were ultimately developed and proposed to the steering committee for further analysis. Customer service using multifunctional teams was the major thrust of both proposed designs, which offered one-stop shopping or clear points for customer contact. Additionally, both designs provided for cross-unit tasks, a generalist orientation, and customer partnerships. Team-based work units were proposed to improve employee skills and morale, to increase customer service, and to maximize resources. The two designs differed in numbers of employee teams or units, the use of a coordinating unit for customer service teams, and the customer contact access points.

The steering committee combined many of the features of the two designs into a single structure. The final proposal focused on customer service teams that would be dedicated to program offices and supported by functional groups that included training, strategic planning and policy development, consulting, and a council for team leaders to share information. The steering committee established detailed design teams to develop a structure for each unit, to determine the level of staffing needed by each unit, and to test the proposed structure with work flow analysis.

Detailed design team leaders who did not have a vested interest in a given area were selected to lead the teams and to lend objectivity during this phase of the design. Volunteers were recruited for each of the teams. While each team focused on their specific areas, the team leaders met weekly to consider common needs, to address questions that were raised, and to prepare a report for the steering committee. Knowing that some areas might be overlooked, the team leaders established a "gaps committee." Several areas and issues were identified as problematic, and those issues were resolved by the leaders. The team leaders then presented their proposed substructure design to the steering committee.

The steering committee reviewed the proposed substructure, added their suggestions, and forwarded it to the HR director. The director, in conjunction with the new managerial staff, made the final design decisions. Only minor modifications were made to the proposals developed by the detailed design teams and the steering committee.

Implementation

In addition to establishing the detailed design teams, the steering committee created a transition team to plan the implementation process and address evolving concerns. The transition team's key responsibilities included planning the employee selection process, developing a communication plan, and developing a supportive training plan. Volunteers for the transition team were selected from all areas of the organization; some were union representatives.

A communication strategy evolved using LAN mail, weekly bulletins, all-employee meetings, suggestion boxes, skip-level meetings with the director, and personal contact by transition team members. Each member of the team was responsible for contacting 10–12 people. Employees also were offered the opportunity to contact the director via e-mail. An employee survey was conducted to determine issues and concerns with the process.

The most significant communication vehicle turned out to be the skip-level meetings with the director. Eight to 12 employees signed up to meet with the director for approximately one to one and one-half hours each week. Questions from the employees led to lively discussions, and employees initiated their own e-mail forum to support the reorganization and to share their excitement about the process and their enthusiasm for the change.

The director also met with customers and field personnel to explain the process and the plans. During a meeting of the HR council, members were overwhelmed. Some people were moved to tears by the consideration given to employees and to the needs of all stakeholders.

During the transition phase, employees were worried about the decision-making process for placing people in the new structure. They also wanted to know who would be the manager of each unit before they identified their unit preferences. The director, therefore, began managerial selection while the transition team developed a plan for employee selection. The employee selection included career counseling and supportive training.

The director's managerial selection process included an employee assessment of managers, personal interviews with managers and senior staff, and a managerial preference process. Each manager was asked to identify three desired jobs in the new structure. Managers were encouraged to select new areas rather than their traditional ones to encourage breadth, stimulate innovation, and demonstrate commitment to cross-training. Many of those selected were placed in new areas.

After managerial selection, employees were offered qualification development clinics to prepare them for their selection process. Knowledge, skills, and abilities for each new unit were identified, and employees were asked to develop capability statements for their three most desired jobs. The clinics were designed to help employees understand how to present their skills and interests in the selection process.

In addition to the qualification development clinics, training sessions were planned to address issues of culture, change, and customer service. The goals of this training were to help people through the change process, to orient people who might select service teams, and to clarify expectations. There was healthy skepticism regarding the likelihood of "real change." Concern existed that this would be a "paper shuffle" without process streamlining, actual service improvement, increased employee input into decision-making, or improved communication flow.

New work groups received follow-up skills training. This training addressed team formation, roles and responsibilities, and performance planning. Using planning guidelines, each new unit developed its own goals, standards, and measures of performance. These sessions also permitted an exploration of member backgrounds and expertise, identified processes that needed streamlining, and determined operating practices.

Career-planning programs were offered on a voluntary basis for people who wanted to explore career paths and options. These sessions included the use of assessment instruments to clarify current strengths. Participants received feedback from others and were encouraged to develop individual development plans.

During the transition phase, preoccupation with internal issues reduced customer contact and bridge-building. The director responded by holding personal meetings with customers to clarify the process and to reassure them that their needs were the focal point of the change. This intervention was received positively because customers knew that they were still being heard and that the future HR organization would be highly supportive of their needs.

Results

Implementation followed in June and moved quickly. Customers knew, through their open communication channels and their involvement in the future search and design conferences, what to expect and what outcomes were being sought. Encouraged by the knowledge that better service was imminent, they were tolerant of the confusion that accompanied the organizational change.

Employees continued to volunteer for special task forces including a celebration task force charged with finding a way to honor the past and to initiate the new organization. There were also teams to work on career development training and facility planning. Not only did employees volunteer, but the type of leadership displayed on the teams was also more democratic than in the past. The flow of information to the whole organization was timely and complete.

With the director spending a great deal of his time in meetings, team members became comfortable making decisions and working without the close guidance that had been a hallmark of the old culture. Teams proposed their decisions to the director for implementation rather than wait for him to initiate activities or processes. Other governmental agencies that learned about the process contacted EPA for detailed information. At a Brookings Institution session on "Streamlining HR," EPA's work was discussed, and attendees of the conferences were asked to visit the organization.

The process was not completely smooth. Unanticipated issues surfaced, including budget reductions and the possible plan to transfer one function from national headquarters to a regional one. The employees were prepared for these additional changes, however, because they were aware of the organization's direction, had confidence in the director's approach, and knew customer's priorities. These issues were discussed openly rather than through rumors. Terms were negotiated and modified to accommodate multiple priorities and needs.

With the continuing need for a balanced federal budget, financial and personnel constraints are likely to continue. Automation is becoming a more critical aspect of the organizational change, as it is crucial to successfully meeting customer needs, but it is also another potential target for budget cutters.

Summary

EPA's strategy for organizational change was both evolutionary and revolutionary. The strategy was evolutionary in the sense that concepts were proposed, analyzed, and selected openly and creatively. The plan was flexible and inclusive of all participants. Additional ideas were incorporated into the plan as they surfaced.

This case was revolutionary in that rapid individual and management change was required and new ways of doing business were developed. People who were specialists became generalists. The number of managerial levels was reduced, and teams were introduced. Key success factors were full disclosure; open information flow; and a clear focus on customer needs, employee concerns, and organizational mission.

Because the employees worked together toward a common goal, their individual knowledge and abilities were maximized for the organization's benefit. This resulted in more efficient and effective use of human resources and in increased job satisfaction for the employees.

Questions for Discussion

1. How can an organization rapidly meet customer needs?
2. How did EPA managers create an environment for learning?
3. What are the three most critical elements in building a learning organization?

The Author

Mary Lippitt, D.B.A., is president of Enterprise Management Ltd. in Bethesda, Maryland, a firm specializing in systems design, change management, team development, quality improvement, and executive development. Lippitt has served high-technology firms, financial service organizations, the health care industry, and government. Lippitt has been active in ASTD for many years, serving as president of the Miami and the Washington, DC, chapters; as a regional director; and as a member of the national conference planning and nominating committees. She is proud to be a second-generation HRD professional. She can be contacted at the following address: Enterprise Management Ltd., 9812 Falls Road, Suite 114, Box 238, Potomac, MD 20854.

References

Axelrod, R. (1992) Getting everyone involved. *Journal of Applied Behavioral Science, 28*(4), 499–509.

Weisbord, M. (1995). *Future search.* San Francisco: Berrett-Koehler.

New York City Civil Service Reform: Parallel Change and Organizational Learning

New York City Bureau of Examinations

Diana D. Woolis and Julia R. Galosy

A newly appointed executive partnered with a consultant to create a learning approach to restructuring and reengineering. This case describes how they supported a move to self-managed work teams, sweeping culture changes, and the development of new leadership skills in managers.

Background

In 1993, Rudolph Giuliani was elected mayor of New York City. He pledged to reinvent city government and appointed a special advisor, Richard Schwartz, to oversee his change agenda, which included the New York City Department of Personnel (DOP) initiative that is the subject of this case study. The DOP's primary mission is to administer the provisions of the State Civil Service Law.

In January 1994, the mayor appointed Lilliam Barrios-Paoli commissioner of the DOP. Barrios-Paoli is a seasoned veteran of New York City politics who is known for her intelligent, no-nonsense, savvy leadership style. When she arrived at DOP, she discovered an organization in which time had stood still in many respects. Policies, practices, and staff had remained relatively unchanged for at least a quarter of a century. Middle and upper managers had carved out fiefdoms, and little that had happened in or outside the agency had affected those relationships and boundaries. The DOP was disconnected in significant

This case was prepared to serve as a basis for discussion rather than to illustrate either effective or ineffective administrative and management practices.

ways from the agencies it served, and dissatisfaction with its quality of service was already high and still rising.

Many of the commissioner's initial efforts were focused on carrying out the mayor's severance and redeployment actions. She knew, however, that DOP, as well as the agencies it serves, could benefit from a major reconsideration of the form and function of its work. She determined that the Bureau of Examinations (bureau) was the core business of the agency. Therefore, reinvention in the bureau could move the agency forward strategically and could provide a model for organizing change in other city agencies.

As one of DOP's operational units, the bureau develops and administers entrance and promotional examinations, promulgates medical standards for public safety positions, and establishes rank-order lists of individuals eligible for appointment. It serves 70 municipal agencies and public authorities. Currently, it receives between 250,000 and 400,000 applications and administers between 150 and 300 exams annually.

In September 1994, Barrios-Paoli hired Diana Woolis to be associate city personnel director. Woolis's charge was twofold: first, to reorganize the current infrastructure to be more efficient and effective; second, to restructure and reengineer. Woolis knew from the beginning that she wanted to deliver, within two years of her appointment, a dramatically changed bureau, one that would be built on an increased capacity to learn. When she arrived, she faced several significant obstacles to change—including the organization's structure, culture, and information systems.

The Change Initiative

To overcome these obstacles, Woolis decided to undertake the following:
- create a compelling reason to change
- change the organization's structure by flattening the hierarchy and creating teams
- change the culture by altering work processes, challenging prevailing assumptions, creating new language, valuing new behavior, and using dialogue and feedback
- help managers to learn new leadership skills as they resolve organizational problems and then use the same process with their own staff.

In November 1994, Woolis hired Julia Galosy, an outside consultant, to help plan the change and to coach and guide the managers. Woolis and Galosy decided to remove the obstacles to change systematically, by changing language first, then behavior, then thinking—and, finally, by enabling critical reframing.

Creating a Compelling Need for Change

In October, Woolis met with each unit and provided a mini seminar that covered the following: the changing nature of work, the workplace, and workers; what that change would mean for the bureau; her goals for change; and the increasing urgency for change given the goals of the new administration. She wrote a brief working paper called "A Blueprint for High Performance Government: 21st Century Civil Service, New York City" and gave it to every bureau employee. Based largely on U.S. Vice-President Gore's report, *Creating Government That Works Better and Costs Less* (1993), it challenged employees' basic assumptions about the form of civil service. While the intent of the working paper was to challenge "how work gets done," it was interpreted by many staff as a recommendation to dismantle civil service and to undermine its ability to assure "merit and fitness." It offended their sense of themselves and their work.

Woolis helped the bureau focus on the need for change. She conducted a short survey of staff that asked 1) What one thing would you change? 2) How would you rate our service? 3) What tasks seem to have no purpose? 4) What skills do you have that you feel are underutilized? and 5) What is the biggest obstacle for change in the bureau? The survey results showed the need for a flatter organizational structure and the elimination of unnecessary work processes. The barriers to change were identified as the bureau's resistance, the law, lack of incentives, and low morale. Benchmarking, customer service, and work process teams were convened in an effort to generate data, dialogue, and insight on the need and the possibilities for change. In addition, Woolis hired a staff person to write a change newsletter, facilitate groups, team train, troubleshoot, and organize and provide "just-in-time" training. It has been critical to successful change to have a capable person in this role.

The commissioner's push for a new structure for the organization and her dissatisfaction with the bureau's "business-as-usual" approach were the key trigger events for change. The commissioner called for and approved the submitted organization plan to dramatically reduce the number of managers. When employees learned of the initiative, morale dropped. They became fearful of an unknown future and of the loss of their jobs, but they also were motivated to take the need for change seriously. The conditions for change that Woolis had articulated to the staff earlier had become a reality.

Flattening the Organization and Moving Toward Self-Managed Work Teams

In just five years, the bureau's staff shrank from more than 200 to 100 people. (The DOP also has shrunk: In 1992, it employed more than 600 people; by July 1995, it employed approximately 379.)

The bureau's structure included a deputy, an associate deputy, assistant directors, unit chiefs, and assistant chiefs—five levels of managers. The top six managers had a collective tenure of over 125 years.

In November, a reduction of managers from 22 to five, and of management levels from five to two, was announced. Woolis requested that an internal search be conducted to select the five managers. She wanted the selection process to be open to all DOP staff and sought a skill set derived from the work of Development Dimensions International (Pittsburgh, PA) instead of from a traditional job description. The commissioner agreed, even though her bias at the time was to handpick the new management staff. Existing managers would have to compete for their jobs. Applications were due in December. The new management team was to take office February 21. Everything went according to schedule. But many staff, especially those who lost their positions, felt that the process (November to February) was painfully long. Others felt that the change occurred too fast.

Several other key decisions needed to be made at this time. It was decided that the salaries of the displaced managers would be reduced to reflect a change in status and that they would not keep their offices. The goal, however, was minimal pain. Every time Woolis imagined a day that the managers would move from their offices onto the floor with all their colleagues watching, she foresaw their humiliation. She deeply wanted to avoid this. The solution was another major change. Because of the downsizing, there was now empty space everywhere. *Everyone* could move. This measure would consolidate the bureau and would save the managers from embarrassment. The commissioner accepted the proposal and made it a department priority. The whole process actually took place over a weekend. By March 10, the entire move had been executed; by March 17, virtually everyone had settled in.

Galosy was hired to help develop a process for the transition of managers who would be displaced. She believed that the bureau first needed to develop a change plan— chronological and articulated— that would include the learning that had to take place to move people through the change. A chronological, phase-specific change plan brings order, language, and structure to the chaos of change. Woolis, however, had to begin the transition process earlier, before such a plan could be completed. Woolis established teams to address work process, benchmarking, communications, customer service, and data analysis. Galosy observed that some of the teams (for example, the benchmarking and communications teams) would have a difficult time moving ahead because they were support teams rather then actual process-change teams. It was imperative to ensure that all teams succeeded. People needed to know what reengineering meant and what they could expect for at least the next two years. The bureau needed a change plan; it needed to lay out some structure and the beginnings of learning to enable the staff to act.

In January, the commissioner promoted Woolis to the position of deputy city personnel director for exams. She was to take office the same day as the new managers. This was a key decision that conveyed to all staff that sponsorship for the change was coming from the top and would be powerful, sustained, and unconditional.

Changing the Culture

In this organization, many employees had tenure and they held the status quo to be sacrosanct. Past lawsuits and the ever-present threat of litigation and union challenge or discontent made employees loyal to traditional psychometrics and to the narrowest interpretation of civil service rather than to customers or innovation. Employees still believed that altering the current approach would compromise the historic mission of assuring "merit and fitness" in the selection system. Total quality management (TQM), personal computers, telecommunications, organization flattening, increased citizen expectations, and other changes had somehow passed by the Bureau of Examinations. Although individual members were cognizant of the outside world, virtually no transference or integration of individual learning and experience was taking place at the organizational level. For example, while many individuals were highly computer literate, little of that knowledge had been applied, or had been permitted to be applied, to the work of the bureau.

Barrios-Paoli had a powerful desire to change the culture to one of innovation and responsiveness. She preferred innovation to avoiding lawsuits, which she felt were inevitable. "If we are going to be sued, let us be sued for trying something different, for strategies to improve service," she said. But Barrios-Paoli wanted those risks to be informed and data driven. This required another shift in the culture from "Well, this is the way we have always done it" or "There was a lawsuit in 1978" to pushing for substantiated reasoning as to why something could *not* be done. Unless such reasoning was tremendously compelling, Barrios-Paoli fearlessly leaped ahead, often to the distress of staff.

Within the bureau, there were no communications systems in place that facilitated the exchange of information, and therefore no guarantee of its validity or accuracy. The value system was heavily steeped in the notion that the "right to know, right to ask" resided exclusively at the top of the hierarchy. People had no idea what the workers sitting next to them were doing. Their information came largely from hearsay and inference.

Consultant Intervention: Helping Managers Learn New Leadership Skills

Galosy was hired to help Woolis and the new managers expand their learning and experience to resolve new organizational issues and begin to craft a shared understanding of the "new" bureau—its form, function, values, and beliefs. The new managers would have to coordinate the work of the new, self-managed work teams and lead the reengineering efforts within their respective "groups" through learning. The new managers were selected based on their potential for leading in a learning organization. To accelerate their learning, a one-day session was set up to explain clearly how managers would move their organization toward self-managed work teams. The resources available to help them included the process reengineering work group, facilitators, experts, customer service, the benchmarking group, and the data analysis team.

The training laid the groundwork for transferring the responsibility for key management tasks to the self-directed work teams over the next six months. The nature of the work within the bureau would not change under restructuring; rather, the work of management would change. Reengineering, however, *would* change the nature of work. The management activities, such as setting schedules and checking and rechecking work, would now be performed by teams. The manager's function was to set up the teams in his or her area and help them to begin to learn to make these decisions—while day-to-day work went on.

During the training session, it became clear that the managers had planned simply to replicate the work that had been done before. They expected, unconsciously, that a shadow organization would grow to perform all of the usual management functions that had been performed by the five layers of management in the past. The trainers' chief obligation was to get the managers comfortable with the new leadership role they had to assume.

Following the one-day meeting, the new managers took over their jobs with a mixture of excitement and dread. Galosy met with them one week later to assess progress. The managers initially expected to be told what to do, how to do it, and when to do it, and felt there was one "right" answer to each situation. However, they began to grow comfortable with the latitude they had to make decisions within a common structure, language, and basic TQM tools. Each of the five group managers worked with his or her group to determine the configuration of the self-managed work team. Each group was different, but each had a good logic for its unique structure.

The managers were given the assignment of coming up with three plans—restructuring, reengineering, and a day-to-day work plan—that would lay out which tasks the groups would address in their move toward self-management, which processes would be the most important to reengineer, and which timelines and resources would be needed immediately. Working with their teams, all the managers created plans that are now being implemented. All plans have been initiated, and each has achieved a measure of success in its efforts. Of the 25 key management tasks identified by the new managers, work groups have assumed, on average, responsibility for 20 tasks. There are approximately 18 reengineering projects under way. A pilot performance evaluation and compensation system for a team-structured public entity is being developed by key staff for submission to the commissioner and mayor.

Lessons Learned

LEARNING. Woolis believes that generative learning is the single most important variable that enables an organization to "catapult" itself over the deep barriers to change. Reengineering and restructuring do not by themselves create generative learning. Neither do changes in behavior and language alone. Generative learning must be built into each step through dialogue, feedback, iteration, reflection, and formal and informal learning opportunities.

RESISTANCE. No matter how noble the effort or how great the improvement, resistance to change must not be underestimated. Even those who want change resist it. Resistance is not in itself a bad thing; it indicates that people are alive and that they care. Resistance is energy that can be used to advance change by engaging in dialogue to develop shared understanding of meaning of what is, can, and should be happening.

COMMUNICATION. Information is oxygen: The less people have of it, the more they feel choked. It must be rapid, rich, and plentiful. A leader of change must talk to people, be accessible, and provide both formal and informal opportunities for dialogue. No matter how many meetings, newsletters, memos, and updates there are, someone feels out of the loop. There is a direct relationship between the effectiveness of communication and trust. Once communication channels open up, all the needed information comes pouring out.

SPONSORSHIP. Sponsorship must be clear, sustained, and unremitting. Commissioner Barrios-Paoli has been an aggressive advocate for change, and she intervenes regularly to remove barriers to change efforts. Further, she has made it clear to all organizational members that the bureau's change initiative is a priority for her and that she views resistance to it (including unnecessary slowness to respond to bureau's requests) as unacceptable work performance.

CHANGE STRATEGY. An organized structure and phased change plan must be created. Galosy and Woolis used a six-phase approach, articulated what each phase was, and communicated it to staff by several methods.

A few key terms that describe the change—restructuring, redesigning, or reengineering—must be chosen, and used consistently and frequently. They must become second nature to all employees in the whole organization. The bureau's new management team began to collectively define its nomenclature, and used the emerging vocabulary regularly.

Finally, leadership for the change must be clear. Workers must know where to get needed help with decisions and resources. The majority of staff who felt they could not live with the new bureau have left through retirement, severance, redeployment, or resignation.

Questions for Discussion
1. What was the significance of the commissioner's role in this change?
2. What resources were necessary to make the change work?
3. What types of learning were necessary for this change initiative?
4. Describe the ways in which this effort does/does not reflect movement toward becoming a learning organization.

The Authors
Diana D. Woolis, Ed.D., is Deputy City Personnel Director for the City of New York. She has been in public administration for almost 20 years and has served in leadership positions at both the state and city level. Woolis has been the primary architect and project administrator of several government change initiatives. Her work and research are focused on creating learning organizations in government and, more specifically, on the relationship between quantum science and chaos

theory and organizational learning and change. She is the author of several articles on these subjects. She can be contacted at the following address: City of New York, Department of Personnel, 2 Washington Street, 18th Floor, New York, NY 10004.

Julia R. Galosy, Ph.D., is a private consultant and is the principal in The Virtual Consulting Company. She has held executive positions at Dun & Bradstreet, Shearson Lehman/American Express, and Union Carbide. She has consulted in change management for New York City Personnel, Nabisco, the U.S. Government, the Canadian Government, and other international clients. Her areas of specialization are change management, leadership development, strategic planning, and networked organizations.

References

Gore, A. (1993). *Creating government that works better and costs less: The report of the National Performance Review.* New York: Plume.

Continuous Cross-Functional Learning

Fowler Products Company

Rob Wood and Linda Gilbert

A small packaging business adopted TQM but found that the organization had to be redesigned to improve work processes and that employees needed new skills to function in the changing environment. The case spotlights changes in structure, culture, and learning support.

Overview

From its single office and plant in Athens, Georgia, Fowler Products Company manufactures machinery for use in the beverage and packaging industry. The business has been in existence since 1952, but was purchased by new owners in 1985 and is currently run by six partners. There are about 80 employees, most of whom have been with the company since its early days.

In the late 1980s, the president of Fowler embarked on a change effort to help the company prepare for the future. Fowler spent much of the 70s and 80s rebuilding beverage industry machinery, but by the early 80s the future seemed doubtful for this type of equipment because the soft drink bottling industry was undergoing a major consolidation. Fowler decided to build its own line of packaging machines and move into the general packaging area. This turned out to be a very wise decision: By the late 80s, less than 50 percent of annual sales was from rebuilt equipment; and by 1992, less than 10 percent.

The capital equipment business is now changing so rapidly that the Fowler structure must be proactive or it will always be playing catch

This case was prepared to serve as a basis for discussion rather than to illustrate either effective or ineffective administrative and management practices.

up. To survive, companies need to move fast and be flexible. This was a problem in the late 80s. The authority structure in place at the time was hierarchical, with only a few people at the top of the organizational chart. The mentality of the workforce was "wait for instruction...don't ask questions." The social element had to change in order for Fowler to remain competitive.

Initial Steps

In 1991, in an effort to obtain resources, Fowler helped fund the Center for Continuous Improvement (CCI). The CCI was established to apply total quality management (TQM) concepts in the pursuit of continuous improvement and to bring world-class manufacturing training to the local area. It included members from an array of local businesses, working in a public-private partnership with the Athens Area Technical Institute.

By 1992 most of the obvious changes had been completed at Fowler. Time clocks were removed, as were "break horns." Supervisors had attended coach training. The tuition program had been expanded. But these were just the first steps in a long-term journey toward cultural change. That year, Rob Wood joined Fowler as vice-president in charge of people development and total quality. He has been in charge of developing and implementing training for Fowler's employees since that time.

After interviewing 80 percent of the employees, Rob Wood determined that a TQM agenda had been evolving for some time. However, the systems in place created functional goals and objectives that were task oriented. Success measurements were highly departmentalized, and only the departments involved in the final stages of project assembly had access to the customers and could gauge their responses. The result of this system was that employees "wiped their hands" after completing their respective tasks. In addition, the limited communication flow from the customers caused ongoing problems. There was tremendous pressure in the production department to satisfy customers, but these pressures permitted—and even encouraged—inordinate waste. At times, quality actually decreased. The production department was commonly called "the fire department"—an indication of the crisis management being practiced. The ownership of project deadlines, promised features, and performance issues often created heated debate. Though all employees wanted to do a good job and satisfy the customers, the process for doing this was unclear. The organization had to be redesigned to improve work processes, and employees had to learn new skills to enable them to function in the changing environment.

Organizational Development

Since the late 80s, Fowler's product designs have undergone a number of changes. The basic organization has remained the same, however. Figure 1 shows the former business model, which was both linear and highly compartmentalized. Each department shown had a supervisor responsible for communication between departments—which slowed the process. The time lag often caused problems in quality and delivery. Employees saw their supervisor as the only person they had to satisfy; the customer was not considered. As a result of this structure, the managerial staff had a very limited perspective of business practices, as did the workforce in general. This led employees to define their jobs narrowly, with no thought for the eventual end product. As Fowler completed its first level of training, employees started to make changes in the way they worked. At first, there was a lot of confusion as the workforce adjusted to changes in the organization.

The current organizational structure is depicted in Figure 2. Instead of isolated departments, there are project teams that operate across functions; instead of supervisors, there is one "coach" per project team. All employees are now either coaches or team members. Though each project team has core people within each functional area, other individuals "flex" as needed, moving up and down—or from side to side—within the matrix as cross-training is completed.

The change in the company's organization resulted in an immediate drop in production-cycle time. Quality rose as individuals working

Figure 1. Original structure of Fowler Products.

Each department shown has a supervisor

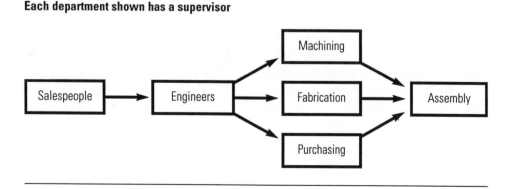

Figure 2. "Flexible matrix" of current organization.

Each project has a cross-functional team and a coach assigned to it

	Sales	Engineering	Machining	Fabrication	Assembly
Project 1	Salespeople	Engineers	Machinists	Welders	Assemblers
Project 2	Salespeople	Engineers	Machinists	Welders	Assemblers
Project 3	Salespeople	Engineers	Machinists	Welders	Assemblers
Project 4	Salespeople	Engineers	Machinists	Welders	Assemblers

on the same project began to communicate better with one another and learned to think about their jobs in terms of their contribution to the final product. At the same time that these organizational changes took place, the plant was physically reconfigured to facilitate communication between project teams.

From the organizational level to the individual level, change and training went hand in hand. One of the first steps on the organizational level was the development of a mission statement and a purpose statement, and a list of core values and beliefs. The core beliefs include a commitment to employees, products, customer service, safety, and quality that is visibly reflected in the current organization.

Training Development Outline and Design Steps

The long-term training plan implemented at Fowler Products began with a development plan, which detailed the phases of planned progress from the initial stage of developing a mission statement and corporate strategic plan through three different levels of training. At this time, level two training is concluding, and preparations are in place for level three training. A separate document—design steps—includes more detailed information about the planning and implementation of this effort, including action items and reasons for each step. The mission statement was important in order to establish a clear direction, a common purpose, and a sense that there was a new way of doing business. Communication and preplanning were emphasized to build trust, to reduce confusion, and to gain individual contribution and commitment. Ongoing reviews and needs analyses helped keep the project on target and created a sense of collaboration. Detailed implementation steps completed the plan. The master plan for overall training throughout Fowler Products was summarized in the development plan and design steps.

Team Development

Currently, most team development is completed by the coaches who have four major responsibilities: 1) people development; 2) team development; 3) linking the team to the bigger picture; and 4) "star management," which helps teams understand performance goals in different areas. People development is individually tailored. Team development promotes rapport among team members and helps them to focus on their tasks. An important part of the coaches' job is to link their teams' tasks to the bigger picture in terms of both the final product and the customer's satisfaction with it. That job is made easier by increased communications with the customer. For example, the assembly personnel now travel to the customer's plant to install the completed machinery and train the customers in its use, a task formerly performed by the representatives.

Star management includes factors that form five points of a star: safety, quality, customer service, productivity, and people. Each team articulates how it will implement and measure progress on these priorities; the responsibility for doing so rotates among team members.

Individual Training

Individual training forms the foundation of Fowler's people-development programs. Employees are encouraged to learn, both on and off the job, and are recognized and rewarded for doing so.

An initial concern that was addressed through their training efforts was the low educational level of the workforce. Twelve people—a high proportion of the staff—lacked a high school education. Fowler implemented a general equivalency diploma (GED) program that provided the employees with both the opportunity to prepare for the test and a $500 bonus for successfully passing it. Ten of the twelve people obtained their diploma; since then, more than half of these individuals have continued their education.

Fowler has instituted a generous tuition reimbursement program that will cover the costs, including books, of courses employees take on their own time. Employees who earn a C in the course get 100 percent of the tuition reimbursed; if they earn a B, 150 percent is reimbursed; if they earn an A, 200 percent. At this point, one out of three employees is involved in this program.

Self-improvement is considered so important that it forms a critical part of each employee's regular evaluations. In addition to offering support for external training, the company offers on-site training at night, partly on company time and partly on employee time. Company-related training is divided into "optional" and "required" courses. The required courses—about six thus far—include communication skills, interpersonal skills, and other topics designed to foster the development of abilities conducive to workforce productivity. Optional courses are open to interested employees who qualify and wish to attend. Both types of training are tracked, and participation is posted publicly.

Underlying the training efforts is the premise that the way to involve employees is to make sure that they understand the mission statement and all it entails, to provide them the training they need, and to reward them for improvement. It's a combination that appears to be working. To the credit of Fowler Products, almost all of the 80 staff members were able to adjust to the ongoing transition from narrowly defined jobs to their new roles as workers in a revitalized organization.

Measuring Change

Fowler Products looks at critical measurements such as safety, warranty costs, on-time delivery rates, and defects per million on in-house assemblies and supplier parts, to name just a few. All have shown favorable trends. For example, consider the area of safety performance. Fowler Products strongly emphasized that each employee was personally responsible for his or her safety and that the company would do everything possible to help. It was important that the employees learn to think about safety and not rely solely on rules, because one cannot write enough rules to protect everyone in every case. In the five years prior to 1993, Fowler averaged seven accidents per year that required medical attention. In the last 18 months, Fowler has had only one accident. This improvement is indicative of what can be done in all areas if employees continue to learn and to help each other in the never-ending quest for continuous improvement.

A change in employee perspective is one of the best indicators of improvement. Each year, Fowler Products holds a Christmas luncheon for all employees and retirees. It is always interesting to listen to the reactions of the retirees when they hear about the progress made over the past 12 months. They make statements like "The housekeeping is great," "The machines look so complex compared with those in the past," and "We can't believe this is Fowler Products." After the yearly meeting with former employees, the progress is more evident than ever.

Conclusion

In one sense, the fact that few previous attempts had been made to institute formal training offered an advantage: Employees had not experienced the phenomena of "truncated learning." When learning efforts are begun and abandoned, cynicism creeps into the workforce (Watkins and Marsick, 1993). "Learned helplessness," however—another organizational barrier identified by Watkins and Marsick—was prevalent. Fowler's generous tuition reimbursement plan overcame this problem by boosting self-esteem through individuals' success in meeting goals they established for themselves. The increase in self-confidence generated by this program, when transferred to the workplace, helped people unlearn their sense of helplessness.

Learning, and the sense of responsibility that comes with it, is a major element of the successes experienced thus far. The very nature of learning, however, dictates that organizational transitions will be a continuing process. As people learn to do their jobs better, individual jobs and the organization as a whole will change to take advantage of new information and skills. This snapshot of Fowler Products captures just one moment in its ongoing development.

Questions for Discussion

1. Fowler's tuition reimbursement plan is sometimes used for courses not directly related to the employees' jobs. Is this a problem? Why or why not?
2. The assembly personnel now install equipment at the customer's site. What are the advantages of this new arrangement? What kinds of training would be needed to enable the employees to fulfill this new responsibility?
3. Compare the former organizational model with the current one. What effects of such an organizational change would influence the quality of the final product? How?
4. The changes described were not undertaken to create a learning organization. Do you think they are consistent with the idea of a learning organization?

The Authors

Rob Wood is vice-president of people development at Fowler Products Company. He has worked in numerous disciplines in the manufacturing environment. Rob spent 12 years in the fiberglass business, working with both Manville and CertainTeed. During that time, he held positions in accounting, manufacturing, organizational development, and human resources. Rob helped to start the Center for Continuous Improvement at Athens Tech, and was its first director. He has consulted with a number of small and large companies in the areas of human organizational design, team development, and process flow. In 1992, Rob joined Fowler Products Company. Rob has a B.B.A. in accounting from the University of Georgia and an M.B.A. from Brenau. He can be contacted at the following address: Fowler Products Company, Collins Industrial Boulevard, P.O. Box 80268, Athens, GA 30608-0268.

Linda Gilbert is a doctoral student in the Department of Instructional Technology, College of Education, University of Georgia. Her interest areas for research include electronic performance support, learning organizations, and information organization. Linda also works full-time for the University of Georgia Center for Continuing Education in the Office of Staff Development. Her prior work experience includes 15 years as a graphic designer, primarily of educational products. Linda is a member of the Association for Educational Communications and Technology (AECT) and the American Society for Training and Development (ASTD). She is on the steering committee of the ASTD regional group in Athens.

References

Watkins, K., and Marsick, V. (1993). *Sculpting the learning organization: Lessons in the art and science of systemic change.* San Francisco: Jossey-Bass.

Steps Toward the Learning Organization

Swiss Postal Service

Matthias Finger and Silvia Bürgin

Consultants describe steps they took to help the top 100 managers of the Swiss Postal Service to collectively identify and address what they saw as impediments to the learning organization. The case illustrates the complexity of large systems change.

Background

In 1992 the Swiss Postal Service (SPS) started to transform itself from part of a public institution into an autonomous, efficient, and competitive public enterprise. We see this transformation as an organizational learning process and conceptualize the outcome to be a "learning organization."

The Swiss Postal Service, with its approximately 39,000 employees, is the second-largest enterprise in the country and one of the largest public sector organizations of the industrialized world seeking to become a learning organization.

There are many reasons for the SPS's transformation. Until 1992 the SPS and Swiss Telecom were integral parts of the Swiss Postes Télégraphes Téléphones (PTT), a public institution with little autonomy from politics and no autonomy for budgeting. Under the pressure of global liberalization of telecommunications—begun in the United States in the seventies—and anticipating the European Community's Telecom deregulation on January 1, 1998, the Swiss government passed a new law on telecommunications in May 1992. This law

This case was prepared to serve as a basis for discussion rather than to illustrate either effective or ineffective administrative and management practices.

liberalizes some sectors of Swiss Telecom and, by the same token, forbids the heavy cross-subsidies of the SPS by Swiss Telecom as of January 1, 1997. Thus SPS, with a sizable annual deficit, was significantly challenged. In 1991, the deficit of the Swiss PTT reached its highest level (U.S. $335 million), despite Swiss Telecom's profits. The results have improved since, but in 1994, the SPS still had a deficit of U.S. $255 million. Moreover, in the context of the crisis of Swiss public finances, and given the shift to the right in Swiss national politics and the corresponding calls for liberalization, deregulation, and privatization, the threat to the SPS was privatization, the decline of public service, or both.

Growing market pressure added to the SPS's difficulties. Not only was the deficit unacceptable, but the SPS also was losing market shares at an accelerated pace, especially in its most profitable businesses—the international express and parcel services that were increasingly being lost to global competitors (TNT, Federal Express, DHL, UPS, etc.). In short, without substantial changes, there was little chance that the SPS would ever become an efficient public enterprise.

With these considerations in mind and a heightened sense of urgency, in January 1992 the newly appointed director of the SPS initiated a profound transformation in order to lead the SPS into becoming a full-fledged learning organization.

Conceptualizing the Transformation of the SPS

We have conceptualized the SPS's becoming a learning organization as a process of profound transformations, taking place simultaneously on three different levels: autonomization from politics, internal structural changes, and cultural transformations (Rey and Finger, 1994). In the case of the SPS, a strategic decision was made to effect internal structural changes first, followed immediately by cultural transformations, while initiating the autonomization from politics three to four years later, as shown in Figure 1.

The structural transformations began in 1992 with an initiative called Optimierung der Führungstrukturen (OFS), the optimization of management structures. This initiative triggered a whole series of structural transformations (a process that is not yet completed) and led to a clearer vision of the changes necessary in the relationship between the SPS and the Swiss political system, as well as the necessary cultural changes. Following are the main structural changes and their corresponding legal and political consequences:

Figure 1. Conceptualization of the Transformation of the Swiss Postal Service.

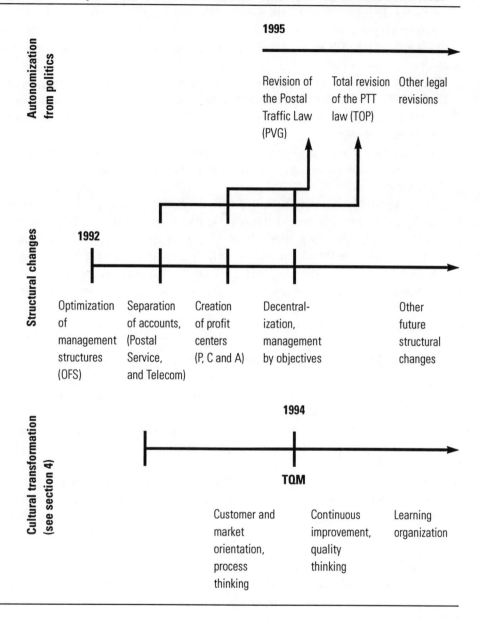

Autonomization from politics

1995

Revision of the Postal Traffic Law (PVG)

Total revision of the PTT law (TOP)

Other legal revisions

Structural changes

1992

Optimization of management structures (OFS)

Separation of accounts, (Postal Service, and Telecom)

Creation of profit centers (P, C and A)

Decentral- ization, management by objectives

Other future structural changes

Cultural transformation (see section 4)

1994

TQM

Customer and market orientation, process thinking

Continuous improvement, quality thinking

Learning organization

- The first step was to separate the bookkeeping for the SPS from that of Swiss Telecom, as both were still operating within the PTT. In 1996 there will be a total revision of the PTT law (TOP), which will create a real holding structure and thus make a clear separation between the two enterprises.
- The second step was to single out the three main profit centers within the SPS and make them independent of each other. These are the post per se (mail, express mail, parcel service), the giro, and the postal car service.
- The third step was to decentralize decision making, introduce management by objectives, and pursue a customer- and market-centered orientation.

The second and third steps led directly to the revision of the Postal Traffic Law (Postverkehrsgesetz, PVG) instituted in 1927. A new law of this kind will bring the SPS in line with the European Community's Green Book on Postal Services, which clearly distinguishes between services open to global competition and "universal services," services the SPS *must* provide. The law will define the small portion of the SPS's activity that will have to be protected by a state monopoly in order to guarantee the public service.

Initiatives Toward the Learning Organization

Immediately after having engaged in internal structural transformations, the SPS initiated substantial cultural changes. Indeed, from the literature on organizational transformation (e.g., Nadler et al., 1995), we know that structural and cultural changes need to go hand in hand. From the literature on the transformation of the public sector (e.g., Auditor General of Canada, 1992), we also know that cultural resistance to change is very important and that, in the case of public enterprises, cultural transformation requires special attention. In conceptualizing this cultural transformation for the SPS, we were inspired by the approach to the learning organization stemming from HRD and training (Dixon, 1994; Watkins and Marsick, 1993), as opposed to the one stemming from systems theory (e.g., Senge, 1990).

Several major initiatives grounded in this conceptualization promoting the learning organization have been undertaken since late 1992 in the SPS. We will describe them here briefly before presenting the most recent initiative in more detail in the next section.

A first initiative targeted at top management was started in Summer 1992 and lasted about eight months. Because a deliberate decision had been made by the SPS to undertake the transformation into a learning organization with the managers in place, particular attention was and still is given to their individual and collective learning. As part of this first initiative, all top managers (approximately 100) of the SPS learned about their fears, anxieties, strengths, and weaknesses in light of the forthcoming changes. As a result, a typology of the SPS managers regarding their attitude toward change was elaborated (Finger and Hofmann, 1995), and corresponding training for the different types was offered. The initiative that will be presented in the next section builds on this one and seeks to identify the collective roadblocks to the learning organization.

A second major initiative was started in 1994 with the organizational unit in charge of implementing the learning organization throughout the SPS—the Personnel and Organization Post (POP). This unit needs to transform itself from a human resources administration and provider of training into a facilitator of organizational learning. In our work with the collaborators of this unit (approximately 40 people), we have elaborated a common vision, identified the main obstacles to realizing this vision, and defined the major steps (including structural changes) necessary to implement that vision.

A third major initiative started in fall 1995. Its first aim was to carry out a companywide capacity-building effort in the areas of total quality and marketing. Its second aim was to set up the structure crucial to the functioning of the learning organization. On the one hand, a group of regionally based full-time trainers, whose role will be to transmit whatever knowledge and skills collaborators at all levels of the organization need, is being put into place. On the other hand, all heads of the various local organizational units (five to 30 employees) are being trained as leaders of the learning organization. Their role will be not only to facilitate organizational learning within their units but also, more specifically, to integrate the transmitted knowledge and skills into their learning organization by means of "quality circles."

A fourth initiative has been started recently and is more technical in nature than the previous three. Through it, we seek to develop the necessary indicators for assessing progress toward the learning organization. Such indicators pertain to individual and collective learning; to cultural and organizational transformation; to emerging leadership capacities; and to the evolution of skills, knowledge, capacities, and motivations within the SPS. Once fully developed, these indicators will serve as powerful tools for the management of the learning organization at all levels.

Identifying Impediments to the Learning Organization

The fifth initiative we will describe is again targeted at the approximately 100 top managers of the SPS, and builds on the first initiative mentioned above, which identifies individual roadblocks to the learning organization. Between spring and summer 1995, we sought to elaborate with these top managers the main impediments to the learning organization as they see them. We will describe first the process by which this collaborative effort unfolded, and then will highlight the major outcomes. We expected that this process would raise the SPS managers' awareness of what was still needed to make the SPS a learning organization.

As part of this initiative, SPS managers gathered in five groups of approximately 20 people within their respective organizational units (e.g., POP, finances and strategy, marketing, logistics, postal network, giro) over two days separated by a month's time. In preparation for the first session, they had filled out a questionnaire listing all the problems in their everyday work. The first session started with a presentation of the conceptual framework of the learning organization as adopted by the SPS. The participants then gathered in small groups to classify their previously listed problems in terms of impediments to becoming a learning organization. This cooperatively generated typology of impediments to the learning organization was then consolidated for each of the five groups. Not surprisingly, these impediments were quite similar for all groups.

In preparation for the second session one month later, the top managers were supposed to form small groups to elaborate, without considering limits of resources, projects that would accelerate the realization of the SPS as a learning organization. During the second session, these projects were deliberately exposed to severe criticism from the participants, as they all had to develop arguments why, given the current state of the SPS, these projects were not feasible. A list of the main obstacles to implementing these projects was thus generated, and only then was this list confronted and compared with the previously elaborated typology of impediments to the learning organization. Not surprising to us, but quite so to the participants, the lists were almost identical, containing mainly cultural impediments. As a result, each of the five groups was able to establish a common list of the main impediments to the learning organization. At the conclusion of the initiative, this list, along with some of the most creative projects, was presented and discussed with the director of the SPS. The discussion was designed and facilitated so that all participants, including the director of the SPS, had to acknowledge that they were part and parcel of these impediments to the learning organization, and that they collectively had to overcome this situation, or as we like to call it, "learn their way out."

Currently, measures are being taken to address each of the following cultural and structural impediments to the learning organization.

Subservience to regulations, the first cultural impediment to the learning organization as identified by the top managers of the SPS, means that everything that is not explicitly mentioned in the regulations is assumed to be forbidden. This impediment inhibits the entrepreneurial spirit necessary for generative learning. It also prevents exploring possible options not regulated by law. Moreover, it generates stable behaviors, praises practices that proved successful in the past, and prevents the generation of information that is not consistent with traditional ways of doing things. More generally, this impediment to the learning organization implies a lack of flexibility and a resistance to change. Consequently, shared assumptions are never questioned, and double-loop learning (the questioning of established values) cannot take place (Argyris, 1992). This subservience to regulations is one of the reasons that, in this case, structural changes need to precede cultural transformations.

Fear of risks, the second cultural impediment to the learning organization, is closely related to the first. This fear is due in part to the promotion system still prevailing in the SPS: The people who are promoted are the ones who never have made a mistake. Such fear of risks impedes the learning organization in two important ways: first, managers are not willing to experiment; second, they are not willing to make decisions that could meet resistance.

Perfectionism is a third widespread impediment to the learning organization as identified by SPS top managers. Perfectionism prevents, among other things, the free flow of information, and thus the very functioning of the learning organization. Perfectionism finds its expression in the medium used for communication, for example, written and copied memos, which have to respect formal constraints, such as perfect presentation, or routing of copies to certain hierarchical superiors. Furthermore, perfectionism means that solutions that are not guaranteed to be successful are not even tried.

Fear of conflict, the fourth cultural impediment to the learning organization, is profoundly rooted in the SPS, as well as in Swiss culture in general. Fear of conflict strongly relates to the fact that managers (and collaborators) of the SPS have difficulty distinguishing between discussing a subject and criticizing a person. As a result, managers avoid expressing divergent opinions in order to prevent conflicts with their colleagues and their superiors. Very often, such divergent opinions are not even raised for fear that they may appear confrontational. It goes without saying that such self-censorship is one of the key impediments to the free flow of information required by a learning organization. Moreover, the fear of conflict is also an obstacle to the questioning of established values.

Linear thinking, the fifth impediment, refers to a series of attitudes that indicate a linear or sequential approach to things and the lack of a global vision. For example, many managers of the SPS said that they had difficulty setting priorities and distinguishing what is really important from what is not. When managers are given a choice, priority is generally given to short-term and operational matters rather than to long-term and strategic thinking and approaches. Such linear thinking especially impedes quick, selective, and efficient information processing. Moreover, the lack of a global perspective is clearly a weakness when it comes to interpreting information and experiences.

Communication problems in general were identified by SPS managers as the sixth most serious cultural and structural impediment to the learning organization. Many of these communication problems are of cultural origin, rooted as they are in the culture described above, and therefore have to be addressed as such. But many other communication problems have structural origins. For example, information is still being generated, in the case of the SPS, in a very bureaucratic way (one authorized source). It is then distributed in a top-down, often secret manner; this information flow takes a long time and often is not user friendly. Because communication is neither rapid nor open, there is a growing risk, with increased interaction as a result of the learning organization, of promoting rumors and creating additional insecurity.

Decision-making processes inherited from public administration were seen by the SPS managers as the seventh impediment to the learning organization. Indeed, decision-making processes in the SPS are particularly long and vague. They therefore impede the learning organization because they distort and obscure the free flow of information. As a result, recommendations for action are often unrelated to the initial interpretation of the information.

Compartmentalization, the eighth impediment, is a primarily structural obstacle to the learning organization. It is inherited from the days when the SPS was a public administration, and becomes a serious problem with the growing customer- and market-centered orientation and corresponding entrepreneurial spirit. Indeed, the self-interests of the organizational units and of their leaders still prevail over the global interests of the SPS. Furthermore, these units traditionally lack confidence in each other and do not collaborate. Because they seldom communicate, they impede the generation and integration of useful information (retaining it, instead, for their own strategic purposes). In each unit, the learning cycle may be functioning, but it does not function for the organization as a whole. In other words, in a dynamic organization that maintains the old compartmental structure, the learning organization might well lead to destructive competition. Thus structural changes are as important as cultural transformations.

Conclusion

This list of key impediments identified by the SPS's top managers is impressive. As a matter of fact, the list is not atypical for a public administration. This list shows that this initiative turned out to be successful. Through it, the top managers of the SPS came to realize that substantial obstacles still prevent the SPS from becoming a learning organization, and that they themselves acted as impediments (for example, when they criticized their collaborators' projects).

This initiative, however, is not without danger. The goal of becoming a learning organization is an ambitious one, and the obstacles identified by the SPS managers can seem overwhelming. If the SPS cannot rapidly demonstrate progress on the road toward the learning organization, or at least show success in the market, this ambitious ideal may well have counterproductive effects, especially on the managers' motivation.

Questions for Discussion

1. Are the reasons that the Swiss Postal Service wants to transform itself into a learning organization different from the reasons usually given by organizations in the private sector?
2. If there is a difference, does this have an influence on the transformation process?
3. The transformation of the Swiss Postal Service into a learning organization implies changes on three different levels—structural, cultural, and legal. Is the sequence of actions undertaken in the Swiss Postal Service (structural, then cultural, then legal) appropriate for the public sector? Why or why not?
4. Are the impediments to the learning organization that are identified in this case specific to the public sector, or can they also be found in large private organizations?

5. Other than the initiative described in this case, what are some means for overcoming these impediments?

The Authors

Matthias Finger holds a Ph.D. in political science and in adult education, and is professor of management of public enterprises at the Graduate Institute of Public Administration in Lausanne, Switzerland. Previously he taught at Teachers College, Columbia University, and at the Maxwell School of Citizenship and Public Affairs, Syracuse University. He is the author or coauthor of nine books and more than 50 book chapters and articles, mainly in the area of social and organizational change. His research interest pertains to the link between individual and structural transformations. He can be contacted at the following address: idheap, 21 Rte de la Maladière, 1022 Chavannes-près-Renens, Switzerland.

Silvia Bürgin holds an M.A. in public administration and is an assistant at the Graduate Institute of Public Administration in Lausanne, Switzerland. She has conducted research in the area of organizational environmental transformation and learning, and is interested mainly in issues of change management in public sector organizations.

The authors are pleased to be closely and actively involved with the transformation of the SPS into a learning organization since its very beginning, both by means of conceptual work and by means of management development and training. They are aware that this is a unique privilege and would like to thank the Director of the Swiss Postal Service, Professor Jean Noël Rey; the director of human resource development, Mr. Alfred Lauber; and many other collaborators for their precious work, their invaluable help, and their patience with the authors.

References

Argyris, C. (1992). *On organizational learning.* Oxford: Blackwell.

Auditor General of Canada. (1992). *Report of the Auditor General of Canada to the House of Commons.* Ottawa: The Learning Organization.

Dixon, N. (1994). *The organizational learning cycle: How we can learn collectively.* London: McGraw-Hill.

Finger, M., and Hofmann, A. (1995). Umgang mit veranderungen in organisationen. In R. Arnold and H. Weber (Eds.), *Weiterbildung und organisation: Zwischen organisationslernen und lernenden organisationen* (pp. 143–158). Berlin: Erich Schmidt Verlag.

Nadler, D., et al. (1995). *Discontinuous change: Leading organizational transformation*. San Francisco: Jossey-Bass.

Rey, J. and Finger, M. (1994). *Die Zukunft der post—die post der zukunft*. Zurich: Orell Fussli.

Senge, P. (1990). *The fifth discipline: The art and practice of the learning organization*. New York: Doubleday.

Watkins, K., and Marsick, V. (1993). *Sculpting the learning organization: Lessons in the art and science of systemic change*. San Francisco: Jossey-Bass.

Section 6:
Lessons Learned and Future Prospects for the Learning Organization

What Have We Learned?

Karen Watkins and Victoria Marsick

The authors draw lessons learned from the cases in this book: what trig-gered the change to a learning organization, the nature of the interven-tions, relationships to other change initiatives, and emerging issues—con-sultants' roles, leaders' roles, interdependency of elements in the process, change groups, spin-offs, informal and incidental learning, metrics for learning, and concrete learning organization tactics.

In our earlier work (Watkins and Marsick, 1993), we concluded that creating a learning organization was a lot like sculpting. Unlike a sculpture, however, the learning organization is always a work in progress. But the creation of a learning organization *is* as much an art as it is a science. Michelangelo, in sculpting, is said to have chipped away at his material until he freed the sculpture that he knew lay with-in. In echoing this sentiment, Henry Moore sounds much like the lead-ers of the learning organization: "I like the fact that I can begin with a block and have to find the sculpture that's inside it. ...It's the quality of the idea and the mind behind it that's important" (Raskey, 1985).

We turn now to a comparison of the cases in this book to identify lessons that we have learned for sculpting the learning organization. Under the auspices of the American Society for Training and Develop-ment, more than 8,500 letters were sent to individuals inviting them to submit a case of a learning organization initiative in their organization or in an organization with which they have worked as an external con-sultant. More than 70 inquiries for case guidelines were received. Of these, 32 individuals or organizations responded with a proposal to write a case. In all, 28 cases were received and 22 cases were selected for inclusion in this volume.

We discuss the following themes: what triggered the change, the type of experiment and the nature of the intervention that supported it, and relationships to other organizational initiatives that bear some resemblance to becoming a learning organization. Finally, we suggest emerging trends and comment on the status of the learning organization initiative.

What Triggers the Learning Organization?

Many of the companies in this book began their journey because they had to do so. Changes in the environment—especially economic shortfalls or projected negative economic consequences due to globalization, shifting markets, privatization, or increased competition—led to awareness that the company soon could be out of business. Internal triggers also drove change. The vision of key leaders was primary. Change was triggered by significantly low employee satisfaction survey results, reading one or more books or seeing a video on the learning organization, executive mandates, or a vision of a better future coupled with the belief that this process would help attain that future.

Half of the cases in this volume explicitly set out to create a learning organization and half later saw a relationship between what they were doing to attain business results and the ideas and concepts of the learning organization.

Triggers for learning may be the same regardless of the level at which the initiative is launched, but the arguments that are used to advocate the learning organization and the design of the initiative itself differ greatly when it is launched from the top or with the top leader's explicit involvement, versus when it is launched from the middle (even if it has the support of the top leader at that level). Mumford (the British subsidiary) and Albert (Ultrasound Coronary Systems), for example, point out that their counterparts were less interested in a learning initiative than in solving a specific business problem. On the other hand, the integrated systems examples and many of the organizational initiatives included the learning organization in vision or mission statements. At the division or other subcompany levels, it may be more important to focus changes on business needs, while at the level of top management or of the whole system, it is appropriate to work at a level that can effect change of the whole organization. *Where* the change enters the organization is clearly significant in determining what is possible.

Depth and Type of Intervention

Table 1 lists key features of each case using the framework by which we organized them in this book—that is, by looking at interventions that emphasize total systems integration or experiments that are driven more by learning at the individual, team, or organizational lev-

Table 1. Overview of the case studies: Individual, team, and organizational learning features.

Case	Individual learning	Team learning	Organizational learning
		Integrated, whole system learning cases	
Intermedics Orthopedics, Inc.	Core competencies are identified that form the basis for training. They continuously ask, "If not, why not?" VisionQuest sessions help new employees reflect and question	Groupware, dialogue, and participation are used to engage everyone in creating a common vision. Compensation and rewards focused on team performance	CEO leads visioning process that emphasizes learning. Linkages are created to support planning, sharing, and learning, across groups or levels
Johnsonville Foods	Contracts stretch people to learn that which is above and beyond day-to-day job requirements	CEO created self-managed, empowered work teams. Leaders set vision and serve as coaches	Great Performance Share created to compensate teams every month based on contract with customers
British Insulated Callender Cables	Learning based on real concerns and issues. Personal development planning and training set in place	New teams are created; teams trained as intact work units	Learning is central to new business strategy and to reorganization in teams. Unions agree to new pay scales and contract that includes learning

Table 1. (continued) Overview of the case studies: Individual, team, and organizational learning features.

Case	Individual learning	Team learning	Organizational learning
	Integrated, whole system learning cases		
Morrison Communications	Learning is integrated with work	People became aware of connections through work on cross-functional and cross-company teams	Leaders model learning Practices named so they could be changed
Land O'Lakes	Learning strategy evolves in response to organizational change initiatives and emphasizes informal learning	Training is provided to intact work teams Cross-functional team empowered to develop learning systems model and practices	CEO identifies and extends new practices to entire company
	Continuous learning cases		
Nortel	Competencies identified as basis for skills development model that enables employees and organization to plan for training	Goal is to train account managers to work in virtual task teams	

Continuous learning cases

Rohm and Haas Company	Competency assessment, 360-degree feedback, and computer-based learning guide enables self-directed learning	Interactive features of computer-based learning guide enables joint problem solving and collaboration
The Virtual School	Individual self-directed learning needs drive the network	Interactive features of network enable joint problem solving and collaboration
Ultrasound Coronary Systems	Engineers used index cards to identify lessons from past experience	Focus group discussion enabled engineers to share learning
AMEV Nederland	System created for people to move in and out of learning: on their own, with coaches, through and after work	Employees used as resources to help one another learn, and create materials to capture learning	New norms were created for systems thinking and work, and for inquiry

Table 1. (continued) Overview of the case studies: Individual, team, and organizational learning features.

Case	Individual learning	Team learning	Organizational learning
Continuous learning cases			
A British multinational corporation	Personal development plans created that emphasized informal learning	Executive group members shared thinking in dialogue sessions	
Fretwell Downing	Personal learning is fed through formal education and relationships	Learning teams at the university emphasize learning from many disciplines/perspectives	Individuals who grow influence company policy
Team and action learning cases			
Volvo Truck Corporation	Managers learn skills to work globally Project work develops critical thinking, dialogue, participatory skills	Global network created to support sharing, collaboration, and sustained learning	Problem solving influences organizational markets/profits and eventually leaders' ability to act globally
Grace Cocoa	Managers learn skills to work globally Project work develops critical thinking, dialogue, participatory skills	Global network created to support sharing, collaboration, and sustained learning	Learning intervention used to change organization's culture and structure to support integrated global company

Team and action learning cases

Ford Motor Company (EFHD) with Washtenaw Community College	Learning course develops skills for dialogue and learning that are tied to real work projects	Collaborative skills developed through training in teams and continued through work reorganization	Partnership exists between EFHD and community groups to improve total quality of community, not just Ford
Coca-Cola	Individuals learn through work on real projects	Action learning teams are used to capitalize on strengths and differences	Problem solving influences organizational markets/profits and eventually leaders' ability to act globally
Middle and Southwest Georgia Communities	Workshop provides skills in visioning and planning	Artist rendering of future vision enables group to collaborate on joint future to which all can commit	Overlapping memberships in different agencies enable success in implementation The community is enhanced and better able to act in the future

Table 1. (continued) Overview of the case studies: Individual, team, and organizational learning features.

Case	Individual learning	Team learning	Organizational learning
	Organizational restructuring cases		
Alberta Labour	Competency profiles inform training Learning is tied to restructuring initiatives	Intact work teams are trained together Teams learn through work in cross discipline and project teams	Customer service restructuring drives change Solutions based on new partnerships with community and industry
Environmental Protection Agency	New mindset is needed to support restructuring that includes ability to challenge existing practices	Learning takes place through large group interventions and team work	Reorganization is driven by future search conference that is integrated with other strategies
New York City Bureau of Exams	Leaders are helped to develop a new mindset and take on new roles	Employees learn to work in self-managed teams Teams and task forces make recommendations for change	Learning strategy is used to develop leadership and employee capacity while downsizing, reengineering, and restructuring

Organizational restructuring cases

Fowler Products Company	Develop individual learning capacity Reward learning through generous tuition reimbursement program	Team-based structure is supported by developing leaders as coaches and by capacity to work in teams	Use learning to enhance ability to think and work systemically for total quality management
Swiss Postal Service	Top management learned about personal orientation to change Training system will be put in place for companywide capacity building	Human resources unit being transformed around common vision	Indicators are being created to assess individual and collective learning, cultural and organizational transformation, leadership capacity

el. Features at the individual level center around the action imperatives of continuous learning and strategies that emphasize inquiry and dialogue. Features at the team level include enhanced collaboration, team learning, and learning among larger groups that might not function as teams, but that create vehicles for collective learning. Features at the organizational level include structures to capture and share learning, empowerment around a vision, connection between the organization and the external community or environment, and strategic leadership for learning. Some features directly address learning, and others highlight structures, policies, procedures, or other organization-level factors that must be in place to facilitate learning.

Table 1 shows differences as the focus on learning moves from the individual to the team to the organizational level. Integrated experiments address all three levels and generally coordinate learning in support of total systems change. They are typically led from the top by charismatic individuals with a vision. By contrast, individual learning experiments are the most limited in their systems impact. They focus on select target groups, are more adaptive than transformative, and are not as closely linked to total system change. Team learning experiments are often used to leverage both individual and organizational learning. They build a critical mass of change agents whose role is to influence larger-scale change. Interventions driven by organizational changes, our third category of experiments, create a widespread infrastructure for change and create impetus within individuals and groups to quickly adapt to a radically new way of working.

Each of these foci involves increasingly deep interventions—from the individual to the team to the organization and finally to the whole systems level—yet these cases are not equally deep. Depth can mean the number of people in the organization involved, the degree of change required to implement the idea, the number of changes required by the intervention, or the way in which interventions are integrated and interwoven.

We compare the skills development model of Nortel (an experiment in its first year involving 108 people of a division of 1,400) with Johnsonville (an organization of 600 people that has more than 10 years of work invested in implementing these principles). Whereas one might think that collaborative learning is neither new nor singularly likely to lead toward a learning organization, in an organization such as Rohm and Haas, where learning has been neither collaborative nor interactive, the shift has the potential to catalyze other important learnings. At Fowler, where members of the organization have low levels of education, a 200 percent tuition reimbursement program can lead to changes in self-esteem that will also catalyze changes in conduct at work. What is significant here is both what is new to the organization and its members and the manner in which the change is carried out. Undergirding all of these changes is a belief that people can unlearn the old and learn the new, that their learning will ultimately make a significant difference to the organization, and that the organization will acknowledge the learning curve and trust that this difference will emerge.

Cases in which the organization is engaged in a number of integrated activities related to creating a learning organization differ from those with a smorgasbord of initiatives that are not as well linked, even if at first glance specific experiments may resemble one another. Thought is given to how activities fit together. Often, these cases point to an evolutionary process that is driven by reflection on learnings from prior steps. For example, the Johnsonville Foods performance contracts grew out of a need to put in place rewards that continued to drive the gains from an earlier initiative. At Intermedics Orthopedics, Inc., the larger vision of systemic integration drove them to create linkages to support planning, sharing, and learning across groups and levels. Intermedics staff continually asked of their efforts, "If not, why not?" The Morrison Communications initiatives were characterized by a high level of conversation among leaders and staff to raise awareness of where they were, where they might want to go, and how they could change their practices to support new goals.

Much has been written on the appropriate sequencing of efforts to move toward becoming a learning organization. Most experts agree that it is best to begin with a vision of where one is headed measured against baseline data about where one is now. On the other hand, these cases suggest that it may be equally important to first make sure that the structure and infrastructure to support the change are in place. Structures can be planned and must also be reconsidered based on lessons learned. The Swiss Postal Service, for example, began with structural changes, assessment and cultural changes, and finally legal or policy shifts. This resulted from a conscious decision to sequence changes in a manner that had the greatest chance of success while ultimately changing all that was necessary to promote a long-term learning and production capacity.

Organizational Changes and the Learning Organization

Some principles embraced by learning organizations overlap with those embraced by several other total organizational change initiatives, particularly total quality management (TQM), business process reengineering, and self-managed work teams. All three involve systemic thinking, teamwork, decentralized decision making, and continuous learning. TQM and reengineering require that work processes be viewed across business functions, and that customer satisfaction drive change. The learning organization, however, differs in that there is less standardization in how it is implemented, as these cases illustrate. The focus is always on learning capacity, whereas other change strategies focus first on changes in work and structures. Changes in work and infrastructure in the learning organization catalyze, support, and reward people and groups for their learning. As the authors of several cases (e.g., Fowler and Land O'Lakes) explicitly point out, the learning organization approach builds long-term capacity, enables people to change mindsets, and creates the ability to think and work systemically in ways that may not be achieved by any of the other initiatives alone.

Senge (1990) said that the TQM movement was the first wave of learning organization initiatives. TQM was a key factor for several cases in this volume. In these cases, a number of TQM principles support the creation of a learning organization, particularly the emphasis on creating appropriate benchmarks against which to measure current versus ideal performance, the use of action teams to solve quality problems, and a customer service orientation. Each of these strategies catalyzes a learning process. In some organizational implementations of TQM, however, the emphasis on control and short-term efficiency improvements may work against a learning orientation.

Recently, a number of organizations have reengineered their work processes to reduce costs. These efforts are often accompanied by a workforce reduction. Because learning is neither an explicit nor an implicit goal of reengineering, it is surprising to see an initiative that couples this intervention with becoming a learning organization. In a climate in which organizations often bungle these types of changes, many will be skeptical of the potential success of this combination. Yet some initiatives are succeeding. Woolis (New York City Bureau of Examinations) argues that by building a learning infrastructure to support organizational reengineering, people learn new skills so that they have the capacity to flourish in the new organization. We are often asked if learning organizations are possible in the face of cutbacks and downsizing. The pain and disruption of such changes typically makes people too fearful to truly learn. The New York City (NYC) experiment leads us to believe that learning organizations can be designed in such an environment. The determining factor is whether—at the end of this painful process—people feel that they and the organization have an increased capacity to both produce and to continue to evolve.

All of the public sector examples in this book, in fact, begin with reorganization, as does the BICC case, which is highly influenced by government regulatory policies. In all these cases, steps are taken to ensure broad-based discussion, some opportunity to influence outcomes (e.g., large group interventions, action teams, new processes for selection based on open access and new job criteria), and efforts to partner with a multiplicity of stakeholders affected by the change (e.g., "third options" with community and business, or negotiations with unions). The heart of bureaucracy is structure, and so the entry point for the learning organization in highly bureaucratic organizations is in changing the structure to enable learning. At the Swiss Postal Service, for example, moving to separate profit centers may allow more rapid changes within each center. Flattening the NYC Bureau of Examinations makes it easier to change outdated procedures.

Size of Intervention

The size of the intervention is also significant. While all of the integrated learning examples involved the whole organization, many also involved whole divisions (e.g., NYC Bureau of Examinations, Alberta Labour) or whole populations (e.g., all of Rohm and Haas's marketing managers, all of EPA's human resources group, or all future global leaders in Coca-Cola or Volvo Truck Corporation). This is a critical factor. At Grace Cocoa, for example, leaders report significant changes during the action reflection learning sessions, but not all are able to translate these learnings into new behavior back at the job. While one can eventually attain a critical mass of individuals implementing a new way of leading and managing, it is much harder to sustain a change when individuals are working alone in nonsupportive environments.

There seems to be an inverse relationship between the size of the organization and the scope of the learning organization experiment: the smaller the organization, the greater the scope of the experiment and vice versa. This is borne out by the cases in this volume. Perhaps because it is so essential to involve all or most of the system in this activity—preferably all at once—there may also be a natural limit to the size of the experiment. It is daunting for most of us to imagine an intervention that would involve, for example, all of the 450,000 or so employees of Ford Motor Company in a long-term learning process. Eliot Jaques (1988) defined an individual's work or cognitive capacity based on ability to project work over a long time period; in other words, the longer the period one could project, the larger would be his or her cognitive capacity. There may also be a correlation between cognitive capacity and the scope of the experiment, both in terms of the number of people involved and the number of changes to manage. Cognitive capacity in these cases is related to one's ability to set in motion a process that exceeds one's immediate span of control.

Emerging Issues

We turn now to emerging issues: consultants' roles, leaders' roles, interdependency of the elements in the process, change groups as learning organizations, spin-offs, informal and incidental learning, metrics for learning, and concrete learning organization tactics.

Consultant Roles

All but six of these cases used an internal or external organizational development or training consultant. Alberta Labour wanted to reduce its reliance on consultants and designed the experiment accordingly, but even so, they did draw on DACUM consultants for expertise in this assessment process. In our earlier work (Watkins and Marsick, 1993), we noted that learning organizations result from new partnerships between line management and a variety of human resource specialists. These cases reinforce our hunch. These consultants couple learning skills with expertise in organizational change technologies that are at the root of organization development. Specialists who build learning organizations transfer their expertise to line managers and others so that everyone in the organization knows how to learn inductively from their work experiences as well as how to predict and manage a change project.

Leaders' Roles

Leaders in these cases emerge as primary gatekeepers of the change and modelers of the learning process. They are often charismatic, risk-taking, visionary change agents—like Ralph Stayer at Johnsonville Foods; Jerry Marler at Intermedics Orthopedics, Inc.; Lilliam Barrios-Paoli in New York's Department of Personnel; Pedro Mata at Grace Cocoa; and Jack Gherty at Land O'Lakes. They have been willing to change themselves—as was seen in Morrison Communications, where Maudie, Richard, and Jadie said that they must first change themselves before they could ask others to change.

Many of these cases identify the first step toward change as changing leaders' roles and capacities. At Land O'Lakes, for example, a cross-functional task force worked first with top managers and supervisors to identify a leader level of the learning organization that emphasized leading through coaching, mentoring, and participatory strategies. Nortel revamped its leadership training programs; Fowler, the NYC Bureau of Examinations, the Swiss Postal Service, and BICC trained new team leaders. Grace Cocoa, Volvo, and Coca-Cola identified changes leaders needed to make in order to create global organizations.

These cases also show that leadership is a shared capacity in learning organizations. Volvo Truck Corporation and Grace Cocoa, for example, developed the capacity of leaders to listen and dialogue with staff when making decisions. Johnsonville Foods and the EPA's human resource group created structures that enabled broad-based participatory decision making. The groupware used by Intermedics involved everyone in technology-mediated decision making and prioritizing. Fowler's star management model prepared everyone within a team to take on new leadership roles. At Tennessee's Virtual School, members drive network decisions by their interests, and at Rohm and Haas users influence the content of the electronic learning guide.

Interdependency of Elements of the Process

Intermedics Orthopedics, Inc. and Johnsonville Foods are mature cases of long-term learning organization experiments that illustrate what happens when one element of the process is overlooked. At Intermedics Orthopedics, Inc., for example, it became clear that middle managers felt that they had been left out of the loop so the company built a system for learning through planning which was consistent at all levels of the organization. At Johnsonville, empowerment of individuals and teams had to be counterbalanced by empowerment of the customer.

Changes at the individual level alone have not led to long-term organizational shifts. Future directions in these cases have consistently pointed toward a higher order change as the next step. Team or action learning experiments look toward means of changing the organizational culture, and continuous learning strategies move toward greater emphasis on teams. "More will be revealed" is a favorite saying of Renee Rogers, organization development specialist at Intermedics Orthopedics Inc. Completion of one step or the launching of a new initiative brings to light other elements or problems that had been hidden or ignored. As the organization evolves, covert problems surface and the change itself creates new problems that must be addressed. The learning organization is an evolutionary process; it is not just one intervention, but many.

Change Groups as Learning Organizations

Although the literature of the learning organization is focused on stand-alone organizations, temporary organizational structures may also share features of the learning organization. The Tennessee Virtual School project and the Georgia community development projects illustrate ways in which temporary structures with a change objective—to develop teachers and transfer technology and to develop communities—may use these ideas to establish norms of continuous improvement, replication and dissemination, and empowerment. New relationships or partnerships also emerge that share learning organization characteristics. For example, Ford and Washtenaw Community College are working to create a community ad hoc coalition for learning through their work with the Ann Arbor community. These developments illustrate the concept of self-regeneration that is fundamental to learning organization theory.

Spin-Offs

Marsick, in her work with Kathleen Dechant, codeveloped the metaphor of the spider plant to describe the way in which these interventions stimulate spin-offs and replications. At Tennessee's Virtual School, one school created its own virtual school. Ford is spinning off its learning organization approach to Washtenaw Community College, Ann Arbor, other divisions of Ford, and even the Small Business Development Center. Grace Cocoa managers who had participated in the Leadership Forum went back and asked to replicate the forum in their locale; participants adopted strategies such as dialogue groups and stop-reflect for work with their back-home teams; meetings and shorter one-week courses were designed around real project work. At Coca-Cola, Mike Grissom found that he could use the global action learning project model for individual development as well.

Informal and Incidental Learning

The learning organization is not the same as a training organization. In some organizations, training hours and opportunities are mandated to meet requirements set by unions or law, but learning may not be meaningful to individuals or add value to the organization. These cases illustrate the value of integrating learning initiatives with business initiatives, reorganization, and change.

A striking similarity of all cases is the move away from primary reliance on formal classroom training and toward capitalizing on the natural learning that occurs informally and incidentally through work.

Many cases build learning around real work issues, integrate learning into work processes, train intact work groups together, institute some form of planning for learning, and include a wide range of informal learning strategies. The initiatives within Land O'Lakes, for example, spurred brown bag discussions and other creative ways to bring people together to talk about their learning. The computer-based interactive technology adopted by both Rohm and Haas and the Tennessee Virtual School enabled people to learn dialogue skills incidentally while they tackled problem solving. Fretwell Downing illustrates the way in which the learning of a key individual outside the organization can effect changes in the organization. AMEV demonstrates the balance between learning initiatives to develop new knowledge and those needed to disseminate knowledge on the job. A key feature of a number of the learning initiatives (e.g., Nortel, Rohm and Haas, Alberta Labour, Intermedics) was a competency study to assess knowledge and skills needed for changing roles. Subsequent training and learning initiatives were then built.

Metrics for Learning

Nuala Beck (1992) draws attention to the fact that every era needs metrics suited to its primary focus, and yet the knowledge age still relies on indicators from a prior industrial era. In our earlier work (Watkins and Marsick, 1993) we attempted to identify metrics that would address knowledge capacity and long-term growth. We find that several cases in this book also seek new ways to measure learning at the organizational level, or as is pointed out in Land O'Lakes, wish that they had paid more attention to doing so. The Swiss Postal Service case, for example, seeks to identify indicators to assess individual and collective learning, cultural and organizational transformation, leadership, and capacity. Nortel, while in the early stages of implementation, used a readiness instrument that we created (Watkins and Marsick, 1995) and gave considerable thought to how it might measure progress toward becoming a learning organization. Boydell lays out indicators of impact for the intervention carried out at BICC.

Concrete Learning Organization Tactics

While all involved with learning organizations would decry the idea that there might be a cookbook of strategies which create these entities, most people would like to know at least a few practical tactics for building a learning organization. Here we draw attention to a few of the more unusual strategies used in these cases:

- The three-tier planning approach at Intermedics can be replicated and shows promise for moving beyond compartmentalization and toward systems thinking.
- Groupware is a promising strategy for involving large groups of people in participatory change. It enables everyone to make his or her opinion known anonymously, gives all an equal vote regardless of hierarchical status, and provides immediate feedback about proposed initiatives.
- The index card activity at Ultrasound Coronary is a useful means of building a data base of critical lessons learned while teaching the organization how to move beyond blame to view mistakes as learning opportunities.
- Large group interventions, although not new, were coupled with other change strategies at the EPA to promote total system change with buy-in from many stakeholders in a relatively short time.
- The artist's rendering of the downtown area in the Southwestern Georgia Community project is an example of making a vision simultaneously visible and influenceable.
- The Virtual School project is a means of transferring technological learning and also of disseminating knowledge to a widely dispersed workforce. The Rohm and Haas electronic learning guide serves a similar purpose. Imagine opening a virtual school on the learning organization!
- The results-based small-group task of budget restructuring at the Alberta Department of Labor is an excellent low-technology strategy for helping everyone in the organization to see systemic interdependencies.
- Using a course on the learning organization as a vehicle to drive work process reengineering and to develop a shared vision is an innovative use of a familiar technology.
- Designing alternative organizational structures through a collaborative future search conference coupled with selection clinics in which individuals bid for three jobs in the new structure is a creative restructuring strategy. This approach builds capacity and commitment.

These concrete approaches offer a variety of starting points for organizations hoping to begin a learning organization initiative.

Conclusion

Those seeking a formula by which to create a learning organization will turn away from this goal for precisely the same reasons that the companies in this book have turned toward it: The learning organization is not a destination, but a journey; it is not a formula, but it does involve some key principles that can be used to tailor a flexible structure to one's unique needs. A learning organization must do the following:

- embed a learning infrastructure—not a training department, but a widespread means of creating, capturing and disseminating knowledge about new products and processes, and about what is working and what is not from both internal and external perspectives
- cultivate a learning habit in people and in the culture so that a spirit of inquiry, initiative, and experimental thinking predominates
- regularly audit the knowledge capital in the organization and progress toward eliminating barriers to learning.

Since we published our earlier book with 18 promising experiments, we have seen great progress toward adopting the idea of a learning organization, in part because of the popularity of this idea. We continue to see few examples of organizations that have been able to develop systemic learning capacity, but many more pockets of experimentation seem to hold promise to make a systemic difference.

What has killed one approach after another has been the superficial implementation of this idea in a piecemeal or compartmentalized fashion. It is also a grave mistake to reduce the initiative to a sterile four- or eight-hour training session and act as if this will change the entire organization. The following disablers, or dysfunctional organizational learning patterns, that we identified in our earlier book still hold true:

- *Truncated learning*—a learned pattern of making changes a mile wide and an inch deep—which is the opposite of a culture of continuous learning
- *Learned helplessness*—a learned pattern of passivity, dependence, and hopelessness around change, which is the opposite of a state of empowerment
- *Tunnel vision*—a learned pattern of compartmentalizing work and life—which is the opposite of interdependence and systems thinking.

The learning organization concept may not survive the assaults made upon it or be able to overcome these deeply embedded norms, but we believe that these cases illustrate what can happen when learning is strategically infused into organizational action. Through these experiences, organizations are gaining a new appreciation of the importance of learning. Human resource persons have begun to broaden their concept of their roles to encourage self-development and team learning, and to take on organizational renewal and learning. Managers have begun to assume new educational roles, including those of coach, mentor, and teacher. Whatever becomes of the current interest in the learning organization, we think that an enhanced learning capacity will remain in these organizations, as will a new appreciation of the role of learning in pulling them toward their desired future. We are optimistic, as we read these cases, that much can be and has been accomplished.

References

Beck, N. (1992). *Shifting gears: Thriving in the new economy.* Toronto: Harper Collins.

Jaques, E. (1988). Development of intellectual capability. In F. Link (Ed.), *Essays on the intellect.* Alexandria, VA: Association for Supervision and Curriculum Development.

Pedler, M., Burgoyne J., and Boydell, T. (1991). *The learning company: A strategy for sustainable development.* London: McGraw-Hill.

Raskey, H. (1985). *The mystery of Henry Moore.* CBC Film Productions.

Senge, P. (1990). *The fifth discipline: The art and practice of the learning organization.* New York: Random House.

Watkins, K., and Marsick, V. (1993). *Sculpting the learning organization: Lessons in the art and science of systemic change.* San Francisco: Jossey-Bass.

Watkins, K., and Marsick, V. (1995). *Readiness for the learning organization. (Unpublished manuscript).* Athens, GA: University of Georgia.

For Further Reading

Argyris, C. (1993). *Knowledge for action: A guide to overcoming barriers to organizational change.* San Francisco: Jossey-Bass.

Argyris, C. (1994). Good communication that blocks learning. *Harvard Business Review, 72*(4), 77–85.

Bauch, R. (1994). *Changing work: A union guide to workplace change.* Washington, DC: AFL-CIO.

Beck, N. (1992). *Shifting gears: Thriving in the new economy.* Toronto: Harper-Collins.

Beckhard, R., and Pritchard, W. (1992). *Changing the essence: The art of creating and leading fundamental change in organizations.* San Francisco: Jossey-Bass.

Brooks, A., and Watkins, K. (Eds.). (1994). The emerging power of action inquiry technologies. *New Directions for Adult and Continuing Education, 63.* San Francisco: Jossey-Bass.

Bunker, B., and Alban, B. (Eds.). (1992). Large group interventions. (Special Issue). *Journal of Applied Behavioral Science, 28*(4).

Campbell, T., and Cairns, H. (1994). Developing and measuring the learning organization: From buzz words to behaviours. *Industrial and Commercial Training, 26*(7), 10–15.

Cohen, M., and Sproull, L. (Eds.). (1991). Organizational learning: Papers in honor of (and by) James March. (Special Issue). *Organization Science, 2*(1).

Dixon, N. (1994). *The organizational learning cycle: How we can learn collectively.* London: McGraw-Hill.

Isaacs, W. (1993). Taking flight: Dialogue, collective thinking, and organizational learning. *Organizational Dynamics, 22*(2), 24–39.

Jacobs, R., and Jones, M. (1995). *Structured on-the-job training: Unleashing employee expertise in the workplace.* San Francisco: Berrett-Koehler.

Jacobs, R. (1994). *Real time strategic change: How to involve an entire organization in fast and far-reaching change.* San Francisco: Berrett-Koehler.

Marsick, V., and Watkins, K. (1990). *Informal and incidental learning in the workplace.* London and New York: Routledge.

Marquardt, M., and Reynolds, A. (1994). *The global learning organization: Gaining competitive advantage through continuous learning.* Burr Ridge, IL: Irwin.

Mumford, A. (1993). *How managers can develop managers.* Aldershot, England: Gower.

Nevis, E., DiBella, A., and Gould, J. (1995, Winter). Understanding organizational learning systems. *Sloan Management Review,* 73–85.

O'Brien, M., and Shook, L. (1995). *Profit from experience: How to make the most of your learning and your life.* Austin, TX: Bard & Stephen.

Pedler, M., Burgoyne, J., and Boydell, T. (1991). *The learning company: A strategy for sustainable development.* London: McGraw-Hill.

Rahim, A. (Ed.). (1995). Organizational learning. (Special Issue). *International Journal of Organizational Analysis, 3*(1).

Redding, J., and Catanello, R.F. (1994). *Strategic readiness: The making of the learning organization.* San Francisco: Jossey-Bass.

Savage, C. (1990). *Fifth generation management: Integrating enterprises through human networking.* Boston: Digital Press.

Schein, E. (1993). On dialogue, culture, and organizational learning. *Organizational Dynamics, 22*(2), 40–51.

Senge, P. (1990). *The fifth discipline: The art and practice of the learning organization.* New York: Random House.

Senge, P., Roberts, C., Ross, R., Smith, B., and Kleiner, A. (1994). *The fifth discipline fieldbook: Strategies and tools for building a learning organization: Lessons in the art and science of systemic change.* New York: Doubleday.

Watkins, K., and Marsick, V. (1993). *Sculpting the learning organization: Lessons in the art and science of systemic change.* San Francisco: Jossey-Bass.

Watkins, K., and Golembiewski, R. (1995). Rethinking organization development for the learning organization. *The International Journal of Organizational Analysis, 3*(1) 86–101.

Wheatley, M. (1992). *Leadership and the new science.* San Francisco: Berrett-Koehler.

Wick, C., and Leon, L. (1993). *The learning edge: How smart managers and smart companies stay ahead.* New York: McGraw-Hill.

Call for Cases for Volume 2

The initial reaction to this publication has been outstanding, both from the potential audience and from the contributors who have provided cases. Consequently, we have decided to develop a second volume, to be edited by Victoria Marsick and Karen Watkins. The number of cases submitted for this volume exceeded our expectations for both quality and quantity. We also discovered during our search for cases that there were many planned or ongoing projects that would not be completed in time to include in this publication. We would like to capture those, and others, in a volume to be published in either late 1997 or early 1998. Anyone interested in submitting a case or needing additional information can contact Performance Resources Organization, P.O. Box 380637, Birmingham, AL 35238-0637.

About the Series Editor

Jack Phillips has more than 25 years of professional and managerial experience, most of it in the human resource development and management field. Currently he serves on the management faculty of Middle Tennessee State University, where he teaches human resource courses at the graduate and undergraduate levels. Through Performance Resources Organization, he consults with clients in manufacturing, service, and government organizations in the United States and abroad. Consulting assignments include a variety of human resource accountability programs, ranging from measurement and evaluation to productivity and quality enhancement programs, with active clients in the United States, Canada, Mexico, Venezuela, Malaysia, Indonesia, South Africa, and Europe.

A frequent contributor to management literature, Phillips has written *Handbook of Training Evaluation and Measurement Methods* (Gulf Publishing, 2d ed., 1991), *The Development of a Human Resource Effectiveness Index* (University of Michigan Press, 1988), *Recruiting, Training and Retaining New Employees* (Jossey-Bass, 1987), and *Improving Supervisors' Effectiveness* (Jossey-Bass, 1985), which won an award from the Society for Human Resource Management in 1986. Phillips has written more than 75 articles for professional, business, and trade publications.